I0256596

composition STUDIES

Volume 43, Number 1

Spring 2015

SUBSCRIPTIONS

Composition Studies is published twice each year (May and November). Annual subscription rates: Individuals $25 (Domestic), $30 (International), and $15 (Students). To subsccribe online, please visit http://www.uc.edu/journals/composition-studies/subscriptions.html

BACK ISSUES

We are in the process of digitizing back issues, five years prior to the present, and making them freely accessible on our website at http://www.uc.edu/journals/composition-studies/issues/archives.html. If you don't see what you're looking for, contact us. Also, recent back issues are now available through Amazon.com. To find issues, use the advanced search feature and search on "Composition Studies" (title) and "Parlor Press" (publisher).

BOOK REVIEWS

Assignments are made from a file of potential book reviewers. If you are interested in writing a review, please contact our Book Review editor at kkinney@binghamton.edu.

JOURNAL SCOPE

The oldest independent periodical in the field, *Composition Studies* publishes original articles relevant to rhetoric and composition, including those that address teaching college writing; theorizing rhetoric and composing; administering writing programs; and, among other topics, preparing the field's future teacher-scholars. All perspectives and topics of general interest to the profession are welcome. We also publish Course Designs, which contextualize, theorize, and reflect on the content and pedagogy of a course. Contributions to Composing With are invited by the editor, though queries are welcome (send to compstudies@uc.edu). Cfps, announcements, and letters to the editor are most welcome. *Composition Studies* does not consider previously published manuscripts, unrevised conference papers, or unrevised dissertation chapters.

SUBMISSIONS

For submission information and guidelines, see http://www.uc.edu/journals/composition-studies/submissions/overview.html.

Direct all correspondence to:

Laura Micciche, Editor
Department of English
University of Cincinnati
PO Box 210069
Cincinnati, OH 45221–0069
compstudies@uc.edu

Composition Studies is grateful for the support of the University of Cincinnati.

Production and printing is managed by Parlor Press, www.parlorpress.com.
ISSN 1534–9322.
Cover art and design by Gary Weissman.

http://www.uc.edu/journals/composition-studies.html

composition STUDIES

Volume 43, Number 1
Spring 2015

Reviewers from March 2014 through February 2015

A journal is only as good as its reviewers. We acknowledge and celebrate the dedication, good will, and expertise of our generous reviewers:

Jennifer Ahern-Dodson, Duke University
Cydney Alexis, Kansas State University
Chris Anson, North Carolina State University
Will Banks, East Carolina University
Charles Bazerman, University of California, Santa Barbara
Joe Bizup, Boston University
Glenn Blalock, Texas A&M University, Corpus Christi
Heather Bruce, University of Montana
Michael Bunn, University of Southern California
Beth Burmester, Georgia State University
Allison Carr, Coe College
Chris Carter, University of Cincinnati
Davida Charney, University of Texas, Austin
Irene Clark, California State University, Northridge
Michelle Eodice, University of Oklahoma
Philip Eubanks, Northern Illinois University
Janice Fernheimer, University of Kentucky
Dana Ferris, University of California, Davis
Kristie Fleckenstein, Florida State University
Moe Folk, Kutztown University of Pennsylvania
Erica Frisicaro-Pawlowski, Daemen College
Gwen Gorzelsky, Wayne State University
Heather Graves, University of Alberta
Jennifer Grouling, Ball State University
Mark Hall, University of Central Florida
Joe Hardin, University of Arkansas, Fort Smith
Susanmarie Harrington, University of Vermont
Joseph Harris, University of Delaware
Bill Hart-Davidson, Michigan State University
Jennifer Hewerdine, Southern Illinois University, Carbondale
Mara Holt, Ohio University
Alice Horning, Oakland University
Jonathan Hunt, University of San Francisco
Brian Huot, Kent State University
Lennie Irvin, San Antonio College
Elizabeth Kalbfleisch, Southern Connecticut State University

From the Editor

Special Issue: Comics, Multimodality, and Composition

Dale Jacobs, Guest Editor

About ten years ago, I was teaching a second-year writing course at the University of Windsor. Several of the students in that class were avid comics readers and, over the course of the semester, began encouraging me to come back to reading comics, a pursuit I had all but abandoned fifteen years earlier. The comics they loaned to me—*Sandman*, *Blankets*, and Brubaker's run on *Daredevil*, among others—pulled me into the narrative in ways that were both familiar from my adolescence and novel in the way they were using the medium. As I read, I began to think about how I had made meaning from comics texts in the past and how I was doing so now, a line of thinking that led to my scholarly interest in comics studies and its intersection with composition and rhetoric.

Over the next several years, I read the occasional article that was published in one of the journals in the field and attended any panels I could on comics at 4Cs. I read the comics studies journals and attended conferences, searching for others who were using the lenses of composition studies to think about comics. As the years went on, I began to see more and more people in composition interested in comics and especially in their potential uses in the classroom. Still, though, those efforts were scattered here and there in journals, in essay collections, in conference presentations, and in informal talk and email exchanges. So when Laura Micciche asked me if I would be interested in guest editing a special issue of *Composition Studies* on comics and composition, I leapt at the chance to bring together composition scholars who are interested in comics and their potential for our field.

I had high hopes for the issue from the start, but I was overwhelmed to receive 24 essay submissions, in addition to all of the other material that I received. Of those excellent articles, four are included here. Gabriel Sealy-Morris's "The Rhetoric of the Paneled Page: Comics and Composition Pedagogy" provides an excellent overview of how comics might be used in the practice of composition instruction, especially as articulated in the WPA *Outcomes Statement for First-Year Composition*. In "Beyond Talking Heads: Sourced Comics and the Affordances of Multimodality," Hannah Dickinson and Maggie M. Werner argue for composing comics in the classroom as a way to help students "expand and demystify the strategies students might use to engage scholarly sources." Kate Comer, in "Illustrating Praxis: Comic Composition, Narrative

Rhetoric, and Critical Multiliteracies," also argues for comics as a medium in our classes, focusing on how narrative and comics theory can combine to offer students a set of heuristics for composition. Molly Scanlon examines the issues and implications of collaborative multimodal composition in her article, "The Work of Comics Collaborations: Considerations of Multimodal Composition for Writing Scholarship and Pedagogy," and, in doing so, pushes the ways that we need to think about collaboration as a field. Taken together, these essays provide a spectrum of possible engagements between comics and composition.

The Course Design section includes two pieces: Leah Misemer's literature and popular culture course on "The Graphic Novel" and Aaron Kashtan's literature and composition course centered on "Handwriting and Typography." Both of these pieces show specific, though very different, ways that comics can be incorporated into the classroom. In our first Composing With piece, Gary Weissman explains how he created the cover of this issue; in the second, Frannie Howes details her own practices as both an academic and comics creator during her time in graduate school. For the "Where We Are" section, I asked three authors whose essays I could not include to contribute a much-abbreviated version of their arguments as a means to show the multiple ways that comics and composition can intersect with each other and with other fields. Susan Kirtley in "The Underdog Disciplines: Comics Studies and Composition and Rhetoric" directly addresses the possible connections between the two fields, while Shannon Walters, in "Graphic Disruptions: Comics, Disability, and De-Canonizing Composition," examines the ways in which comics and disability studies can help to critique normative assumptions about multimodality in Composition. In "Comics and Scholarship: Sketching the Possibilities," Erin Kathleen Bahl traces the possibilities and current state of scholarly publishing in comics form. Finally, Aaron Scott Humphrey offers a fascinating comic (inked by John Carvajal) entitled "Visual and Spatial Language: The Silent Voice of Woodstock" in which he challenges us to consider how comics can help us to think about multimodality in new ways.

I want to thank Laura Micciche for inviting me to edit this issue and for all the support throughout the process. Working on this special issue has been a pleasure. I hope that you find it reading it as exciting and productive as I have.

Windsor, Ontario
January 2015

Composing With

A Comic Strip Cover Story

Gary Weissman

I created the cover for this special issue of *Composition Studies* with elements poached and reworked from various sources. The banner bearing the words "comics, multimodality, and composition" and the small bird perched atop it are hand-drawn approximations of clipart I found online. For the head of our guest editor, I plucked a photo from Dale Jacobs's Facebook page, altered it in Photoshop, printed the image, and traced over it with marker. I then scanned the drawing, reduced its scale, added a drop shadow, and arranged the arched lettering. It was editor Laura Micciche's idea to feature Dale in this way. His shrunken head speaks to how the cover took shape through dialogue, the pitching and fine-tuning of ideas.

The key element I reworked was a six-panel comic strip I drew as an undergraduate college student, sometime in the late 1980s. Back then I did comics for the campus newspaper and humor magazine, but this strip never saw print. Rather than crumple it up, I stored it away in my files where it remained for a quarter of a century, until Laura asked me to make a cover for this issue on comics. My old strip came to mind because it is a comic about the process of composing comics.

Titled "The Creative Process, Illustrated," the strip features a well-dressed gentleman sitting silently at a desk for three panels before an idea for a one-panel gag cartoon occurs to him in the fourth panel, appearing in a thought bubble over his head. The sophomoric gag, scatological in nature, does not bear repeating here. That it shows a sketchily doodled figure, naked and expressing excitement ("Hot dog!") over his belly button's orificial transformation, need not concern us. The strip's fifth and sixth panels essentially match the cover's bottom two panels: the cartoonist drawing his idea followed by the cartoonist going "back to the drawing board," the crumpled ball of paper indicating that the opening provided by the blank page has led to a dead end.

Part of the strip's humor lay in the contrast between the inanity of the lowbrow gag and the dapperness of the suit- and sweater-vest-wearing cartoonist (whose visage I adapted from a 1930s comic book). A similar contrast is drawn between the vulgar gag, no sooner envisioned than abandoned, and the grandeur of a romantically conceived creative process. Somewhere in the course of rendering his idea on paper—namely, in the gap between the fifth and sixth panels—the cartoonist realizes it's crap. Unlike the excitable figure

Composition Studies 43.1 (2015): 13–14

in the gag he pictured, though, he responds with near indifference. Failure punctuated by delusive moments of inspiration is the norm.

Repurposed for the cover of this journal, the comic employs different humor and conveys different meaning. The idea shown in a thought bubble no longer concerns a one-panel gag cartoon; instead, it depicts a cover design for this special issue: the decorative banner with Dale's head beside it. In the third panel that idea dissipates, replaced by what the artist is able to put on paper. Does the crumpled paper ball in the fourth panel represent the artist's rejection of his idea upon seeing it realized, or his inability to capture what he envisioned? I imagine the latter (it's a better joke) but don't know for sure.

In composing these words I approach the vanishing point of my own creative process, poking at those places where my understanding of the comic on the cover starts to fray. Choosing and revising my language with as much care as I drew and erased and copied and pasted pixels in Photoshop, I find words for what hardly concerned me while I worked on the cover. I theorize that in repurposing my old strip I replaced the juvenile humor of the poop joke with more mature wit. But, I wonder, what exactly is witty about the comic I made for the cover?

That comic is like the cover of an old punk song cleaned up for radio play on an adult contemporary station. It's a cover version of the strip I drew as an undergraduate, with the filthy part taken out and replaced by something else. The name for that something else is irony. It's ironic that the comic shows the very cover design that the artist is unable or unwilling to show. It's ironic that the design he rejects makes it onto the cover. It's ironic that the design appears in the strip as an idea in a thought bubble and not as a drawing, when the idea in a thought bubble is itself a drawing. It's ironic that the banner the artist fails to draw to his satisfaction succeeds at presenting the title of this special issue. It's all very ironic, or at least I think it is. And in thinking about the easy way in which this humor substitutes for the gag I drew twenty-five years ago, I come to appreciate that irony is scatology for grown ups.

Composing the Uncollectible

Franny Howes

I am both an academic and a comics creator: these writing selves have grown up together and are deeply intertwined. The indie comics creator in me drives my academic work to move between analysis, autobiographical reflection, and cartoon art, and the academic in me theorizes how comics work or could work as they pour out of me.

I've published my comic series, *Oh Shit, I'm in Grad School!*, in print and online since 2008. While to some people comics might be fetishized artifacts to be collected, I have developed a rhetorical strategy of creating *uncollectible* comics.

An uncollectible comic takes a decolonial approach to the relationship between the collector and the collected. In his book *The Darker Side of Western Modernity*, the decolonial theorist Walter Mignolo asks the question, "Who establishes criteria of classification?" and, who gets classified (83)? His critique suggests that the act of collecting and classifying is a colonizing gaze—a position of power where you impose order and control on something you possess. This critique implicates scholars and comic geeks alike, and I have used the tropes of one group to challenge the practices of the other.

Uncollectibility doesn't mean you shouldn't buy comics or own them, or that I don't want people to buy or own my comics. It's more that I have over time developed a strategy of making things *that fail to be collectible.*

An uncollectible comic is fundamentally incomplete, implying a greater whole that is not actually attainable. It deliberately sabotages attempts to create "absolute" or "ultimate" editions or knowledges about itself. Uncollectibility as a strategy recognizes that comics are ephemeral, and that this is a virtue and not a flaw. A comic is a moment in time as well as a material artifact. It refers to a larger whole (in my case, by being part of my series) but that whole may not exist or may never be attainable: the series is never complete because completeness is always deferred. My comics' numbering scheme and irregular schedule make it difficult if not impossible to know exactly how many there are and whether or not you'll ever get any more. Some gaps in numbering suggest the existence of "missing issues" that I never actually drew.

I make hybrid comic book—coloring books that explicitly ask you to permanently alter the text, and comics with activity pages that leave part of the content of the book up to the reader. This began as a take-off on "Mad Libs" that I never expected anyone to fill out. But they did complete them, and then shared their responses with me. The inclusion of an activity page as a joke (because, who would ever actually write in their comic books?) then grew into deliberate blank panels, where the reader is instructed to draw themselves in, and blank dialogue and thought balloons, where readers are asked to write their own content (see fig. 1). Seeing my readers interact with my comics (literally watching people color them in) has taught me that comics are both things and happenings. Comics have multiple selves.

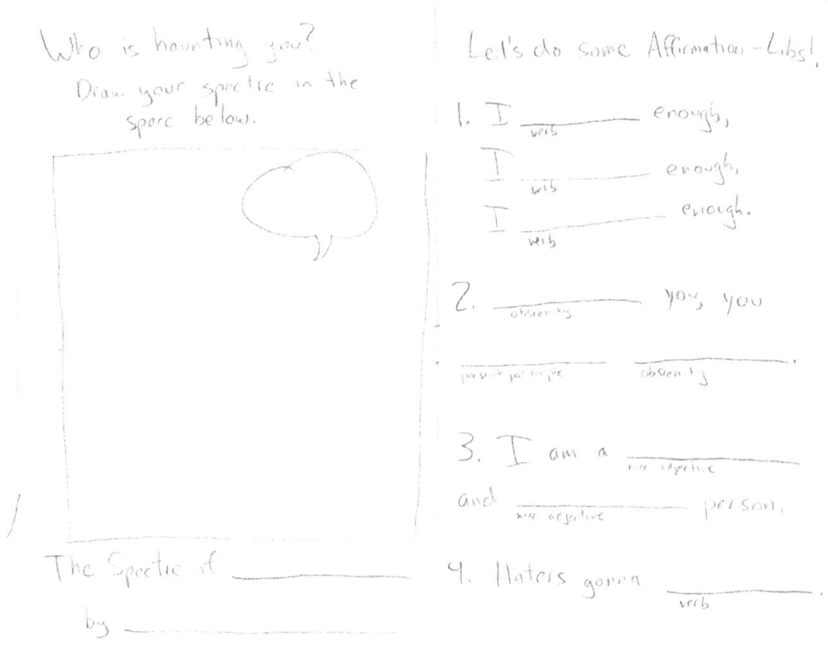

Fig. 1. Activity pages from *Oh Shit, I'm in Grad School!* Coloring and Activity Book, 2012.

I realize that I don't need to tell the field of writing studies to be careful about the power dynamics of a mint condition copy of *The Death of Superman*. But what I do want to say is that to collect a comic means more than just to be a fan and have a collection that you keep in pristine condition. The gaze of the collector is one of mastery. It is a judging gaze that evaluates what belongs and what does not belong. We collect comics all the time when we assemble them into bibliographies or syllabi or "essential" editions.

I have worked to disturb this relationship. The rhetorical practice that surfaces in *Oh Shit, I'm in Grad School!* is ultimately about challenging my audience's notions of how to value a text, how to compose a text, how to interact with a text, and what a text is in the first place. My comics are by design unassimilable into Western ways of scholarly knowing, although this is an ironic thing to realize from having literally just finished writing a dissertation about them.

Finally, an uncollectible comic says this: don't collect comics, attend comics. "Attention" is a way of knowing that doesn't presume mastery or ownership. Attending comics emphasizes space and time, seeing comics as something you go to rather than something you study and read. It implies listening, watching, and actively relating. As Shawn Wilson writes, in an indigenous research paradigm, knowledge is relational, and truth is a form of right relationships (80, 114). What I have learned from decolonial feminist thought and research is that all scholars can benefit from rethinking (and decolonizing) the knower's relationship to the known. But furthermore, as a rhetor you can design a text to emphasize these ideas. If its materiality challenges the reader, if its serialization challenges the collector, if its absence of seriousness challenges the scholar, if its seriousness challenges the nonscholar, if its interactivity challenges the book lover, the relationship between the audience and the comic is brought to the foreground.

Attending comics is a different way of being: it is phenomenological. One reads a comic, but attends comics. Attending looks at a comic as part of a web of relations: connected synchronically and diachronically to other things and people. Attending comics recognizes that any one comic we hold is only a thread: not a discrete or masterable text, but both a window into a place and a place in itself. When we attend comics, we listen with our eyes.

Works Cited

Mignolo, Walter. *The Darker Side of Western Modernity: Global Futures, Decolonial Options*. Durham: Duke UP, 2011. Print.

Wilson, Shawn. *Research Is Ceremony: Indigenous Research Methods*. Black Point: Fernwood, 2008. Print.

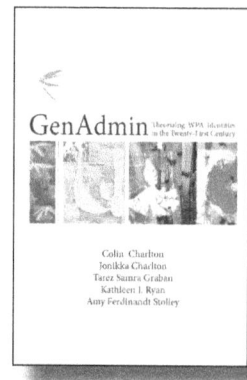

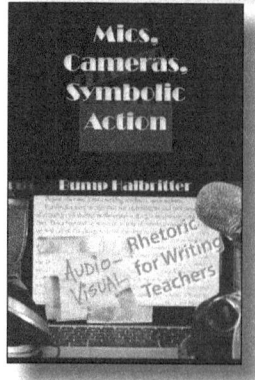

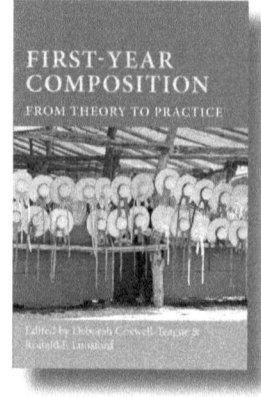

VISUAL AND SPATIAL LANGUAGE: THE SILENT VOICE OF WOODSTOCK

BY: AARON HUMPHREY INKED BY: JOHN CARVAJAL

MULTIMODAL LITERACY[1] CHALLENGES US TO THINK ABOUT LITERACY AND THE BOUNDARIES OF TRADITIONAL "ALPHABETIC" TEXTS, AND TO CONSIDER HOW MEANING IS CONVEYED THROUGH THINGS LIKE T.V. SHOWS, VIDEO GAMES, WEBSITES AND COMIC BOOKS.[2]

BUT **ALL** TEXTS ARE MULTIMODAL—EVEN TRADITIONAL "ALPHABETIC" TEXTS CONVEY MEANING THROUGH A WHOLE RANGE OF MODALITIES...

WHEN WE OPEN UP LITERACY TO INCLUDE OTHER SETS OF SIGNS—

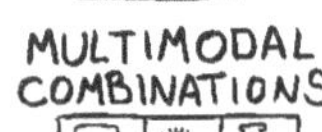

—WE CAN EXPOSE NEW MEANINGS IN ALPHABETIC TEXTS THAT WE MIGHT OTHERWISE TAKE FOR GRANTED.

COMICS CAN ASSIST US IN THIS PROCESS BY DENATURALISING WRITING'S [visual icon] AND [spatial icon] MODALITIES.

Composition Studies 43.1 (2015): 19–30

FOR EXAMPLE,
WRITTEN LANGUAGE IS OFTEN LINKED TO SPEECH—(IN FRENCH, LANGUE MEANS BOTH "LANGUAGE" AND "TONGUE") —BUT COMICS CAN EMPHASISE THEIR DIFFERENCES.

CAN WE SEPARATE OUT THIS **IMPLIED VERBAL MODALITY** OF WRITING FROM ITS **VISUAL AND SPATIAL** MODALITIES?

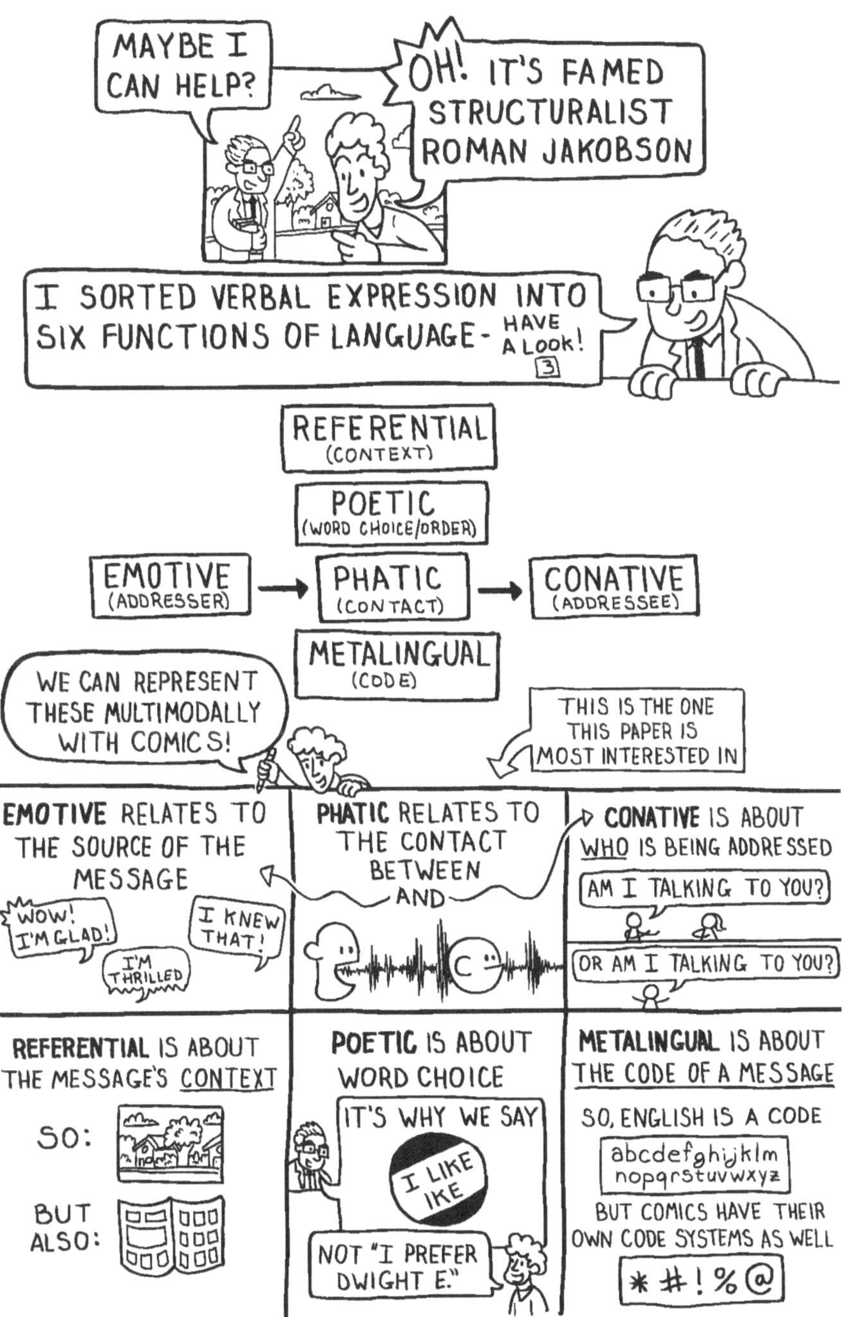

PHATIC COMMUNICATION HAS BEEN DESCRIBED AS THE "SOCIAL GLUE" THAT CHARACTERISES "SMALL TALK" AND "TALK ABOUT THE WEATHER"

HOWEVER, THE **PHYSICAL PROPERTIES** OF SPEECH ALSO WORK TO BIND BOTH PARTIES TOGETHER IN TIME + SPACE

SOUND WAVES LITERALLY SURROUND US AND PASS THROUGH US ALL IN AN INSTANT — (EVEN VOCALISATIONS WE CAN'T UNDERSTAND PERFORM THE PHATIC FUNCTION!)

ALTHOUGH JAKOBSON'S OTHER LINGUISTIC FUNCTIONS SURVIVE THE TRANSLATION FROM [speech] TO [eye] MORE OR LESS INTACT, THE PHATIC MODE OF CONTACT IS ENTIRELY **TRANSFORMED**

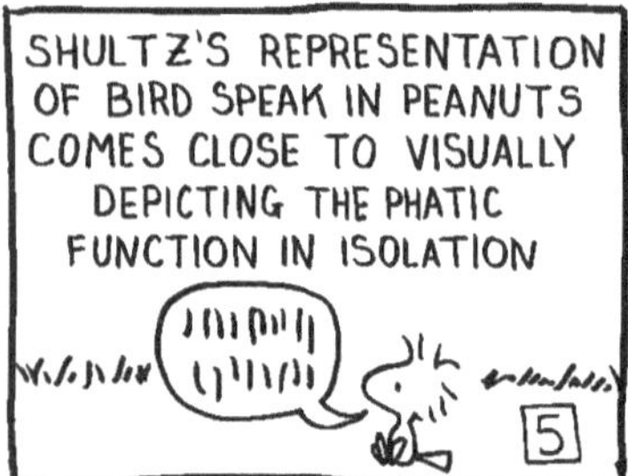

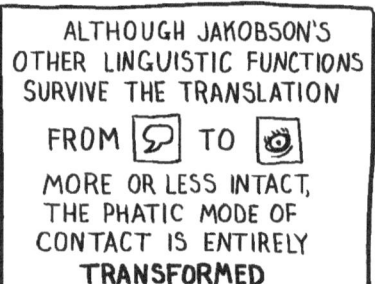

I THINK THIS IS A GOOD WAY TO REPRESENT THROUGH A **VISUAL MODALITY** THE QUALITIES OF **VERBAL MODALITIES** THAT ARE LOST IN TRANSLATION TO WRITING.

JAKOBSON FIRST PRESENTED HIS WORK ON THE SIX FUNCTIONS OF LANGUAGE AS AN ORAL CONFERENCE PRESENTATION...

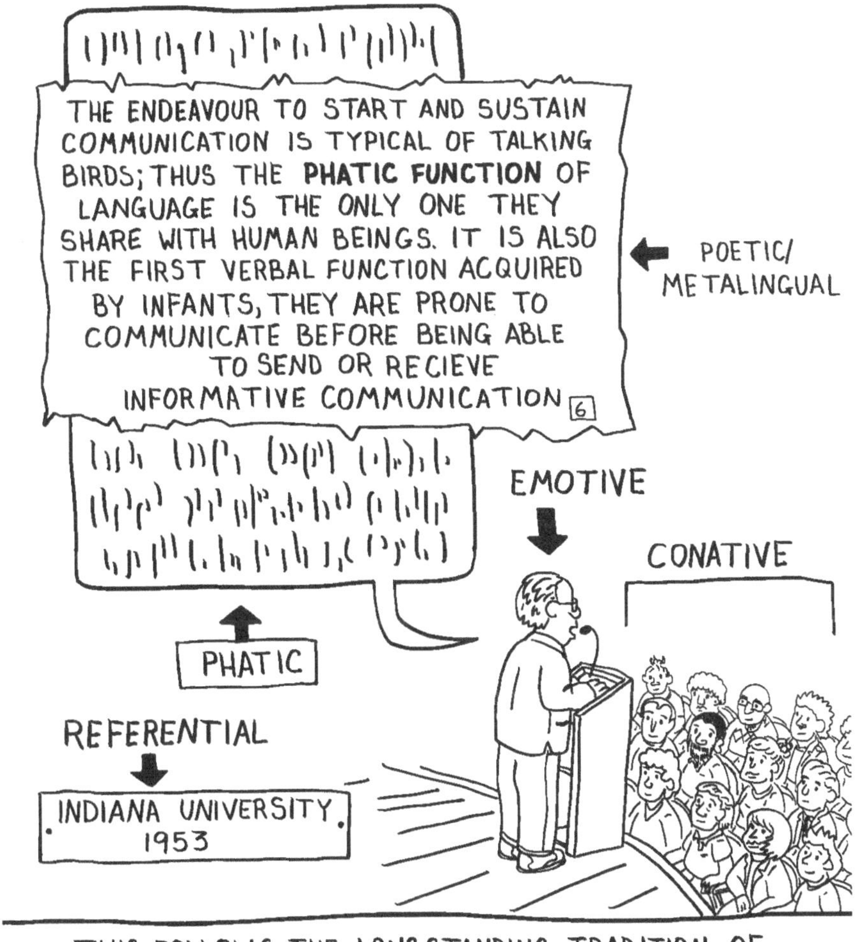

THE ENDEAVOUR TO START AND SUSTAIN COMMUNICATION IS TYPICAL OF TALKING BIRDS; THUS THE **PHATIC FUNCTION** OF LANGUAGE IS THE ONLY ONE THEY SHARE WITH HUMAN BEINGS. IT IS ALSO THE FIRST VERBAL FUNCTION ACQUIRED BY INFANTS, THEY ARE PRONE TO COMMUNICATE BEFORE BEING ABLE TO SEND OR RECIEVE INFORMATIVE COMMUNICATION [6]

POETIC/ METALINGUAL

EMOTIVE

CONATIVE

PHATIC

REFERENTIAL

INDIANA UNIVERSITY 1953

THIS FOLLOWS THE LONGSTANDING TRADITION OF PHILOSOPHICAL, ACADEMIC AND RELIGIOUS TEXTS BASED IN AND COPIED FROM SPOKEN LANGUAGE – WE HAVE COME TO LINK SPEECH & TEXT

THIS IS WHY WOODSTOCK'S CHICKEN SCRATCH WORKS-

IF YOU SQUINT, THIS
LOOKS LIKE

AND SO, WE ARE SURROUNDED BY "VOICES" EVEN WHEN WE ONLY SEE WRITING AND DO NOT READ IT—BECAUSE THE VISUAL FORM OF WRITING HAS COME TO BE SYMBOLIC OF THE VERBAL MODALITY.

THE BOUNDARIES OF THIS THEORY ARE EXPLORED IN THE FIELD OF ASEMIC WRITING WHERE WRITERS & ARTISTS CREATE TEXTS THAT MIMIC SOME OF THE QUALITIES OF PRINTED WRITING, BUT WHICH HAVE NO PRESCRIBED LINGUISTIC MEANINGS.

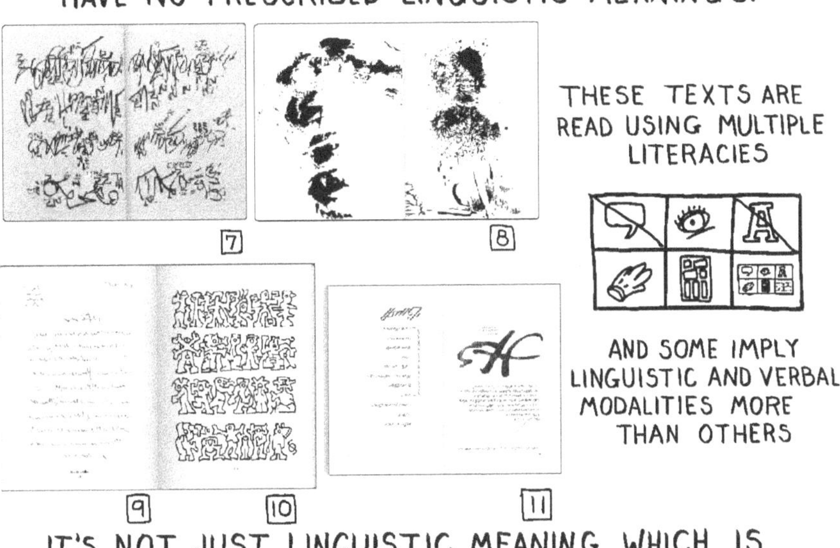

7
8
THESE TEXTS ARE READ USING MULTIPLE LITERACIES
AND SOME IMPLY LINGUISTIC AND VERBAL MODALITIES MORE THAN OTHERS
9
10
11

IT'S NOT JUST LINGUISTIC MEANING WHICH IS CONSTRUCTED MULTIMODALLY, BUT ALL THE FUNCTIONS OF ADDRESS –

JUST AS WRITTEN TEXTS STILL COMMUNICATE MANY MESSAGES WHEN THEY HAVE NO CLEAR LINGUISTIC MEANINGS, MUCH OF THE INFORMATION CONVEYED IN SPOKEN COMMUNICATION RELATES TO JAKOBSON'S FUNCTIONS OF LANGUAGE, EVEN IN CASES LIKE THE ANIMATED PEANUTS CARTOONS, WHERE ADULTS ARE ONLY HEARD MAKING SOUNDS OF A MUTED TRUMPET, RATHER THAN WORDS. →

WHAT DO THESE MODALITIES SAY ABOUT THE FUNCTIONS OF ADDRESS?

THE SOURCE OF THE MESSAGE?

THE RECIPIENTS OF THE MESSAGE?

THE CONTACT BETWEEN THEM?

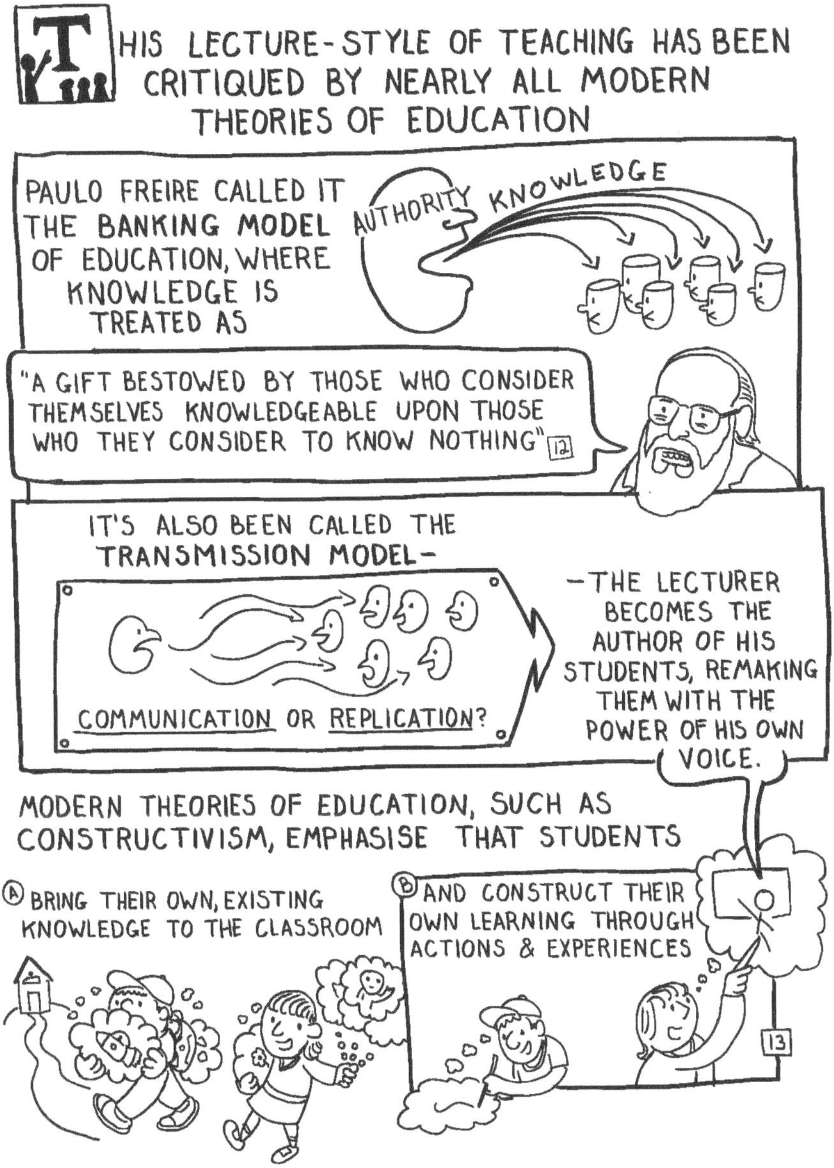

HIS LECTURE-STYLE OF TEACHING HAS BEEN CRITIQUED BY NEARLY ALL MODERN THEORIES OF EDUCATION

PAULO FREIRE CALLED IT THE **BANKING MODEL** OF EDUCATION, WHERE KNOWLEDGE IS TREATED AS

AUTHORITY

KNOWLEDGE

"A GIFT BESTOWED BY THOSE WHO CONSIDER THEMSELVES KNOWLEDGEABLE UPON THOSE WHO THEY CONSIDER TO KNOW NOTHING" [12]

IT'S ALSO BEEN CALLED THE **TRANSMISSION MODEL**–

COMMUNICATION OR REPLICATION?

–THE LECTURER BECOMES THE AUTHOR OF HIS STUDENTS, REMAKING THEM WITH THE POWER OF HIS OWN VOICE.

MODERN THEORIES OF EDUCATION, SUCH AS CONSTRUCTIVISM, EMPHASISE THAT STUDENTS

(A) BRING THEIR OWN, EXISTING KNOWLEDGE TO THE CLASSROOM

(B) AND CONSTRUCT THEIR OWN LEARNING THROUGH ACTIONS & EXPERIENCES [13]

Despite this, lectures remain central to academic discourse, as exemplified by how closely lectures and conference papers are linked with published journal articles, book chapters and textbooks. For example, Jakobson's 1953 lecture was transcribed into text and turned into a frequently cited piece of writing.

This is underscored by the fact that academic conference presentations, which are essentially lectures, are called 'papers' even if they are never published in print.

AS THE MULTIMODAL FORMS OF LECTURES ELEVATE THE SPEAKER'S VOICE
AND AS THE VISUAL AND SPATIAL MODALITIES OF WRITING IMPLY A VERBAL MODALITY...
FIG 2.6.1
...SO TEXT BOOKS, JOURNAL ARTICLES AND OTHER ACADEMIC DISCOURSE IMPLY BOTH THE IDEA OF A LECTURE AND ALSO ITS POWER STRUCTURES...
TAKE THIS TEXT BOOK FOR EXAMPLE:
THE WRITER'S "VOICE" IS WHAT IS MOST IMPORTANT EVEN WHEN THIS IS VISUALLY OR SPATIALLY INCONVENIENT
As seen in Figure 7.3.1, this phenomenon is
IMAGES ARE NUMBERED AND QUARANTINED, SEPARATE FROM THE WRITER'S "VOICE"
NO SIGN OF FIGURE 7.3.1, TWO PAGES LATER...
AND STILL NO SIGN OF IT...
FIGURE 7.3.1! THERE IT IS!
...ALONG WITH FIG. 7.3.2, WHICH WILL NOT BE DISCUSSED IN THE TEXT FOR SIX PAGES.
MEANWHILE, THE WRITER'S "VOICE" CONTINUES AS IF IT WAS NEVER INTERRUPTED
FIG. 7.3.3: READER DESPERATELY FLIPPING BETWEEN PAGES
YES, FIGURE 7.3.1 IS STILL BEING DISCUSSED DOWN HERE, IN INTRICATE DETAIL THAT NECESSITATES FIGURE 7.3.3

HOW CAN PRINTED DISCOURSE MOVE BEYOND THIS LOGOCENTRIC AND LECTURE-CENTRIC CONSTRUCTION?

...EITHER WITH CAPTIONS OR BY DRAWING IN A LECTURER!

THE ABILITY OF CARTOONS TO *FOCUS* OUR ATTENTION ON AN IDEA IS, I THINK, AN IMPORTANT PART OF THEIR SPECIAL POWER, BOTH IN COMICS AND IN DRAWING GENERALLY.

14

Our enemies are not the digital bits that dance across our screens but the neural impulses that animate our lizard brains.

15

IN THE LAST VOLUME WE MET THE GREEKS: THEIR LEGENDS, CUSTOMS, AND THOUGHT! NOW WE FOCUS ON THEIR GREAT WAR WITH THE *PERSIAN EMPIRE!*

16

HOW CAN WE MAKE THIS TABLE MORE MEANINGFUL?

HMM.

MAYBE YOU CAN MAKE THIS INTO A GRAPH?

CORRECT!

17

UNLIKE -A- LECTURE

IN WRITING, THE PHATIC MODE OF CONTACT IS NOT DRIVEN BY THE WRITER'S VOICE & PRESENCE

BUT BY THE WAYS

READERS INTERACT WITH THE PAGE! **

MAPS

CHARTS

GRAPHS

DIAGRAMS

ILLUSTRATIONS

COLLAGES (LYNDA BARRY)

COMICS

COMICS CAN DO ALL OF THESE!

SO COMICS CAN BRING THE VISUAL AND SPATIAL MODALITIES TO THE FOREFRONT OF WRITING?
I WOULD ARGUE THAT THEY ARE ALREADY AT THE FOREFRONT OF WRITING, BUT COMICS CAN MAKE THAT MORE APPARENT...
AND WRITING WITH COMICS ALLOWS US TO MANIPULATE THOSE MODALITIES IN INTERESTING WAYS!
THEY GIVE US A WAY OF SHOWING WHAT WE MEAN
RATHER THAN JUST TELLING IT!
AND GIVE US TOOLS TO DO DIFFERENT THINGS IN REGARDS TO THE FUNCTIONS OF LANGUAGE
REFERENTIAL
POETIC
PHATIC
EMOTIVE
IN WRITING THIS PAPER, I'VE TRIED TO LAY OUT SOME TOOLS FOR ANALYSING THE MULTIMODAL QUALITIES OF COMICS & OTHER TEXTS
I'VE ALSO TRIED TO USE DIFFERENT TECHNIQUES AND MULTIMODAL COMBINATIONS ON EACH PAGE
WHICH CAN IN TURN CHALLENGE THE POWER STRUCTURES COMMONLY EVOKED IN ACADEMIC WRITING & PUBLISHING.
SO IF YOU WANT, YOU CAN GO BACK AND TRY TO FIGURE OUT HOW DIFFERENT MODALITIES & FUNCTIONS OF LANGUAGE WORK ON EACH PAGE!
OR EVEN BETTER - YOU COULD TRY WRITING THIS WAY YOURSELF!

Articles

The Rhetoric of the Paneled Page: Comics and Composition Pedagogy

Gabriel Sealey-Morris

While comics have received widespread acceptance as a literary genre, instructors and scholars in Rhetoric and Composition have been slower to adopt comics, largely because of a lingering difficulty understanding how the characteristics of the form relate to our work in the classroom. Using as guides the *WPA Outcomes Statement for First-Year Writing*, and the *NCTE Position Statement on Multimodal Literacies*, this essay seeks to establish the conditions necessary for a pedagogically sound, functional use of comics in composition instruction, not only in readings and textbooks but also in practice.

In "Trudy Does Comics," Chris Anson's contribution to *The WAC Casebook*, an art major challenges her philosophy professor's newfound commitment to student expression by turning in comics pages for her assignments. Howard, the professor, grades the first comic a C-, arguing that only one of the characters talks, and not enough. Though Trudy includes more dialogue in the second, Howard gives it a C- as well, because there is "simply less text here than in the other students' papers" (31). Trudy objects, arguing that the professor's resistance to her comics contradicts his nominal support for student creativity and expression. While *The WAC Casebook* is primarily designed to provoke conversations about pedagogy, classroom practices, assignment development, and other practical and theoretical aspects of teaching composition, Anson's story points out another salient fact: comics, and the students who read, write, and think about them, have reached academia, and they are not going away.

This essay seeks to establish the conditions necessary for a pedagogically sound, functional use of comics in composition instruction, not only in readings and textbooks but also in practice. As one of the most accessible forms of multimodal text (insofar as no computing, audio, or video expertise is necessary), comics complicate notions of authorship, make sophisticated demands on readers, and create a grammar and rhetoric as sophisticated as written prose, while also opening up new methods of communication often disregarded by conventional composition instruction. This discussion is organized around two guiding documents in the field: the Council of Writing Program Administrators (WPA) *Outcomes Statement for First-Year Composition* and the National Council of Teachers of English (NCTE) *Position Statement on Multimodal Literacies.* I examine how comics literacy dovetails with the goals of compositionists, as made visible in these two statements.

Comics in the Tower and the Trenches

In the last decade, comics have made significant inroads in literary studies: peer-reviewed journals, including *The International Journal of Comic Art, Studies in Comics, The Journal of Graphic Novels and Comics,* and the web journal *ImageTexT*, specialize in scholarly studies of comics. In 2008, *Modern Fiction Studies* devoted an entire issue to comics, and journals as prestigious as *PMLA* regularly include major articles on comics literature. Discussions of the graphic novel canon are in full swing, as books like 2009's *Teaching the Graphic Novel,* edited by Stephen Tabachnik, enter the academic conversation. In *PMLA* Hillary Chute, one of the most prolific comics theorists today, argues that "now is the time to expand scholarly expertise and interest in comics" because the comics medium "opens up some of the most pressing questions put to literature today" (462). In the twenty-first century, as humanities scholarship turns more interdisciplinary and definitions of art and literature become less genre- and medium-bound, a greater acceptance of comics as art and literature seems inevitable.[1]

In composition studies, on the other hand, the optimistic (yet somewhat disappointing) pedagogical program suggested by Paul Buhle in a 2003 *Chronicle of Higher Education* article seems typical of critical approaches to comics pedagogy.[2] After wondering aloud whether comics "represent something like the last horizon of the professor or student in pursuit of an unexhausted topic," Buhle's program finally settles on the reductive "connect with the students" model: "In one format or another, they [comics] will reach the kids. That should be our cue as well." Buhle, widely recognized as a "prodigious force of this evolving movement's left wing" (Dooley), retains with his enthusiasm a hint of the sighing pedagogue. As Buhle says in a 2008 interview, "In one sense, it's my response to the fact that my students, undergrad and grad alike, read fewer 'regular' books each year" (Dooley). Buhle's dedication to comics is obvious; he started *Radical America Komix* in 1969 and edited both a comics history of the Students for a Democratic Society (SDS) and a comics adaptation of Howard Zinn's *A People's History of the United States.* Considering his career, one wonders why such hedging is necessary.

While comics scholarship has developed legitimacy in narratology, deconstruction, and feminist and queer rhetorics, rhetoric and composition instructors are still a step behind and have yet to integrate fully comics into classrooms. Many instructors are willing to accommodate comics into composition, as attested by the abundance of *Calvin and Hobbes* strips or pages from *Maus* in new composition textbooks. But as of yet, conference presentations and articles focused on the practical and theoretical uses of comics in composition instruction remain in their beginnings. A number of textbooks have appeared that seem promising: Jeffrey Kahan and Stanley Stewart's *Caped Crusaders 101: Composition Through Comic Books*, James Bucky Carter's edited volume *Building Literacy Connections With Graphic Novels*, and Nancy Frey and Douglas Fisher's *Teaching Visual Literacy: Using Comic Books, Graphic Novels, Anime, Cartoons, and More to Develop Comprehension and Thinking Skills*. But these titles continue the trend of treating comics as pedagogical tools for building conventional literacy, only hinting toward an expanded view of multimodal literacies.

More promising, *Understanding Rhetoric: A Graphic Guide to Writing*, written by Elizabeth Losh and Jonathan Alexander, and illustrated by Kevin and Zander Cannon, deploys the comics essay form originated by Will Eisner (*Sequential Art*) and Scott McCloud (*Understanding Comics*) to teach students the basics of rhetoric. Like McCloud's *Understanding Comics*, *Understanding Rhetoric* exemplifies the pedagogical potential of comics by including the authors as characters, providing an energetic, Socratic dialogue; two student characters to address the anxieties and challenges of real students in social and educational contexts; and a fully-developed overview of the history of rhetoric, the uses of rhetoric in real life, and the prevalence of multimodal rhetoric in modern culture. *Understanding Rhetoric* not only demonstrates the pedagogical uses of comics as texts, but also begins to answer the question posed in Anson's "Trudy Does Comics"—namely, how can instructors help students use visual literacy to create their own texts?

Rhetorical Knowledge

The WPA places "rhetorical knowledge" at the head of its *Outcomes Statement*. To gain rhetorical knowledge, students "focus on a purpose," "respond to the needs of different audiences," and "respond appropriately to different kinds of rhetorical situations." Rhetorical knowledge is indeed relevant to understanding comics. In many ways, the terms for the conversation were set in nonscholarly books by two practitioners, Eisner and McCloud. Eisner's 1985 *Comics and Sequential Art* remains an invaluable textbook for aspiring artists, while McCloud begins the rhetorical conversation with *Understanding Comics*, an influential study of the storytelling, aesthetic, and rhetorical potential of the comics medium that he expands upon in *Reinventing Comics* and *Making Comics*. Both practitioners realize that comics require a radically different kind of literacy than does conventional prose literacy. As Eisner explains, writing comics "is a special skill, its requirements not always in common with other forms of 'writing' for it deals with a singular technology" in which writing and image-making "are irrevocably interwoven" (*Comics* 122). McCloud emphasizes the disconnect between the two modes, explaining, "Our need for a unified language of comics sends us toward the center where words and picture are like two sides of one coin. But our need for sophistication in comics seems to lead us outward, where words and pictures are most separate" (*Understanding* 49). While McCloud has deepened and complicated his definition in subsequent volumes, the terms introduced in *Understanding Comics* have largely stuck.

McCloud's definition has emerged as the baseline among comics scholars, intellectuals, and practitioners, as much out of convenience as conviction; not everyone who comments on comics knows Thierry Groensteen, or Chute, or Charles Hatfield, but they are likely to have read *Understanding Comics.* However, in a 2001 reconsideration of *Understanding Comics*, Dylan Horrocks (another comics creator and author of the acclaimed *Hicksville*), cautions against comics theorists' willingness to readily, and often uncritically, accept what he calls McCloud's "nation-building," the attempt to effectively create a single, monolithic understanding of what constitutes comics. Horrocks is concerned with the danger of "adopting [*Understanding Comics*] as a manifesto," when it is more helpful as a map, one of many, for "an infinitely complex landscape." "Sequential art" suffers from the prioritization of art over words, he writes, though McCloud and Eisner argue for their equality. Horrocks, however, points out McCloud's underlying lexophobia, arguing that McCloud essentially distrusts the ability of words to express ideas precisely, and "seems to be exploring a possible solution: replacing words with his own invented vocabulary of pictograms," an experiment "doomed to fail" as all artificial attempts to purify language have failed. Horrocks' preference would seem to be a graced state of free play, or an artistic anarchy, free of artificial borders and the compulsion to define.

Other theorists continue to refine the definition of comics. Ian Hague presents the "Definitional Program" in *Comics and the Senses*, differentiating between elemental, knowingly incomplete, and social definitions of comics. Elemental definitions seek to "identify comics on the basis of specific, observable characteristics" such as format or genre, construct "knowingly incomplete definitions" that refuse to draw hard boundaries between comics and other text/image hybrids, and empower "social definitions" that accept as comics anything identified as such by creators or readers (12-18). Robert Harvey insists on defining comics as the "static blending of word and picture for narrative purpose" (3), while Dale Jacobs deepens the definition by adding the qualifications that "comics are a rhetorical genre, comics are multimodal texts, comics are both an order of discourse and discrete discursive events" ("Marveling" 182). Groensteen denies the necessity of words altogether, arguing that "those who recognize in the verbal and equal status, in the economy of comics, to the image, begin from the principle that writing is the vehicle of storytelling in general," an assumption that wordless comics and film deny (8). As the many definitions indicate, comics, as a medium and form, present significant rhetorical challenges for instructors and teachers. Comics are not prose. Nor are comics image. And yet, comics are also not merely a combination of the two. According to Chute, "comics doesn't blend the visual and the verbal—or use one simply to illustrate the other—but is rather prone to present the two nonsynchronously" (452). By linking two communication codes, comics potentially express a rhetorical richness beyond what either can accomplish alone. The NCTE, referring to multimodal forms in general, recognizes this effect: "All modes of communication are codependent. Each affects the nature of the content of the other and the overall rhetorical impact of the communication event itself."

This hybrid form may be at once a more complex, and more natural, form of literacy. The NCTE *Position Statement* claims, "Young children practice multimodal literacies naturally and spontaneously," further explaining that from "an early age, students are very sophisticated readers and producers of multimodal work," needing help "to understand how these works make meaning, how they are based on conventions, and how they are created for and respond to specific communities or audiences." Similarly, McCloud, in Chapter 6 of *Understanding Comics*, argues that "show and tell" is an essential part of literacy learning. He shows a child demonstrating the workings of his toy robot to his elementary school class. While the boy limits his explanations to "It's got one of these things," showing one of the toy's features without naming it, the teacher insists on substituting words for gestures: "What is that, Tommy?" (138). As the episode progresses, Tommy again demonstrates an action the robot performs, while the teacher adds a verbal explanation, "The head flips back" (139). As McCloud explains, "We all started out like this, didn't we? Using words and images interchangeably" (139).

In McCloud's scene, the teacher represents the separation that culture maintains between word and gesture or between word and image, insisting on the primacy of word over gesture just as culture at large insists on the priority of word over image. McCloud illustrates a deep truth: that the division of word from image is synchronous with the division of word from gesture, and that both are instances of a sophistication that at once makes critical thinking and abstraction possible, and simultaneously limits our ability to communicate in other ways. In a sense, the "growth" or "maturity" from picture books to printed, pictureless text is the first instance of a specialization that continues throughout the education process and extends into the academy itself. The education system maintains artificial divisions between image and word, just as it maintains artificial distinctions between science and humanities.

Though the WPA *Outcomes Statement* somewhat diminishes the role of the author in the text, limiting mentions of authorial presence to "adopt appropriate voice, tone, and level of formality," authorial identity and presence are central to rhetorical knowledge. Developing an effective authorial *ethos* is often key to responding "to the needs of different audiences" and responding "appropriately to different kinds of rhetorical situations," as the outcomes outline. The comics medium offers numerous models for developing *ethos*. Many comics writers, particularly those of the autobiographical genres so prevalent in indie comics, picture themselves in their works. Harvey Pekar, Art Spiegelman, Alice Kominsky-Crumb and R. Crumb (often in collaboration), and others have made careers of caricaturing themselves in revealing, often scandalous fashion. McCloud, too, includes himself as a character frequently (see fig. 1), as do the authors of *Understanding Rhetoric*.

Fig. 1. Scott McCloud, in *Understanding Comics* (57) and *Making Comics* (5). Notice the graying temples in the later self-portrait.

Visuals make the writer transparent in a very different way than the writing of the prose memoirist. The comics writer may use images, including images of himself, to signify gestures, moods, and expressions that cannot be adequately conveyed in prose. Further, by portraying himself, "the inward vision takes on an outward form" (Hatfield 114). As Hatfield explains, the use of caricature in cartooning allows authors to "recognize and externalize his or her subjectivity" (115). By both revealing and objectifying oneself, the author creates "a sense of intimacy and a critical distance"—precisely the kind of tension that makes comics reading a uniquely multimodal experience.

Critical Thinking, Reading, and Writing

The second section of the WPA Outcomes Statement, "Critical Thinking, Reading, and Writing," suggests that students completing first-year writing should be able to "use writing and reading for inquiry, learning, thinking, and communicating." In comics, the media structure demands a particularly active kind of reading, and thus a particularly engaged kind of reader. Eisner believes that "in comics the imagining is done for the reader. An image once drawn becomes a precise statement that brooks little or no further interpretation" (*Sequential Art* 122). However, precisely the opposite is true: the mixture of images with words presents no less than a whole new set of interpretive tasks. The reader is no longer required to interpret only a set of words, nor is the viewer required to interpret only an image; the comics reader must interpret these two sets, as well as the relation between them, while also deciphering the relation of the whole panel (words and images) to the meta-panel of the page. David Punter tells us that reading comics "invites browsing, the taking of time to form multiple connections, time to re-read and see new depths in the connections between pictures, time to allow visual representations to sink in" (132). That is, comics demand a reading that takes time and effort different than prose reading.

Comics reading differs from prose reading in a number of key ways. While prose reading is linear and sequential, the comics page presents itself immediately as a whole; the comics reader has the option of scanning the whole page first to view the elements as a structural unity and thus intuit one level of meaning before reading a single word or panel. One school of thought, derived from Eisner and McCloud, conceives the "action" of comics as occurring in the spaces between panels (commonly called the "gutter"), filled in by the reader's imagination, but later theorists have critiqued this notion. Hatfield, for instance, points to the "synchronic" panel in which time "blurs" as multiple actions take place over one panel—that is, unlike the most common panel in which a single action is rendered, a synchronic panel presents actions that could not take place simultaneously in the same panel (53). As Groensteen argues, in comics, "the codes weave themselves inside a comics image in a specific fashion, which places the image in a narrative chain when the links are spread across space, in a situation of co-presence" (7). The links, or actions, are co-present on the page, with the space between and surrounding panels taking the place of time, creating a unique interpretive challenge. Yet even in sequence, there can be no prescribed order, as a comics reader may start with words, with images, or with various combinations—reading a caption, studying the image, then reading dialogue balloons, for instance.

Further, while Eisner asserts that "what goes on INSIDE the panel is PRIMARY" (*Sequential Art* 63; emphasis in original), Chute explains that in actual practice "a reader of comics not only fills in the gaps between panels but also works with the often disjunctive back-and-forth of reading and looking for meaning" (Chute 452). Like Chute, Hatfield argues that, rather than fixing meaning, comics are "texts that require a reader's active engagement and collaboration in making meaning" (33); the fragmentation in the comics form is its strength, encouraging "different reading strategies, or interpretive schema, than [readers] would use in their reading of conventional written text" (Hatfield 36). Jacobs too argues that comics readers are active creators of meaning rather than passive consumers, interacting with "paratextual elements, [. . .] using literacies acquired through the reading of not only comics but also written texts, visual texts, and people's bodies and facial gestures" (200).

Because of their multimodal nature, comics dictate a critical distance, whether in response to their visual distortion of reality, their collision of words and images, their potential openness in reading, or their static rendering of temporal experience. Immersion in a comics page is more difficult than in prose, which is temporal and necessarily sequential, or in the presence of image only, which is static and visible within a self-created context. As Groensteen suggests, in comics "the story is possibly full of holes, but it projects me into a world that is presented as consistent, and it is the continuity attributed to the fictional world that allows me to effortlessly fill in the gaps in the narration"" (11). In short, reading comics well requires work that closely resembles the work of interpreting real life—with its cacophony of images, words, sounds, and states (emotional, mental, physical). A reader cannot read comics on one level only (say, the efferent, or superficial, gleaning only data), as the juxtaposition of codes requires mental negotiations. As the NCTE statement explains in the context of multimodal literacy, "It is the interplay of meaning-making systems (alphabetic, oral, visual, etc.) that teachers and students should strive to study and produce." Comics literacy need not replace or damage prose literacy, but rather enlarge literacy in all its forms.

Knowledge of Conventions

Perhaps the primary objection to using comics in the composition classroom, either as reading assignments or as projects for evaluation, is the objection raised by the professor in Anson's example: the writing is not equivalent to an essay. That objection stands in for a number of similar objections, all growing from the same, pressing question: Can comics present complex ideas in a rigorous, academically appropriate way? One of the tasks of the composition classroom, as defined by the WPA *Outcomes Statement*, is to provide students with knowledge of the "conventions of usage, specialized vocabulary, format, and documentation in their fields." There are two ways in which comics can help students begin to master these conventions: first, through engagement with comics textbooks such as *Understanding Rhetoric;* and second, by asking students to make their own comics essays. As a textbook in the comics medium, *Understanding Rhetoric* provides possibly the only existing, appropriate example for using comics in a writing classroom. One of the unique features or capabilities a comics textbook provides (often exploited by McCloud in *Understanding Comics* and the sequels that follow) is the capacity to both explain and demonstrate conventions of argument and academic inquiry simultaneously, as opposed to an explanation followed by a separate illustration or example, as in a conventional textbook. In the comics form, explanation and example are one: the example is the explanation.

In "Issue 5," which is how *Understanding Rhetoric* organizes chapters, mimicking serial comics, the authors provide an excellent example of the potential for a comics textbook while discussing research and source usage. In "Coming Clean with Citation," authors Losh and Alexander cover plagiarism in a way only a comic could. In the scene, artists Kevin and Zander Cannon attempt to finish the chapter with characters plagiarized from the internet, explaining "The panel just wasn't working—and we didn't have time to start all over" (203). The artists, characters in the story, show themselves literally taping a cut-out figure over the images of the authors that have been used previously for the book (see fig. 2).

This comical scene motivates a discussion in which the Cannons, playing the part of naïve students, attempt to argue that "these characters were just there for the taking on the internet [. . .] so we figured it would be okay" (204), and enter into a dialogue with the authors, who explain the reasons for citing quotations: "Even material you find online was created by somebody," "what about your credibility as an artist?," and, "if you are going to quote someone else's work, have a good reason for reproducing it exactly" (204-05). Through the use of characters, and the device of the cut-out figures, the book succeeds in demonstrating plagiarism visually, explaining the concepts in a conversational manner for verbal learners, and performing the conventions it is explaining by citing the source of the cut-outs ("Tom Gammill, creator of The Doozies") in a footnote.

Fig. 2. Plagiarism made visible in *Understanding Rhetoric* (203).

Processes

According to the WPA *Outcomes Statement*, by the end of first-year writing a student should have a functional sense of process, understanding that "it usually takes multiple drafts to create and complete a successful text," and that writing is "an open process that permits writers to use later invention and re-thinking to revise their work." Drafting and revising are among the most crucial skills composition instructors instill in students, along with an understanding that writing, at least at an academic level, is frequently less raw talent and genius than planning, time, and work. For the individual creator, writing comics is a labor-intensive task, requiring a long development of craftsmanship and skill and a long process of writing, drafting, drawing, and finishing that unites the recursive process of composing with the equally recursive process of image-making. While an artist such as Charles Schultz may draw a daily strip consistently for fifty years (with short breaks), another artist such as Spiegelman may take weeks or months to produce a single page.[3] Writing a comic may begin with sketches, with a script, with a desired page design, or even with a conceptual or formal experiment (as in many of the early comics collected in Spiegelman's *Breakdowns*). Numerous comic artists, including R. Crumb and Spiegelman, have published their notebooks and sketches, demonstrating the planning, drafting, and revising that build their work.

In *Making Comics*, McCloud depicts the creative process as a series of rhetorical choices (see fig. 3) shaped by moment, frame, image, word, and what he calls "flow," or how panels transition (37). McCloud further develops his explanation of the process by creating a comic story on the fly, with a set of four stock characters set in a parodic crime story (involving an apparent drug deal, a surprise shooting, and a high-speed chase). McCloud narrates his choices, demonstrating how framing, detail, and panel-to-panel transitions affect the reader's experience. Then, after establishing the story, McCloud puts three different versions side-by-side to compare: a straightforward, basic version, and two revisions of increasing intensity and complexity (48-49).

In this sequence, McCloud demonstrates not only how different choices create rhetorical effects but also the importance of drafting to experiment with these effects. Further, McCloud demonstrates that no medium explains how comics work as well as comics do. McCloud acts out process on the page, consistent with the WPA's call to help students learn to "build final results in stages," creating a form that students can easily return to as they work to understand it.

Comics are an ideal site for collaborative work, an element of composition instruction that finds its way into both the WPA and NCTE statements. In the introduction to their *Outcomes Statement*, the WPA calls learning to write "a complex process, both individual and social," as is the writing process itself. The section on processes requests that students learn to "understand the collaborative and social aspects of writing processes," including learning how to "critique their own and others' works" and "balance the advantages of relying on others with the responsibility of doing their part." Collaboration has been a cornerstone of composition studies from the beginning of the discipline, whether in peer review and group projects in the classroom, or the collaborative studies of pioneering compositionists like Andrea Lunsford and Lisa Ede.

The authors of *Understanding Rhetoric* comment on their collaborative process in the introduction, explaining, "We knew that we would have to revise what we wrote based on what the illustrators drew," and that "if we hadn't all been willing to work with others' suggestions, we would have had a very limited and unsatisfactory book" (13). All four appear as speaking characters in the book, providing different perspectives and combining talents as the book demands.

Fig. 3. McCloud's three examples, each gaining in intensity (*Making Comics* 48-49).

As compositionists shift to multimodal rhetoric, collaboration becomes more crucial, as noted in the NCTE *Position Statement*: "Because of the complexity of multimodal projects and the different levels of skill and sensitivity each individual brings to their execution, such projects often demand high levels of collaboration and teamwork," a fact the authors realize will be somewhat distressing to instructors. As such, the NCTE authors reassure instructors: "Teachers of the English/Language Arts already have models for this type of collaboration, such as those for producing a play." Further, the statement provides examples of "other kinds of more traditional multimodal projects" requiring collaboration, such as "brochures, literary magazines, books, videos, or greeting cards." Any upcoming revision to the *Position Statement* would ideally include comics in that list.

It is a practical reality that many comics are created collaboratively. Collaborative authorship is true especially of commercial, popular comics, such as newspaper comic strips and superhero comics, which must meet daily and monthly deadlines that would strain the capacity of a single writer/artist. The division of labor in comics has often been a function of the demands of the publishing industry, with writers, pencilers, inkers, colorists, and others necessary to speed production. But the collaborative possibilities of comics also offer a richness of voices and perspectives. As Punter explains, with multiple artists working on the same text, "the visual representation of a character is allowed to run through a series of changes, held together not by imagistic coherence but by a free-flowing set of pictorial changes secured only by a style and material representation of dialogue" (132). Such multiplicity is not restricted to commercial superhero comics; it has also been used to great effect in Harvey Pekar's ongoing *American Splendor* series, as numerous artists present vastly different perspectives on Pekar's appearance, environment, and life experiences, united by Pekar's idiosyncratic voice (Hatfield 46-47).

While Eisner, characteristically, presents comics authorship in the Great Man model, asserting that "the departure from the work of a single individual to that of a team is generally due to the exigency of time" (*Sequential Art* 123), he recognizes the commercial reality of comic-book production. *Graphic Storytelling and Visual Narrative* includes an amusing page from Kevin Huizenga on the process of making a comic (see fig. 4). From initial idea to finished product, including such stages as scanning artwork, silk-screening color covers, and assembly, a different character performs each of these. Significantly, considering the previous discussion of drafting and revising, Huizenga presents the creative process of writing and drawing within an arrowed circle, alongside an empty thought balloon, all bracketed by "thinking."

The process in Huizenga's cartoon is moderately scaled in comparison to the major commercial operations McCloud discusses in *Reinventing Comics*—the covers are silkscreened one by one, and the "assembly" involves a photocopier and stapler—but even such a small-scale operation would be outside the means of students, except perhaps art majors with access to equipment. In today's digital environment, however, production of a comic is more within reach than ever. As the NCTE explains, "With the development of multimodal literacy tools, writers are increasingly expected to be responsible for many aspects of the writing, design, and distribution processes that were formerly apportioned to other experts." Authors routinely self-publish, in purely digital formats, even designing their own digital covers and layouts with simple, user-friendly tools. Students collaborating at all stages—writing, drawing, and composing pages for themselves in a digital environment—practice multiple rhetorical, invention, and composing skills within the scope of first-year composition.

Fig. 4. Eisner likely approved of the same character writing and drawing (*Graphic Storytelling* 21).

Composing in Electronic Environments

Both the WPA *Outcomes Statement* and the NCTE's *Position Statement* underscore the necessity of composing in digital environments, the WPA recognizing that "writing in the 21st-century involves the use of digital technologies for several purposes, from drafting to peer reviewing to editing" and arguing that teachers must prepare students for "common expectations." Two of the WPA's "common expectations" are worth considering in regard to comics: that students "use electronic environments for drafting, reviewing, revising, editing, and sharing texts" and "understand and exploit the differences in the rhetorical strategies and in the affordances available for both print and electronic composing processes and texts."[4] Since the outcomes statement was adopted in 2000, the first of these two has become moot; students use electronic environments for drafting, reviewing, and so on, beginning in elementary school. Using digital technology is not a goal for first-year writing, but is now the norm. Effectively using the technology to its potential may remain an area of instruction, but using technology more effectively is always an area of instruction, even if that technology is print books and pencils for taking notes. By now, in the middle of the second decade of the twenty-first century, students are accustomed to using electronic environments for composing texts.

In this area, the NCTE's 2005 statement is more relevant. The *Position Statement* explains, "there are increased cognitive demands on the audience to interpret the intertextuality of communication events that include combinations of print, speech, images, sounds, movement, music, and animation." Further, "Skills, approaches and attitudes toward media literacy, visual and aural rhetorics, and critical literacy should be taught in English/Language Arts classrooms." NCTE anticipates the current reality of digital media, recognizing in 2005 how essential multimodal literacy would become. But, more significantly, the statement recognizes the need for students to create multimodal texts. And those multimodal texts may easily look like comics.

Working from similar assumptions, Richard Lanham's descriptions of contemporary digital texts in *The Economics of Attention* can be applied to the generations-old comics medium. While warning that words "create one order of meaning, images another, and we don't want them too close together" (85), Lanham sees that "the digital expressive space moves [...] toward a more energetic oscillation between conceptual thought and behavior" by combining the sequential reading of alphabetic letters with the immediate apprehension of the picture plane (102-03). Print, according to Lanham, is marked by "fixity" and "invisibility," as it delivers meaning without calling attention to itself as a medium. But in comics, as in digital media, that "fixity comes unglued [. . .], and in the process we come to see the expressive surface, typography and style, to look at it rather than through it" (Lanham 80). The work involved in making comics goes hand in hand with its freedom, lending the medium a unique self-consciousness similar to that which Lanham argues is encouraged by digital texts. This openness extends not only to the forms of words, as in the choice of font in word processers or hand-drawn letters, but to the page itself; when the writer creates and selects every image and word in the meta-panel, s/he has options unavailable to either the prose writer or the image-maker.

But what use is an awareness of comics' special qualities to composition students? Simply put, comics literacy situates students within modernity's radically changing communication systems. Comics literacy can play a part in preparing students for the complex work of making meaning in an increasingly fragmented and multivocal rhetorical world. Jacobs' "Marveling at *The Man Called Nova*: Comics as Sponsors of Multi-Modal Literacy" argues that comics have "the ability to create meaning with and from texts that operate in print form and in come combination of visual, audio, and spatial forms as well" (181). A multimodal literacy is essential for intellectual survival in contemporary culture, as we find ourselves "navigating the world around us in complex ways that go well beyond functional print literacy or even an expanded, social constructivist version of print literacy" (183). By the combination of words and images, and of words as images (with images as synesthetic expressions of not only vision but also sound and texture), comics provide a practical and active training for navigating the world of mass media, advertising, and government propaganda, in domains from the digital to the freeway.

One barrier to students creating basic, functional comics—the skill set and difficulty involved—has been effectively leveled in recent years. The kind of comics-making described in Eisner's books as well as the tools that go along with traditional comics require years of practice, as anyone who has tried to draw with quill pens and brushes can attest. However, digital technology has rapidly replaced pen and paper. As far back as 2000, in *Reinventing Comics*, McCloud speculates on the future of comics creation, imagining that digital drawing slates and CPUs "can and probably will be combined, laptop-style, into a single wireless all-purpose drawing tool" (151). McCloud draws himself in a grassy field, drawing on something that looks an awful lot like a large iPad, ten years before that device's introduction.

Just as digital technology has made it easier for students to create effective, professional recordings, videos, and presentations, so tablets and comics-creating apps are making it easier for students to communicate using the comics medium, even without drawing talent. Popular webcomics like *The Oatmeal*, *Hyperbole and a Half*, and *XKCD* have made a virtue of their simple, even crude use of digital tools. For students, the drawing tablet–CPU hybrid McCloud imagined back in 2000 is an everyday reality, as is the capacity to create comics with a level of sophistication that required expensive, intimidating equipment even as recently as 2006, when McCloud warned readers that "a full suite of hardware and software can cost thousands" (*Making* 204). While professional cartoonists use more complex programs such as Photoshop or Sketchbook, students have a range of simpler and cheap or free apps and web programs to choose from for making functional (if not Eisner Award-winning) comics. Comics-making apps for tablets range from the crude and ridiculous (at least a half-dozen apps for making rage comics) to fairly sophisticated programs such as *Comic Book!*, an iPad app that lets users edit photos into a comic book format, with many options for altering images, adding texts, and designing the page, or *Comic Life*, a program that does the same for Mac or PC. While such programs offer more limited means of expression than ink and paper, they allow students who do not draw the ability to communicate in a medium they could not access otherwise.

Conclusion: Let Trudy Do Comics (and Presentations, and Photo-essays, and Websites. . .)

While digital humanists like Lanham look to the new literacy of digital technology, we have largely missed the fact that the generations-old comics medium offers the composition instructor an incredibly powerful tool for widening the literacies of her students and preparing them for the multiplicity of codes, rhetorics, messages, and manipulations that the contemporary world presents to them. Incorporating comics into the curriculum alongside other conventional and unconventional media enriches students' literacies enormously, preparing them for the world of discourse that surrounds them. Forward-thinking compositionists are incorporating digital literacy into the classroom, dealing successfully with all of the technical challenges that go into making students conversant in photo-processing, presentation, and web design programs. For those who are as expert in digital production as in rhetoric and composition, such advances are only logical. The fields in which students do and will produce texts in their lives are nothing like the traditional models of production and publication that have shaped writers' habits for generations. Writers are their own editors; authors self-publish without embarrassment; scholars turn from the dense, tiny print of bound journals to the interactive screen.

It is no longer necessary for an instructor who asks students to produce a photo-essay to justify her decision, nor should it be necessary for an instructor who wishes to assign a comic strip. The problem Trudy presents, to return to Anson's essay, is how to assess comics in a composition class. The problem is twofold: first, the problem of a student who refuses to write the assignment placed in front of her; and second, the problem of a professor who has difficulty imagining how to craft an assignment in any other form than an essay. As the NCTE *Position Statement* warns, "The complexity of multimodal work suggests that an assessment process must be developed and refined collaboratively by students, teachers, administrators, parents, and other stakeholders over time," a difficulty that "may prevent some teachers from attempting this kind of work." The statement's language makes it clear that such a process, however, must be collaborative—the instructor does not shoulder the burden alone. Understanding the rhetorical complexities of the comics form, Howard and Trudy can negotiate. That is, Trudy can make an effort to understand that writing situations require different kinds of forms and genres appropriate to the situation (one of which is comics, though not when an essay is required), while Howard can practice writing assignments that allow students more latitude in choosing their forms. Howard need not allow every assignment to be done in any form; rather, he may offer assignments in which comics (or other text-image forms) may be one appropriate product, and offer these assignments alongside more traditional essay-based assignments.

Permitting, or encouraging, students to produce their own comics, however, opens up a whole new understanding of authorship and authority that may have transformative effects. One of our greatest challenges as writing instructors is convincing students to own their authority as authors, to move from reluctant consumers of texts to producers. As Jared Gardner notes, we produce texts in an environment in which, for writers, the "choice of tools (pen, typewriter, laptop) have become irrelevant: the achievement of the author seems wholly independent of the tools or the act of making" (54). For students, this displacement makes the prospect of authorship even more distant; words are something generated out of the ether, read on an illuminated, unstable screen and immediately forgotten. As their reading, so their production—hurried, impersonal, and ephemeral. Comics-making, however, is a labor-intensive production, physically and mentally. Encouraging students to produce comics as essays is another means of encouraging students to slow down, to consider the power of their rhetorical productions, and to own their authorship in a more palpable way than typing glowing dots onto a screen.

Notes

1. As I am revising this essay, Nick Sousanis, a doctoral candidate at Columbia University, has completed a dissertation written and drawn entirely in comics. Excerpts have already appeared on his blog, *Spin, Weave, and Cut.* A comics essay on the endeavor has appeared in *Juniata Voices.*

2. Charles Hatfield gently criticizes Buhle in *Alternative Comics: An Emerging Literature,* calling the essay "underresearched" and lacking a "full acknowledgement" of the growing work of new conferences and publications (xi).

3. Working on *In the Shadow of No Towers,* many pages took longer than Spiegelman's monthly deadline, as much as five weeks according to the introductory essay, "The Sky is Falling!"

4. In the interest of space, I will save discussion of the relative advantages of web comics and conventional print comics for a subsequent article. In the meantime, I would direct readers to Dale Jacobs's recent article, "Webcomics, Multimodality, and Information Literacy," which lays out the issues.

Works Cited

Anson, Chris. "Trudy Does Comics." *The WAC Casebook: Scenes for Faculty Reflection and Program Development.* Ed. Chris Anson. New York: Oxford UP, 2002. 28-32. Print.

Buhle, Paul. "The New Scholarship of Comics." *The Chronicle of Higher Education* 49.36 (16 May 2003): B7. Print.

Carter, James Bucky, ed. *Building Literacy Connections with Graphic Novels: Page by Page, Panel by Panel.* Urbana: NCTE: 2007. Print.

Chute, Hillary. "Comics as Literature? Reading Graphic Narrative." *PMLA* 123 (2008): 452-65. Print.

Council of Writing Program Administrators. *WPA Outcomes Statement for First-Year Composition.* WPA, 17 July 2014. PDF file. 3 Dec. 2014. <http://www.wpacouncil.org/positions/outcomes.html>.

Dooley, Michael. "Power to the Panels: An Interview with Paul Buhle." *AIGA Journal of Design.* Amer. Inst. of Graphic Design. 17 June 2008. Web. 3 Dec. 2012. <http://www.aiga.org/content.cfm/power-to-the-panels-an-interview-with-paul-buhle>.

Eisner, Will. *Comics and Sequential Art.* Tamarac: Poorhouse, 1985. Print.

---. *Graphic Storytelling and Visual Narrative.* 1996. New York: Norton, 2008. Print.

Frey, Nancy, and Douglas Fisher. *Teaching Visual Literacy: Using Comic Books, Graphic Novels, Anime, Cartoons and More to Develop Comprehension and Thinking Skills.* Newbury Park: Corwin, 2008. Print.

Gardner, Jared. "Storylines." *SubStance* 40.1 (2011): 53-69. Print.

Groensteen, Thierry. *The System of Comics.* Jackson: UP of Mississippi, 2009. Print.

Hague, Ian. *Comics and the Senses.* New York: Routledge, 2014. Print.

Harvey, Robert C. *The Art of the Comic Book: An Aesthetic History.* Jackson: UP of Mississippi, 1996. Print.

Hatfield, Charles. *Alternative Comics: An Emerging Literature.* Jackson: UP of Mississippi, 2005. Print.

Horrocks, Dylan. *Hicksville.* Montreal: Drawn & Quarterly, 2014.

---. "Inventing Comics: Scott McCloud's Definition of Comics." *Comics Journal* 234 (2001): n. pag. Web. 3 Dec. 2014. <http://www.hicksville.co.nz/Inventing%20 Comics.htm>.

Jacobs, Dale. "Marveling at the Man Called Nova: Comics as Sponsors of Multimodal Literacy." *CCC* 59 (2007): 180-205. Print.

---. "Webcomics, Multimodality, and Information Literacy." *ImageText* 7.3 (2014): n. pag. Web. 20 Oct. 2014. < http://www.english.ufl.edu/imagetext/archives/v7_3/jacobs/>.

Kahan, Jeffrey, and Stanley Stewart. *Caped Crusaders 101: Composition Through Comic Books.* Jefferson: McFarland, 2006. Print.

Lanham, Richard A. *The Economics of Attention: Style and Substance in the Age of Information.* Chicago: U of Chicago P, 2006. Print.

Losh, Elizabeth, Johnathan Alexander, Kevin Cannon, and Zander Cannon. *Understanding Rhetoric: A Graphic Guide to Writing.* Boston: Beford/St. Martin's, 2013. Print.

McCloud, Scott. *Making Comics: Storytelling Secrets of Comics, Manga and Graphic Novels.* New York: Harper, 2006. Print.

---. *Reinventing Comics: How Imagination and Technology are Revolutionizing an Art Form.* New York: Harper, 2000. Print.

---. *Understanding Comics*. New York: Paradox, 1993. Print.

National Council of Teachers of English. "Position Statement on Multimodal Literacies." *NCTE*. NCTE, 18 Aug. 2008. Web. 3 Dec. 2014. <http://www.ncte.org/positions/statements/multimodalliteracies>.

Punter, David. "Postmodernism, Criticism and the Graphic Novel." *Authorship in Context: From the Theoretical to the Material*. Eds. Kyiaki Hadjiafxendi and Polina Mackay. New York: Palgrave MacMillan, 2007. 131-44. Print.

Sousanis, Nick. "Comics as a Tool for Inquiry: Concerning a Dissertation in Comic Book Form." *Juniata Voices* 12 (2012): n. pag. Web. 30 Nov. 2014. <http://www.juniata.edu/services/jcpress/voices/pdf/2012/jv_2012_162-172.pdf>.

Spiegelman, Art. *In the Shadow of No Towers*. New York: Pantheon, 2004. Print.

Tabachni, Stephen, ed. *Teaching the Graphic Novel*. New York: MLA. 2009. Print.

Beyond Talking Heads: Sourced Comics and the Affordances of Multimodality

Hannah Dickinson and Maggie M. Werner

This article analyzes the genre of the sourced comic as an important pedagogical tool in the development of both alphabetic and multimodal literacies. We argue that sourced comics provide multiple design elements with which students can explore their complex relationships with scholarly sources, make visible various power relations informing students' source engagement, and expand and demystify the strategies students might use to engage scholarly sources in their future multimodal and alphabetic writing practices. Based on these affordances, our analysis suggests that sourced comics have pedagogical value as a form of multimodal academic writing.

Among teachers of writing, it has become *de rigueur* to speak early and often of academic conversations. Our conferences are grand conversations; our journals professionalize them; our talks with colleagues in the halls and on listservs perpetuate them, redirect them, and complicate them. And—most importantly for our purposes here—our pedagogies enact them. While the metaphor of conversation is tossed around innocently enough, in the last fifteen years it has become systematized. Conversation no longer refers only to the practices of our scholarly lives, it has come to be a paradigmatic metaphor for teaching students in composition classrooms how to relate to and engage with academic sources, debates, and discourses (Bruffee; Ellis; Graff and Birkenstein; Harris; Lynch; Olson). Yet, it is also a metaphor that seems to baffle our students: "What do you *mean* I should be in conversation with my sources?" In an attempt to remedy this confusion, we introduced an assignment that requires students to depict imagined conversations with and among published scholars. Using the desktop publishing program Comic Life 2 by plasq, students created comics in which they were directed to engage in "conversation" with scholars. With the support of a teaching and learning grant from our institution, we piloted the assignment in three different composition classes and studied the efficacy of employing comics as a tool for deepening students' engagement with source material.

When we began this study and introduced this assignment to our students, we viewed the genre of the sourced comic merely as a vehicle for teaching students how to engage with academic sources. Yet, the comics students produced took up traditional academic scholarship in such innovative ways—in terms of design, power, and knowledge production—that we were compelled to consider the sourced comic not just as a means to an alphabetic end, but as a powerful pedagogical genre in its own right. The sourced comics provided us, as well as our students, with important insight into how undergraduate writers engage scholarly sources and authors, making visible the range of roles available to students as they negotiate their own power and authority in relation to source material. Thus, we suggest that the sourced comic—a visual, linguistic, audio, gestural, and spatial genre explicitly concerned with the use of scholarly source material—is a valuable pedagogical tool because it (1) affords students a much wider range of design elements with which to articulate their understandings of and relationships with scholarly sources than traditional textual genres, (2) makes visible the variety of power relations that inform students' engagement with scholarly sources, providing valuable opportunities for metacognition and formative assessment, and (3) simultaneously expands and demystifies—through invention, play, and reflection—the strategies students might use to engage scholarly sources in their future multimodal and alphabetic writing practices.[1]

These conclusions about the value of the sourced comic as a pedagogical genre are drawn from our analysis of forty-two students' sourced comics. The comics were created by students at Hobart and William Smith Colleges, a selective, small liberal arts institution. Of the students whose comics we analyzed, 60% identified as women and 40% as students of color. The race and gender of the student authors (and perhaps of the scholars they cite) may well be a factor in how students chose to position themselves in relation to the scholars in their comics. Indeed, we argue that one of the benefits of using the sourced comic as a pedagogical tool is that it provides opportunities for both students and professors to analyze and reflect on the ways undergraduate writers negotiate complex networks of power, which undoubtedly include race, gender, education, and other factors. In the analysis that follows, however, we were careful not to make assumptions about how students' racialized or gendered identities might have impacted their authorial choices; given our small sample size and the fact that we did not interview students, this seemed like the most ethical way to proceed.

Two of the classes we studied, introductory composition courses, created sourced comics as a prewriting assignment in preparation for a persuasive research essay, for which students were required to include images of the authors. The third class, a 300-level course in composition theory and pedagogy, asked students to synthesize four readings from the course and offer their own intervention into the imagined conversation. In this version, students were invited to depict the four scholars in an imaginative setting and were permitted to use representational images of the scholars, rather than their actual photographs.

The assignment sheet provided in both courses offered no instructions about how to use the comic form or how to relate to the scholars. Instead, we simply instructed students to "put four sources in conversation with each other and yourself." While a more specific assignment might help students engage their sources in a more dialogic and egalitarian fashion, our less directive assignment gave us valuable insights into the multiple ways in which students make sense of the notion of engaging in "conversation" with sources.

In addition to the flexible boundaries of our assignment, the multimodal nature of comics also encouraged the various relationships we saw our students forging with and among sources. Multimodal compositions, like comics, are those that "take advantage of a range of rhetorical resources—words, still and moving images, sounds, music, animation—to create meaning" (Anderson et al. 59). Moving from strictly alphabetic texts to ones that communicate through multiple modes necessarily extends the boundaries of literacy. This expanded literacy "includes understanding and competent control of representational forms . . . such as visual images and their relationship to the written word" (New London Group 61). Thus the multimodality of comics—a genre that combines "sequential art and text in order to create narrative meaning for the audience"—means that they function as a critically engaged "multiliteracy" rather than a "debased form of print literacy" (Jacobs, "Marveling" 182). When we understand comics as more than just picture stories with simple text, they can be integrated into the composition curriculum as a critical part of, not adjunct to, literacy learning. Through our assignment, we found support for Dale Jacobs' claims that comics encourage an expansive form of literacy and that examining the literate practices surrounding comics can enlighten writing teachers to the many ways that all multimodal texts "can and should affect our pedagogies" ("Marveling" 183). Through our students' comics, we found that we not only gave students new ways to engage with sources but also gave us new insight into how our previous pedagogy obscured the resources students already *had* for engaging with sources.

We were able to understand the varied ways students interact with sources by applying Jacobs' method for analyzing comics' multimodal meaning-making features to our students' sourced comics. We also analyzed students' uses of sequencing, attending especially to issues of narrative, redundancy (Groensteen 115), action (Postema 58), mise-en-page (Kukkonen 19), and closure (McCloud 67). Throughout our analysis, we were especially struck by the care students took to differentiate themselves from the scholar-characters in their comics; while students were often willing to take up positions of power or authority in their comics, they very rarely occupied the same role or position as the scholar-characters they depicted. Indeed, students almost universally circumvented the task of "having a conversation" in either a casual or academic way. Instead they found ways to interact that often highlighted the power inequities between themselves and published scholars. By taking on the role of "interviewer" or "conference organizer" and the attendant gestures, language, and sounds of those positions, students used the design elements of comics to enact complex, in-progress, and highly personalized relationships with their source material that exceed and complicate the requirements of textual literacy practices, which tend to insist that students control their sources. Across all three classes, students positioned themselves in multiple and unpredictable ways. Here, we suggest that it is precisely because comics are a multimodal genre that they can help students and educators think more expansively and critically about the complex networks of power that shape students' engagements with academic sources.

Affordances of Comics in the Classroom

Initially, we brought to the sourced comic assignment some troubling attitudes about the value of comics and multimodality. We imagined that the sourced comics might provide a high interest, accessible approach to understanding the use of source material with the goal of improving students' alphabetic literacy practices. In some cases the sourced comics did improve students' production of alphabetic texts. We also discovered, however, that, because comics are such "complex textual environments" (Jacobs, "More Than Words" 22), they presented our students with powerful opportunities to articulate and reflect on their own relationships with academic sources that moved well beyond the sourced comic's value as an invention activity in the service of alphabetic literacy. Our initial understanding of the role of comics in students' literacy practices is far too common. As Jacobs argues, "in the development of children's and adolescents' literacies, reading comics has almost always been seen as a debased form of word-based literacy, albeit an important intermediate step to more advanced forms of textual literacy, rather than as a complex form of multimodal literacy" ("More Than Words" 20). As our analysis makes clear, it is precisely because of comics' complexities that students were able to articulate and reflect on relationships to and among the scholars they cite. In other words, the sourced comic should not be understood as a tool for improving students' essays, but as itself a pedagogical genre.

Sourced comics provide students with an opportunity to "hear" themselves and their scholarly sources. Jacobs argues that "we are better able to 'hear' the voice of the narrator because we can see what words are emphasized by the bold lettering and we associate particular kinds of voices with the narrative voice" (*Graphic Encounters* 14). A similar dynamic was at work in students' sourced comics. They were better able to "hear" their own voices and the voices of the cited scholars because the range of representational possibilities was both extensive and complex. While not all of the students' sourced comics included narrators, they were all compelled to confront the questions: What kind of voice does this speaker have? How can I best represent that voice not only through words, but also through images, typography, and sequencing? The requirement that students represent scholarly voices, as well as their own, within the genre of the sourced comic allowed students to draw on a wide variety of meaning-making strategies, which extend far beyond words and paragraphs.

If comics help students to "hear" their sources, they also afford students the opportunity to "see" as and with their sources. The kinds of engagements with academic source material that comics make possible—possibilities that support and exceed those allowable in alphabetic texts—reflect Kristie Fleckenstein's theorization of the affordances of polymorphic literacy, in which "reading and writing . . . draw on verbal and nonverbal ways of shaping meaning" (613). Describing the impact of polymorphic literacy on students' understandings of place, Fleckenstein writes: "Too frequently place is transparent, a taken-for-granted reality outside of our control that escapes our conscious attention. Requiring students to create verbal images of place engages them in what Berthoff calls *seeing as*. We do not see; we see as or see with" (629; emphasis in original). We make a similar argument about academic source material, which can also too often be viewed by students as a static, "taken-for-granted reality out of [their] control." Requiring students to render academic source material in multiple modes allows them to "see as or see with" their sources. The comics students produce—artifacts of seeing as and with their sources—provide students and educators with meaningful opportunities to analyze the constraints and affordances that scholarly sources, and their associated power relations, bring to bear on their speaking, reading, writing, and thinking.

Comic scholarship across a variety of disciplines has argued for the usefulness of comics in teaching because they can provide students with multiple modes of communication in one genre that together build critical and multiliterate competencies (Bitz; Carter; Cary; Frey and Fisher; Jacobs, *Graphic Encounters*; Monnin; Versaci). Comics are layered with diverse symbolic forms that work together to "break down the barriers that text is often thought to erect: Image and text, visual and verbal, author and reader, content and form," making them a valuable pedagogical tool (Helms). Students confront significant barriers when finding, citing, integrating, and developing academic source material. While the sourced comics students produced did not always break down boundaries between scholars and students, it did help to reveal them, allowing our students and ourselves an opportunity to question both the unspoken and explicit divisions we experience between scholarly sources and student voices.

Entering the Conversation...about Conversation

Within composition studies, the conversation metaphor is typically traced to Kenneth Burke's imagined parlor as described in *The Philosophy of Literary Form*. Burke invites his readers to imagine a parlor filled with people engaged in a "heated" discussion that has long preceded their arrival and will persist after their departure. These "interminable" discussions are ones the new arrival must carefully listen to and assess before joining (110-11). Burke's parlor conversation has become a dominant metaphor for teaching composition students how to engage with academic source material.

We do not acknowledge often enough, however, the complex networks of power that inform the ways that scholarly conversations take place and are taken up by students. While we might teach students how to integrate, agree, disagree, or build on a scholarly source, we rarely ask students to consider how they might situate their own power, authority, and knowledges in relation to these sources. The sourced comic makes such meta-critical moves possible because it both broadens the range of allowable design elements and offers an opportunity to think critically about the assumptions embedded in alphabetic literacies.

That our students' comics didn't clearly depict common interpretations of academic conversation suggests that the genre provided them with an opportunity to articulate their skepticism of a metaphor that imagines we all—intellectual giants, professors, graduate students, and undergraduate students—have been invited into the same space *and* invited to participate equally. Through the affordances of the comic genre, students in our study interpreted and even reimagined conversation in ways that differed from the parlor metaphor as we understood it, showing that "academic conversation" is neither as argumentative nor as egalitarian as common interpretations of the parlor metaphor might suggest. For even if new participants are able to grasp the tenor and formulate a perspective, they might not—considering the power of the company in the parlor—be able to "put in [an] oar" (Burke 110).

Likewise, conversation exists in both casual and academic modes and these modes can be confusing for students. Textbooks like Gerald Graff and Cathy Berkenstein's *They Say, I Say* and Joseph Harris's *Rewriting* provide models for learning the "moves" of academic conversation in an attempt to demystify the process. Erik Ellis argues, however, that pedagogical treatments of the conversation metaphor ignore the unrehearsed nature of conversation and suggest that academic conversations follow rules that cannot be broken, ignored, or altered. This may be true of claim-driven, alphabetic texts, but the sourced comic makes space for students to include the full range of features that make up conversation: inflection, gesture, interruption, spatial positioning, and visual cues.

Furthermore, meaningful engagement with sources extends beyond an understanding of academic discourse; students must also negotiate power imbalances that arise from differences in knowledge and experience. The genre of the sourced comic allows students not only to practice reading and understanding sources but also to figure out where they stand in relation to them. In doing so, the comics show the creative ways in which students negotiate power relations and stake out arguments. In their comics, many students demonstrated delight at holding ideas in common with published authors. Yet, when it came to enacting dialogic turn taking—which the genre of the comic supports and the assignment required—students, for the most part, imagined other kinds of interactions. They called scholars on the phone for "help with a paper"; they facilitated academic conferences; they interviewed scholars; they rarely, however, created conversations in which they participated in the kind of egalitarian exchange that the parlor metaphor imagines. Thus the genre of the sourced comic provided students with the opportunity to engage sources in ways that include, and go beyond, egalitarian dialogic exchange and to reflect on these choices in ways that highlighted the power discrepancies they felt in their imagined talks with scholars.

"I'm Only a College Student!": Negotiating Roles in Comic Conversations

Students adopted a variety of roles in their sourced comics, yet they almost always emphasized the differences between themselves and scholars. The three most common roles students took up were as follows: (1) learner in the conversation (while the scholars were the experts); (2) someone with first-hand experiences (while the scholars reported on the experiences of others); and (3) organizer of the conversation (while the scholars were participants). Because comics offer a wide array of design elements, students can engage with sources in creative ways that are often seen as markers of faulty academic writing, a genre that encourages students to make claims with authority and to position themselves as equals in a conversation they are just entering. Thus, these roles demonstrate the options students embraced while negotiating power differences. By allowing students the opportunity to work through source engagement without requiring them to speak with expertise, sourced comics can provide a window to "see" how students are negotiating their relationship to scholarly sources.

One of the most common roles that students inhabited was that of learner. The multiple design opportunities afforded by comics not only enabled this role, but also made it an appropriate and important way for students to participate actively, even though they do not possess the same power and authority as their scholars. Chelsea D., for example, insists on her novice status through audio and linguistic strategies, allowing her to dramatize and explicate the ways in which she learns from her experts.[2] After her college president introduces the speakers and each is given a chance to make a claim, Chelsea finally appears, as do her thoughts in a bubble: "I haven't done a study yet. I'm only a college student and I don't have a PhD" (see fig. 1).

Fig. 1. "Impacts of Texting on Literacy and Spelling Skills." 2012. Chelsea Dunay.

In this thought bubble (an audio design element that shows what is "unheard" in her comic), Chelsea D. makes explicit the ways in which students and scholars enter academic conversations on fundamentally unequal terrain. Scholars have empirical data to back up their claims, while students have rarely done first-hand "scholarship, analysis, or research"; thus, taking on the voice and persona of an authority can be difficult for students and frustrating for readers (Bartholomae 136). The sourced comic, however, provides students with an opportunity to make visible these complex negotiations with scholarly authority. Chelsea D. uses the thought bubble to build her *ethos* not as a scholarly equal, but as a learner. She acknowledges her limitations and considers the reason she might not know the answer to her research question: she hasn't studied it enough, but she also suggests later that she is open to new information provided by trustworthy sources and to changing her mind. Chelsea situates herself as distinct from the scholars and in need of their expertise. Her design choices show her as a thoughtful learner, doing what learners do, assessing what they do not know, seeking information, and developing a stance.

Other students also strategically employed gestural strategies to emphasize their roles. Kristin doesn't explicitly clarify her student status, but includes photographs of herself making faces that alternate between a thinking expression in which she looks up and holds a finger to her chin and a perplexed one when she asks questions. While no doubt exaggerated, this gestural design choice dramatizes Kristin's thinking, questioning, and learning processes even when her linguistic design doesn't explicitly articulate these positions. Kristin also uses audio design to articulate her own perspective in a thought bubble, showing that she does indeed "get it," but that she's unwilling to share her knowledge with the scholars, although she shows it to the audience (see fig. 2)[3].

Fig. 2. "Creative to Academic Writing." 2012. Kristin Ressel.

Kristin illustrates that she is considering, not just accepting, what the scholars are saying, and she makes a perceptive connection between what she is studying and Bloom's taxonomy. While her gestures show her as an uninformed student, the multiple design elements working together demonstrate that she understands the arguments of her sources and how to use them to support her own ideas. As the two examples in Figure 2 illustrate, Kristin's comic exemplifies the design flexibility students used to create their roles in the comics, which allowed them ways to tentatively make assertions (often in the form of a thought bubble) that they did not feel authorized to own fully. As readers of the sourced comic, we can appreciate the meanings that students craft in multiple modes.

Anna also strategically uses gestural design elements in her comic to illustrate her role as a learner, as she plays with her authority/lack of authority. She explicitly embodies her position and seems to relish the options afforded by the comic genre and the humor with which she can begin to articulate her thoughts on a topic through her design. Anna is particularly playful in her gestures, using pictures of herself reacting to the scholars, who stay frozen in the same image as they pose various claims. She is alone in the first panel with a thought bubble that reads, "Hmm…I wonder if class size has a positive effect on student achievement. I think it does!!" In the next panel, an expert on class size appears, and Anna gasps in surprise (see fig. 3).

Fig. 3. "Class Size versus Student Achievement." 2012. Anna Miano.

The panels that follow are all long rectangles in which Anna always appears on the left and additional scholars are added on the right side of the panel; by the end of the comic, Anna is pictured in a panel with four scholars. Figure 3 shows Anna's shifting facial expressions in subsequent panels as each new scholar is added to the conversation.

While Anna does not provide significant ideas of her own within the comic, she suggests that meaningful intellectual work is occurring through her sequencing strategies. Throughout the comic, Anna plays with her spatial design and sequencing as scholars continue to appear out of thin air, suggesting that control is an important part of the learner role. While she selected these authors, the serendipity of the scholars' appearances helps make visible the ways in which, as researchers, we rarely have full control over our sources. We can stumble upon a valuable source or an interesting idea; scholars and texts we have forgotten or misunderstood can be reanimated by the right question or the right moment. Anna emphasizes this through her gestural, linguistic, and audio design choices: the scholars make claims (linguistic), she shows us her surprise, interest, confusion, thoughtfulness (gestural), and she accentuates her words with rhetorically appropriate punctuation so we better "hear" her (audio). Further, Anna's use of sequencing suggests that her reactions to new information are important actions even if she does not yet find herself in a position to contribute her own ideas to the scholarship she is encountering. By repeating the same panel shape and structure over and over, Anna adds further emphasis to her shifting facial expressions; Anna's face provides the only action in the sequence (aside from the word and thought bubbles). The actions represented by Anna's face help her to enhance her *ethos* as a learner.

Sourced comics also afforded students opportunities to reference their own experiences in order to apply—and even extend—the theories of scholars. As with the role of learner, academic texts—spaces for authoritative declaration based on research—often do not explicitly valorize the role of "experiencer." In Michael's comic, he positions himself as experiencer to explore the relationship between socialization and language, and his gestural, linguistic, and spatial choices emphasize his personal authority. In the text, he introduces vocabulary specific to the scholars' discourse —"code-switching"—and while he doesn't credit this term to an author, he verifies it by referring to his own experiences. We can see Michael's attempt to participate in the conversation as an equal; to do so, however, he can call on no original research. He strategically applies concepts he's learned in class to his own experience, a kind of evidence that he *does* have authority to use in this genre. Michael reinforces the personal authority he is claiming linguistically through the gestural mode. He is often called on to participate by the scholars: they ask him to describe certain concepts, like literacy sponsorship, and, on one occasion, ask him to describe his own experiences with discourse. When he answers, he looks directly at the reader to emphasize his control over his own experiences. He also uses spatial design to equalize his position. He gives himself as much (or more) space as his scholars, at one point filling a whole page with his own speech bubbles, creating a sequence in which his experiential authority is central to the narrative (see fig. 4).

Fig. 4. "When Minds Collide." 2012. Michael Ortiz.

The ways in which students used the design elements provided by comics to position their experiences were not always as explicit as Michael's use. Scarlynn, for example, identifies herself as being part of the constituency her sources are discussing, yet in the first three pages of her comic, she asks the scholars questions and summarizes their comments without revealing her stake in the discussion. She makes the gestural design choice to use the same picture of herself each time she speaks. In this photograph, she looks directly into the camera with a slight smile on her lips. Her arms are up as she pulls her long, straight hair back with a pair of sunglasses (see fig. 5). Linguistically and gesturally she positions herself as a learner. However, on the fourth page, when she begins to articulate her own experiences, we're introduced to a new image of Scarlynn, and a new voice as well (see fig. 5). In this picture, she looks down, frowning, as she holds her head in her hand and exclaims, "This is so frustrating!! I want to see future generations of minorities with primary discourses that are acceptable!" Scarlynn continues to move back and forth between these two photos throughout the rest of the comic. The smiling "learner Scarlynn" asks the scholars questions and synthesizes answers, while the frowning "experiencer Scarlynn" expresses growing frustration with comments like, "I guess we are set up for failure everywhere we go." Scarlynn's design—in particular the linguistic (she speaks differently depending on her role), the audio (she uses capitals and multiple exclamation points to underscore her frustrations), and the clear gestural differences illustrate that she is constructing her comic to push at inequality, which she is excruciatingly aware she inhabits. Scarlynn cleverly uses the alternating modes of learner and experiencer to suggest that the reality of the differences in power, experience, and knowledge are reflected in her as a "student body." When she attempts to assimilate—to mimic the normal discourse of the authorities—she is smiling, polished, confident, yet this position continues to come into conflict with her experiential knowledge, leaving her frowning, frustrated and holding her head as if she is in pain.

The distinction Scarlynn creates between her roles as learner and experiencer is enhanced by her sequencing choices. Rather than using multiple photos of herself, as Anna does, Scarlynn uses only two photos of herself in her comic. The repetition of the same two photos reinforces the idea that Scarlynn's narrative is not strictly linear or progressive. She does not simply assimilate new scholarship and find her ideas have changed; rather, the reader returns to the same images again and again, foreclosing the possibility of narrative closure. The repetition of the frowning and smiling Scarlynns suggests that the conflict between the scholars' research and Scarlynn's experience is perhaps unresolvable, and her comic points to the ways in which academic conversation might just as often be a frustrating return as a dialogic progression.

Fig. 5. "Minorities' Literacy." 2012. Scarlynn Gutierrez.

Even though all the students had to create a conversation to fulfill the assignment, some chose to make their role as conversation-creator explicit in the action of the comic itself, while also affirming the authority of the scholars they were citing by taking on the role of organizer. Stephanie organizes a conversation that is designed to help a struggling exchange student by imagining herself as the president of her college rather than as a student. Stephanie takes linguistic and gestural authority to bring scholars together, pose the problem they must solve, synthesize their answers, and come to a final and informed conclusion. While she creates power for herself, she also positions herself as different from the scholars, because they are able to offer ideas. Indeed, while in the comic Stephanie suggests that it is she who will come to a final decision, it is actually "Muriel Harris" who proposes the solution that Stephanie elects to adopt (see fig. 6). Stephanie plays with power and authority in multiple design modes, but her comic makes clear that scholars are the ones with the answers that she seeks. She imagines interaction, but does not pose her own claims, as academic conversation requires. Figure 6 shows Stephanie (on the right side of the page) in dialogue with the character of Muriel Harris. While the images and the dialogue show interaction, Harris occupies more physical space than Stephanie and backs up claims with citations. It is here, on the ninth page of the comic, that Stephanie speaks for the first and only time. At this point in the comic, Stephanie zooms in on the speakers. While Muriel Harris's first utterance and both of Stephanie's are depicted in boxes, Harris's second utterance is not framed. This adds to the sense that it is Harris's conclusions that are most central to the narrative action of this sequence. She is also pictured standing; while we do not actually see Harris standing up, we can imagine—through the act of closure—that Harris has stood up in order to make this final, crucial comment. The rest of the comic is narrated by Morgan Freeman, who provides exposition, and by Lad Tobin, Paulo Freire, Donald Murray, and Muriel Harris, the four scholars debating how to best help the exchange student. So, while Stephanie casts herself in a role of power (college president), her design choices emphasize that she is not an equal participant in the conversation. She is able to organize and synthesize, and we know from the importance given to Harris linguistically, spatially, and gesturally that Harris is the scholar Stephanie most agrees with. "Organizer" offers Stephanie a role in which she can be a learner, but also design a space that shows not only that she is learning, but also that she is able to evaluate information and imagine herself as having authorial power to select, organize, and evaluate sources.

Like Stephanie, Afrika calls a conference on the topic of her research paper, "The Crime of Illiteracy," and also makes clear her power in selecting the scholars, asking follow-up questions, and synthesizing. She leaves almost no space to articulate her own opinion, which she saves for her thought bubbles (see fig. 7). Yet, given the roles she set up—conference organizer and conference attendees, student with a research question and scholars with research—it is perfectly reasonable that she would not articulate a position on this occasion. Afrika negotiates power through strategic design that shows her as a student with a developing perspective. Through her linguistic choices—quoting, paraphrasing, and summarizing the scholars—she demonstrates that she is capable of understanding and intervening in the topic. She does so in a nuanced way by controlling the claims of her sources in order to reach the result she believes in and by showing her thoughts to readers. Her comic simultaneously demonstrates her learning process, ability to synthesize sources, and the thought process that leads to her eventual thesis.

Fig. 6. "The Truth About the Writing Colleagues Program." 2012. Stephanie Nieves.

Like Stephanie, who took the role of college president, Afrika professionalizes herself to equalize her position. She poses dressed up in the faculty dining room, a spatial and gestural choice to claim authority. Unlike the learner role, which emphasizes student as novice, or the experiencer role, which emphasizes student as personal authority, the role of organizer demonstrates a move toward a position we are more likely to find in an alphabetic essay. By explicitly acknowledging the authority of the scholars, Stephanie and Afrika demonstrate a hallmark of academic discourse: building *ethos* by showing credible support for one's own claims. But the reluctance to make explicit their own claims illustrates that students may not feel authorized to engage directly with sources. Sourced comics, therefore, provide creative options for students to negotiate those difficulties in order to better understand sources, their own thought processes, and how to develop and pose claims.

Fig. 7. "The Crime of Illiteracy." 2012. Afrika Owes.

The design options afforded by the sourced comic not only make visible the many ways that students position themselves in relation to published scholars but also enable students to rethink scholarly conversation in ways that both allow and encourage their participation in varied roles. In each of these cases, whether they take up the position of conversation learner, experiencer, or organizer, students strategically position themselves as *authorized* to participate in the conversation while also making explicit the asymmetrical power relationships they are working within. Comics and the multiple design modes they afford, therefore, help us to illustrate alternative visions of the conversation metaphor.

The sourced comic also provides opportunities for students and instructors to analyze and reflect on the strategies undergraduates use when they engage scholarly sources. Often the design choices our students made visualized the metaknowledge that is part of the research and writing process: choosing sources, finding sources, figuring out how to bring them in, how to learn from them, and how to move beyond them. These additional clues provided us, as composition instructors, insight into undergraduate writing choices that we might otherwise have understood simply as error. For example, students who tend to bury their own claims in summary and rhetorical questions generally positioned themselves as "organizers" in their sourced comics. Based on this observation, we were able to discuss with our students the limitations and affordances of positioning oneself as a conversation organizer in multiple forms of literacy, including academic essays. The sourced comic allows students a space to work through multiple roles and in doing so, instructors and students can learn much about how to negotiate the very real power that separates a composition student from a composition scholar.

Implications

The sourced comic opens up possibilities for academic writing to be realized in the multimodal genre of the comic. While most of our students' comics helped to problematize the—often invisible—assumptions of equality associated with the parlor metaphor, one student demonstrated that the kind of academic conversation suggested by the parlor is indeed possible in the sourced comic. Chelsea B., in "Coffee with Educators" is the only student in our study who makes her position equal to the scholars as she directly engages them, a position she enhances through the visual and spatial gestures of the comic. Her design, however, suggests that even in cases where students are able to position themselves as dialogic equals in an academic conversation, they might only be able to do so by repositioning the scholars as potentially less authoritative than they really are. She imagines a scenario very close to Burke's parlor: she and the scholars are chatting over coffee. In the excerpts shown below (these are in order, but not continuous), each of the scholars is represented by an image of one of Chelsea's friends whom she posed and photographed around a table in the dining hall, sitting at the same level. Enhanced by such design choices, Chelsea's comic demonstrates that she is an active participant in the conversation (see fig. 8). The example below shows various moments in the comic in which Chelsea engages in a version of academic conversation. She openly disagrees with a scholar of note (Lad Tobin) and thinks that Paulo

Freire is "a little dramatic." She shows that she can linguistically stake out a position, and uses the thought bubble—not as a way to bury a claim—but to show her thought, like a note one might make while annotating a text. Chelsea also directs the conversation on two levels, one within the comic as the character who both begins and ends the conversation, and one outside the narrative as its composer. Chelsea's dual role as conversation participant and narrative composer is emphasized by her sequencing choices. We move from an image in which all of the scholars are pictured actively speaking and gesturing, to close-ups on the scholars. Yet between each close-up, we return to Chelsea, suggesting that her comments and reactions make up the central action of the comic. Chelsea's use of thought bubbles helps us to see that the move from scholarly comment to student response is not automatic; internal thoughts and reactions are a key component in moving to a fully articulated argument. Like the other students, Chelsea turns her internal reactions into key comic actions, but does not stop there. She continues the sequence, playing out ways that a student might move from the internal to the articulated. Yet in order to make all of these moves, she must recast Tobin, Freire, Murray, and Harris as not just college students, but as her friends. Chelsea B. demonstrated one of the many ways that students were able to take control of their sources by recasting the scholars, and she went further by incorporating moves typical of an academic essay in comic form.

Fig. 8. "Coffee with Educators." 2012. Chelsea Begg.

Chelsea's sourced comic demonstrates academic conversation as we might imagine it happening: a student does research and is able to use that research to articulate a position, one that is the primary argument in the text. But the comic assignment puts a spin on teaching students source integration and interaction. Rather than offering students the option to try on the language of their sources, assignments like the comic conversation afford students the opportunity to make their *sources* code-switch to speak the students' language and enter their spaces, rather than the other way around. Such control over how sources speak might be especially important for students from underrepresented groups. The sourced comic also helps us to tease out the complications and contradictions of the conversation metaphor itself. How is academic conversation like and unlike everyday conversation? How might we communicate that academic conversation requires students to simultaneously perform authority and appropriately acknowledge their positions in relation to published scholars? How does the conversation metaphor address or elide issues of race, class, gender, nationality, and linguistic diversity? One way to help students interrogate these questions is through the sourced comic, a valuable pedagogical tool that helps instructors identify students' specific challenges engaging scholarly texts *and* that makes more visible to students the complex networks of power and knowledge they must negotiate when engaging with scholarly sources. Thus, the sourced comic assignment, when accompanied by reflective and critical discussion, may actually help instructors and students trouble the assumptions that depict academic conversation as egalitarian and natural. Examining our assumptions about the nature of academic conversations may help our students to be more self-aware scholars, and may also contribute to a pedagogy of social justice by compelling students and teachers alike to consider how identity, authority, and academic discourse interact.

Sourced comics reveal that, for undergraduates, academic conversations take place within complex networks of power in which students must carefully situate themselves and their ideas. The systemization and simplification of the conversation metaphor suggests that academic conversations are simultaneously egalitarian spaces where differences in power and authority are erased *and* spaces with rules and codes that must be followed in order for participants to be included. Yet, students in our study, no matter their level of privilege, rarely imagined that they were participating in an equal exchange of ideas. Instead they positioned themselves as learners, experiencers, and organizers. As students negotiate the tricky terrain of their own authority, they must also negotiate the codes of academic discourse. Thus, the sourced comic does not represent a *solution* to students' difficulty with integrating source material; instead, it helps to reveal the complex choices that students are always already negotiating when we ask them to engage with sources. These are choices that traditional alphabetic texts can sometimes disguise as error in the forms of patchwriting, quote-mining, and stilted academic prose. The sourced comic, while a potentially valuable tool for students, may be an even more valuable tool for instructors, helping us to see where and even why our students struggle to enter and negotiate academic conversations.

Acknowledgements

The Comic Conversation assignment was inspired by a teaching presentation given by Steve Engel at the University of Michigan; Steve also provided invaluable insights in early stages of this project. We also wish to thank the Center for Teaching and Learning at Hobart & William Smith Colleges, which funded this research study with a teaching grant in 2012.

Notes

1. In "A Pedagogy of Multiliteracies: Designing Social Futures" The New London group identifies "six design elements in the meaning-making process: those of Linguistic Meaning, Visual Meaning, Audio Meaning, Gestural Meaning, Spatial Meaning, and the Multimodal" (65). Dale Jacobs applies these elements of design to analyze the complex ways that comics make meaning ("Marveling"; *Graphic Encounters*).

2. Students are identified by their real names, reflecting their wishes indicated on permission forms we collected. All comic dialogue is reproduced as it appears in the original text, including errors and typos.

3. Figures 2,3,5, and 8 contain images taken from various places in the comics and do not represent the complete narrative sequences.

Works Cited

Anderson, Daniel, Anthony Atkins, Cheryl Ball, Krista Homicz Millar, Cynthia Selfe, and Richard Selfe. "Integrating Multimodality into Composition Curricula: Survey Methodology and Results from a CCCC Research Grant." *Composition Studies* 34.2 (2006): 59-84. Print.

Bartholomae, David. "Inventing the University." *When a Writer Can't Write: Studies in Writer's Block and Other Composing-Process Problems*. Ed. Mike Rose. New York: Guilford, 1985. Print. 134-65.

Begg, Chelsea. "Coffee with Educators." Writing Colleagues Seminar. Fall 2012. PDF file.

Bitz, Michael. *When Commas Meet Kryptonite: Classroom Lessons from the Comic Book Project*. New York: Teachers College Press, 2010. Print.

Bruffee, Kenneth A. "Collaborative Learning and the 'Conversation of Mankind." *College English* 46.7 (1984): 635-52. Print.

Burke, Kenneth. *The Philosophy of Literary Form: Studies in Symbolic Action*. Berkeley: U of California P, 1941. Print.

Carter, James Bucky, ed. *Building Literacy Connections with Graphic Novels: Page by Page, Panel by Panel*. Urbana: NCTE, 2007. Print.

Cary, Stephen. *Going Graphic: Comics at Work in the Multilingual Classroom*. Portsmouth: Heinemann, 2004. Print.

Dunay, Chelsea. "Impacts of Texting on Literacy and Spelling Skills." Writers Seminar. Fall 2012. PDF file.

Ellis, Erik. "Shushes in the Parlor: Reclaiming the 'Conversation' Metaphor." *Disrupting Pedagogies in the Knowledge Society: Countering Conservative Norms with Creative Approaches*. Ed. Julie Faulkner. Hershey: IGI Global, 2012. 60-76. Print.

Engel, Steve. "Teaching with Technology." English Department Writing Program Colloquium, Ann Arbor, MI. 30 October, 2008. Lecture.

Fleckenstein, Kristie S. "Words Made Flesh: Fusing Imagery and Language in a Polymorphic Literacy." *College English* 66.6 (2004): 612-31. Print.

Frey, Nancy, and Douglas Fisher, eds. *Teaching Visual Literacy: Using Comic Books, Graphic Novels, Anime, Cartoons, and More to Develop Comprehension and Thinking Skills*. Thousand Oaks: Corwin, 2008. Print.

Graff, Gerald, and Cathy Birkenstein. *"They Say/I Say": The Moves That Matter in Academic Writing*. 2nd ed. New York: W.W. Norton & Company, 2010. Print.

Groensteen, Thierry. *The System of Comics*. Trans. Bart Beaty and Nick Nguyen. Jackson: UP of Mississippi, 2007. Print.

Gutierrez, Scarlynn. "Minorities' Literacy." Writers Seminar. Fall 2012. PDF file.

Harris, Joseph. *Rewriting: How To Do Things With Texts*. Logan: Utah State UP, 2006. Print.

Helms, Jason. "Helenistic Encomium: A Reflection on Comics and Rhetoric." *Kairos* 13.2 (2009). Web. 5 Jun. 2014. <http://technorhetoric.net/13.2/disputatio/helms/index.html>.

Jacobs, Dale. *Graphic Encounters: Comics and the Sponsorship of Multimodal Literacy*. New York: Bloomsbury Academic, 2013. Print.

---. "Marveling at 'The Man Called Nova': Comics as Sponsors of Multimodal Literacy." *CCC* (2007): 180-205. Print.

---. "More than Words: Comics as a Means of Teaching Multiple Literacies." *English Journal* (2007): 19-25. Print.

Kukkonen, Karin. *Studying Comics and Graphic Novels*. Malden: Wylie-Blackwell, 2013. Print.

Lynch, Paul. "Composition's New Thing: Bruno Latour and the Apocalyptic Turn." *College English* 74.5 (2012): 458-76. Print.

McCloud, Scott. *Understanding Comics: The Invisible Art*. New York: Harper Perennial, 1994. Print.

Miano, Anna. "Class Size versus Student Achievement." Writers Seminar. Fall 2012. PDF file.

Monnin, Katie. *Teaching Graphic Novels: Practical Strategies for the Secondary ELA Classroom*. Gainesville: Maupin House, 2010. Print.

New London Group. "A Pedagogy of Multiliteracies: Designing Social Futures." *Harvard Educational Review* 66.1 (1996): 60-92. Print.

Nieves, Stephanie. "The Truth About the Writing Colleagues Program." Writing Colleagues Seminar. Fall 2012. PDF file.

Olson, Gary A. "Publishing Scholarship in Rhetoric and Composition: Joining the Conversation." *Publishing in Rhetoric and Composition.* Ed. Gary A. Olson and Todd W. Taylor. Albany: SUNY, 1997. 19-33. Print.

Ortiz, Michael. "When Minds Collide." Writers Seminar. Fall 2012. PDF file.

Owes, Afrika. "The Crime of Illiteracy." Writers Seminar. Fall 2012. PDF file.

Postema, Barbara. *Narrative Structure in Comics: Making Sense of Fragments.* Rochester: RIT P, 2013. Print.

Ressel, Kristin. "Creative to Academic Writing." Writers Seminar. Fall 2012. PDF file.

Versaci, Rocco. "How Comic Books Can Change the Way Our Students See Literature: One Teacher's Perspective." *The English Journal* (2001): 61-67. Print.

Illustrating Praxis: Comic Composition, Narrative Rhetoric, and Critical Multiliteracies

Kathryn Comer

Thus far, pedagogical discussions about comics in the college classroom have focused primarily on *reading*, with less attention paid to the complementary potential of *composing* comics. This essay advocates using narrative theory alongside comic studies to provide students and teachers with a flexible, transferable vocabulary compatible with literacy-focused pedagogies. For support, I draw upon the contributions of undergraduate students in an advanced composition course centered on graphic memoir, in which the combination of medium and genre provided a user-friendly but sophisticated environment for rhetorical experimentation and multimodal literacy development. Three core concepts—narrative gaps, narration, and focalization—are offered as helpful heuristics for rhetorical design; their application in two students' memoirs illustrate the insights and skills that can result from a theory-driven approach to comic composition. Ultimately, I suggest that such an approach holds significant potential for generating critical engagement, refining rhetorical consciousness, and fostering critical multiliteracies.

Thus far, pedagogical discussions about comics in the college classroom have focused primarily on *reading*, with less attention paid to the complementary potential of *composing* comics. This essay advocates using narrative theory alongside comic studies to provide students and teachers with a flexible, transferable vocabulary compatible with literacy-focused pedagogies. For support, I draw upon the contributions of undergraduate students enrolled in an advanced composition course centered on graphic memoir; the combination of medium and genre provides a user-friendly but sophisticated environment for rhetorical experimentation and multimodal literacy development. The students' graphic memoirs presented here illustrate the insights and skills that can result from a theory-driven approach to comic composition. Before examining these texts, I offer some context for this research and delineate the key concepts that informed this course's conversations and students' resulting praxis. These literary techniques—narrative gaps, narration, and focalization—serve as heuristics for rhetorical design, as evidenced in two sample student graphic memoirs. Ultimately, I suggest that such a pedagogical approach offers opportunities to enhance students' critical engagement with literacy development while fostering a transferable rhetorical perspective.

Multimodal Pedagogy and Graphic Memoir

Comics align remarkably well with composition's pedagogical commitment to fostering students' multiliteracies. Comics rely on more than just linguistic and visual modes of communication; they combine words and images with gestural, spatial, and even audio modes into a truly multimodal experience.[1] Moreover, they do so within a form that is familiar and accessible while still challenging and innovative. Surprisingly, despite the surge of academic interest in comics, there has been a relative neglect of comics in published scholarship within composition studies, though ongoing experimentation is evident in online resources and conference programs. Most research to date has occurred in early education, where comics are believed to appeal to resistant students and provide creative alternatives to conventional writing assignments (e.g., Crilley; Schwartz and Rubinstein-Avila; Handsfield, Dean, and Cielocha; Morrison, Bryan, and Chilcoat). In several influential articles, Dale Jacobs highlights comics' compatibility with contemporary literacy pedagogy in middle school, college composition, and biography studies, arguing that "(1) reading comics involves a complex, multimodal literacy; and (2) by using comics in our classrooms, we can help students develop as critical and engaged readers of multimodal texts" ("More" 19). Like Jacobs, Laura Micciche and Hillary Chute each persuasively argue that working with comics can expand our own and our students' definitions and practices of reading. My experiences support these arguments and suggest the logical next step: in addition to the benefits gained by reading comics, the act of composing comics has a great deal to offer students and teachers at the college level. By asking students to produce as well as read comics, we can energize processes of invention, problem solving, design, and revision that may fundamentally influence their attitudes toward and abilities with diverse literacies.

My own approach to comics in the classroom has focused on the genre of graphic memoir. I chose this angle for several related reasons. First, graphic memoirs served as my own introduction to comics, and I am now hooked; I suspected they might hold a similar power over students. Second, their autobiographical approach suits my ongoing pedagogical agenda of encouraging heightened awareness of the rhetorical construction of narrative texts. Composition students and teachers tend to be rather familiar with the conventional "personal narrative" assignment, which is ripe for revision.[2] Too often, autobiographical writing is used as an expressive exercise without audience or exigency, an approach that deemphasizes the persuasive power of personal narrative. Comics productively complicate students' relationships to personal narrative. Adding "graphic" to "memoir" emphasizes the rhetorical nature of storytelling: the texts are produced and published with such effort and effect that they resist being deemed a wholly self-oriented or private act. The comics medium offers a remarkably rich set of resources to illustrate authors' processes of self-narration and subjective representation of "real" events. Finally, as Joseph Witek notes in "Seven Ways I Don't Teach Comics," one needs to establish some boundaries in order to teach comics effectively; it's neither possible nor productive to cover all eras, genres, and texts in a single course. Selecting a particular focus allows for more precision in both critical concepts and rhetorical considerations.

For these reasons, graphic memoirs' combination of familiar but likely underexamined media and genre characteristics contribute to a rhetorically conscious approach to multimodal composition. This focus utilizes theoretical concepts from both comics and narrative studies that serve as valuable resources for fine-tuning students' rhetorical and critical awareness. In the course described below, I borrow liberally from these traditions, providing students with a rhetorical framework for analyzing and then composing graphic memoirs. Three intertwined concepts—narrative gaps, narration, and focalization—proved most valuable in this pedagogical experiment and students' resulting comic compositions. Though they are certainly not the only tools available for a critical approach to comic narratives, they provide a solid foundation for students' rhetorical analysis and production of graphic memoirs.

In the sections that follow, I offer a narrative of my own first experiment with comics in the classroom. I organize the story of this pedagogical design according to the New London Group's recursive process, described as available designs, designing, and the redesigned. The New London Group's process is a useful heuristic for outlining students' multiliteracy development because it emphasizes "the fact that meaning-making is an active and dynamic process, and not something governed by static rules" (74). The next section, "Available Designs," provides a brief description of the resources with which the class started: students' previous experiences and the critical terminology I provided. In "Designing," gaps, narration, and focalization are illustrated in two students' memoirs. Finally, "The Redesigned" argues for the value of graphic narrative in sharpening students' critical consciousness, along with their literacy skills. Throughout, I rely on students' contributions—both their graphic memoirs and their reflections—as the most persuasive evidence of comics' potential in composition pedagogy.

Available Designs

Situated Practice

The course under discussion was offered in 2010 at a large public state university. Students who enrolled in the class to fulfill an upper-level writing requirement had no way of knowing that it would focus on graphic memoir or include multimodal composing.[3] They were surprised but receptive when I explained the graphic memoir focus. Their enthusiasm no doubt arose from an expectation of fun rather than any investment in the topic, confirming the commonly held belief that comics work well to engage students' interest. However, introductory surveys and discussions revealed a lack of exposure that contradicts common scholarly assumptions about young people's previous engagement with the medium. In this case, students associated graphic texts with cartoons, "funny pages," superheroes, and, most of all, childhood. Most knew of graphic novel series, like *The Watchmen* and *Sin City*, but only through their movie adaptations. Overall, students saw themselves as neither fans nor experts when it came to comics. Despite this, students quickly realized that they already knew many of the conventions of comics. They easily recognized comics conventions like dialogue balloons, panel layout, and action and sound cues, and therefore felt comfortable interpreting the rhetorical effects of conventional and unconventional variations in different comics. On the whole, however, they were more confident in their ability to read than to write in multiple modes, a tension that remained throughout the course. Regarding memoir, students also reported a lack of experience with the genre, and while they expressed a good understanding of storytelling strategies, they did not have the vocabulary to articulate their ideas.

Overt Instruction and Critical Framing

I offered students a set of tools from narrative theory and comics studies to supplement our conversations and secondary readings.[4] Though not exhaustive, this vocabulary not only made it "easier to *talk about* particular features of texts, it [made] it easier to *see* them"—and therefore to *use* them (Case 7, emphasis in original). To that end, I focused on three major concepts that became the most useful for rhetorical analysis and production: narrative gaps, narration, and focalization. Taken together, these concepts provide a critical vocabulary that helps students understand the rhetorical negotiations that lie at the heart of graphic memoir.

Narrative Gaps

Probably the most frequently noted characteristic of comics is the work they demand of audiences to decode their multimodal cues. This participation is at the heart of comics' power. By demanding that audiences literally read between the lines to achieve what Scott McCloud calls "closure," comics enlist audiences as "willing and conscious collaborator[s]" (*Understanding* 63, 65). This emphasis on author-audience collaboration aligns nicely with Wolfgang Iser's concept of narrative gaps—moments of ambiguity, unreliability, or inscrutability in the story—that serve as "the switch that activates the reader into using his own ideas in order to fulfill the intention of the text" (*Prospecting* 28). Just as authors assemble elements to guide readers' experiences, audiences must work to interpret those cues; neither author nor text fully determines meaning-making, "for the text only takes on life when it is realized" (Iser, "Reading Process" 279). By extension, the construction of narrative gaps is essential to a rhetorically effective story. Because "reading is only a pleasure when it is active and creative," Iser argues, successful storytellers construct narrative gaps to prevent "the boredom which inevitably arises when everything is laid out cut and dried before us" ("Reading Process" 280).

Comics make this interactivity visible on the page through the interplay of panels and gutters. The presence of gutters, or what Barbara Postema calls "the gap between fragmented moments," may not require an explicit "filling in blanks… [but] they create the conditions for the process of signification"—or, often, "retroactive resignification" (49, 50). Indeed, the act of reading comics is not linear or smooth. The eye skips around the page, directed but not controlled by the author's design: "The fractured surface of the comics page, with its patchwork of different images, shapes, and symbols, presents the reader with a surfeit of interpretive options, creating an experience that is always decentered, unstable, and unfixable" (Hatfield xiii–xiv). As Micciche notes, the reading process demanded by comics can disrupt students' passive reading habits; the necessarily recursive process that results demands that audiences "read and re-read, absorbing new details each time and comprehending the significance of a page, for instance, only after the words and pictures in each panel have sunk in" (9). When students in this course engaged the primary texts, the initial idea that comics are faster and easier to read shifted as students realized that "in order to get the full message from the story I had to go back and slow down my reading, grasping the full image before proceeding" (K.S.). Reading practices in the course focused on authors' construction choices, their strategic manipulation of shifting responses in the service of the culminating closure, as well as on the effort demanded by the conscientious, critical audience.[5]

The rhetorical strategies afforded by gaps and closure accorded well with the students' stated aversion to having everything spelled out for them; an effective memoir in this view was one that requires a little work, prompting audiences "to see the light for themselves rather than being talked down to and being told what to think" (I.M. 4). Others agreed, up to a point: "On the one hand I don't want to be overly obvious, to where I don't put any faith in my reader to fill in the gaps and make connections but I don't want to be so obscure that meaning is lost in too many possibilities of interpretation" (A.B.). In this way, students' experiences as audiences brought home the importance of creating narrative gaps in their own memoirs, inviting their audiences to co-create meaning.

Narration[6]

Both the primary and secondary work in what Gillian Whitlock has termed "autographics" highlights the affordances of comics for self-representation. If the constructed nature of comics illuminates the mutuality of meaning-making, autobiographical comics further spotlight the layered subjectivities on both sides of the page. As Jared Gardner suggests, "graphic memoir provides a space to theorize and practice new ethical and affective relationships and responses" (1). The comic form illustrates and complicates the core tension in autobiographical writing: the relationships among the different personae of "the self" as author/narrator/character. Within the text itself, the conventions of comic narration clarify an essential distinction between the "narrating-I" and "experiencing-I" by placing them in separate spaces (Bruner; Lejeune; Olney). In most graphic memoirs, the voice of the storyteller appears in the text boxes above, below, or between the panels where the story unfolds, in which the character's voice and thoughts appear within balloons. When this convention is followed, it visually distinguishes the present day identity of the narrator from the version of that self who acted in the past. Students recognized that authors do "a lot of work… to differentiate between [his/]her present day self and the person that [he/]she was at the time" of the events depicted (V.A. 2). When this conventional separation of narrating-I and experiencing-I is flouted, the resulting disruption causes readers to reassess their interpretive assumptions.

Throughout, these negotiations also draw attention to the author him- or herself, who stands outside and orchestrates textual performances.[7] In this way, the standard moves of comics narration reflect a social constructivist view of identity: "The comic book memoir reminds us at every turn that the retelling of one's personal history is, in part, an act of invention. . . . To read such a work is to understand at a fundamental level the 'truth' of a memoir is something that cannot be tied simplistically to the facts" (Versaci 58). Graphic memoirists become ventriloquists of their narrators and previous selves, a process that layers past and present perspectives, voices, and personalities. This presentation of multiple selves is a process of deliberate editing, not wholesale disclosure, and the audience's interpretation is also necessarily complex. As Whitlock suggests, comic self-representations "might produce an imaginative and ethical engagement with the proximity of the other" (978). Throughout their work with comics narration, students' negotiations of these others—within as well as outside themselves—challenged their beliefs about identity, authenticity, and representation.

Focalization

Like narration, the concept of focalization enables a nuanced discussion of memoirists' strategies for representing subjective memories. A term coined by Gerard Genette, focalization refers to an important difference between who "speaks" and who "sees" an unfolding story. In comics, of course, the viewer looks directly at the text, but that text is filtered and focused through panels, balloons, layout, styles, colors, and so on. These design choices shape the audience's interpretation of and relationship to the story and its teller. When authors illustrate their own lives, they make manifest their own interpretive lenses. An impulse toward autobiographical accuracy can just as often take the form of emotional as literal truth, which may produce exaggeration or distortion. Hatfield considers the creation of a graphic self—"the self-caricature"—the most important rhetorical move in a comic because it dictates the relationship between author and audience (114). The self can be drawn as it once seemed or now appears, or with a (literal or figurative) filter/mask, or with variations according to mood. Such expressions communicate complex psychological realities: "In brief, the outward guise reflects inward attitudes: objectification enables self-understanding and self-transformation" (Hatfield 116). As a result, focalization calls into question notions of honesty in self-representation and objectivity in any representation.

The memoirist's textual incarnation aside, focalization also addresses the sometimes subtle, sometimes overt means of guiding not just what the audience sees, but how. As Rocco Versaci explains, "by their very nature, comic book memoirs present the world as seen through their artists' eyes, and those 'visions' become the memoirists' powerful and evocative worldview" (45). Illustrations may present the narrating-I's retrospective, mature gaze or the experiencing-I's immediate, in-the-moment perspective; the author-character may be viewed from the outside, or the audience may see the story through his/her eyes; settings may be specific or impressionistic; and so on. The rhetorical resources of focalization are extensive, as are the ways in which authors use them "to manipulate the reader's orientation . . . [or] to manipulate and produce various emotional states in the reader" (Eisner 89). Students' negotiations of focalization required attention not only to memoirists' subjective experiences but also to the ubiquity of filters in representations of reality. The idea that autobiographical texts accurately represent reality cannot withstand the clearly constructed nature of comics.

As this brief overview of narrative gaps, narration, and focalization demonstrates, graphic memoirs can work well to immerse students in rich theoretical investigations of identity, subjectivity, and rhetorical self-representation—investigations that also demand attention to practical issues of multimodal communication. Although these concepts constitute only a small sampling of the tools available, this critical vocabulary provides a strong foundation upon which students can build.

Designing: Transformed Practice

By the time we got to the final project,[8] the students had begun to feel comfortable with the interpretation of comics, but they were far less sanguine about creating their own. To different degrees, they were concerned about both selecting a worthwhile story and presenting it graphically. Indeed, most nerves revolved around insecurity over their visual literacies; while visual analysis had felt somewhat familiar, visual composition was a fresh challenge for many. During this process, students spent a fair amount of time fretting and reassuring each other and themselves: "[I]t doesn't matter how terrible the pictures look as long as they get your point across. Don't let your lack of artistic talent hold you back from drawing if that's what you would prefer to do" (M.S.). Some discovered unknown or long-forgotten talents for drawing; some considered staging scenes; many used a combination of photos, sketches, and maps (often manipulated by Photoshop or ComicLife or both) to create mixed-media memoirs.

According to our individual and collective conversations, students' decisions were based on their preference for participatory rhetoric: as authors, students wanted to offer their audience the right balance of cues and gaps to ensure active engagement in the meaning-making process. The two very different memoirs I present here reflect some of their resulting decisions. In addition to assessing and adapting existing options from their developing knowledge of conventions of graphic memoirs, students also necessarily generated new strategies as they negotiated particular agendas and practical constraints like available resources and their own literacies. In this way, students consciously participated in genuine design, acting as "both inheritors of patterns and conventions of meaning and at the same time active designers of meaning" (New London Group 64). These students' graphic memoirs, as well as their reflections on the project, provide evidence of the strategic invention, creative problem-solving, and rhetorical awareness fostered by that experience. Although these designs deploy an impressive range of comic resources, my analysis here focuses on students' use of narrative gaps, narration, and focalization—their informed illustration of those theories in practice.

Illustrating Life Lessons: "Always Wear Your Helmet"

Like many other students' memoirs, Axel K.'s "Always Wear Your Helmet!" recounts a vivid childhood memory, in this case a major snowboarding accident in which he broke his femur: "[This event] definitely stands out as one of the defining moments in my short existence on this planet. This experience drastically altered my life not only during the injury but shaped my life as a whole and continues to affect me" ("Analysis" 1). He knew the story was well suited to the comics medium: "For one, the whole breaking a bone story is one that many people have experienced in their lives. Also, due to the physical nature of the event, many of the elements would be more interesting if depicted graphically rather than purely with word" ("Proposal" 1). Whereas many students struggled to come up with a tale worth telling, Axel felt fairly confident that "one of the most terrible and life-changing events" of his life would make an entertaining story with a clear moral ("Analysis" 1).

Axel's confidence, however, did not extend to his technical ability to create the memoir: "Yet, with all the excitement comes some anxiety too because I am a terrible artist" ("Illustration"). He did not have access to family photos, and they would not have provided the visuals he needed, so he ultimately decided to "to draw so I can express more with people's bodies and faces but am afraid that people will discredit my work because of the terrible artistic quality" ("Illustration"). The question of stick figures was the subject of several blog conversations in which students brought up McCloud's notion of "amplification through simplification," the idea that audiences can more easily identify with abstract visual representations than detailed realism (*Understanding* 30). According to the students, as "[t]he most general interpretation of the human form possible," stick figures were deemed a valid option (Q.K.). So, like a few others, Axel drew his comic and thereby, like many, discovered unexpected benefits resulting from supposed constraints.

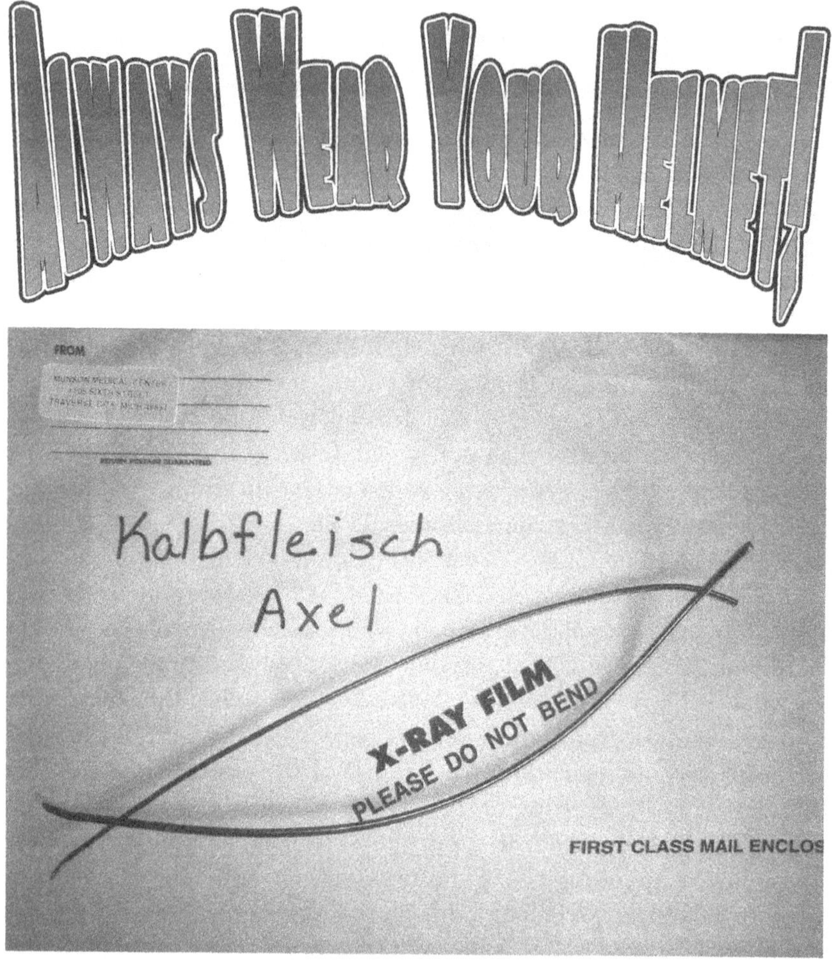

Fig.1. The title page for "Always Wear Your Helmet!"

"Always Wear Your Helmet!" serves as one example of student authors' attempts to balance open interpretation with an overt message. The moral of the story is placed right up front on the title page, which also features a photo of an x-ray folder and two curved metal rods that, we will discover, ended up in the author's leg (see fig. 1). These cues are both clear—there will be an injury and lesson learned—and incomplete. Axel strategically delays the revelation of their cause, incorporating what he called "an element of suspense and foreshadowing" designed to maintain audience interest ("Analysis" 1). On the first page, the present-day author/narrator appears, reflecting on his youthful feelings of invincibility before "that fateful day I finally learned the truth" ("Always" 2). The following few pages are devoted to setting the scene (a skiing trip to Michigan) and establishing character (two excited adolescent boys and a tolerant father); these details include a moment in which Axel considers lending his helmet to his friend instead of wearing it himself, only to remember his mother's repeated warnings and changing his mind: "This time I actually listened" (4). As Axel explained in his analytic reflection, "The audience is left wondering what is going to happen, why is this helmet so important… and wanting to read to find out what happens next" ("Analysis" 1-2). The dramatic climax comes midway through the memoir, when the young Axel attempts a risky ski jump.

This turning point is designed for maximum audience involvement as events unfold (see fig. 2). The layout creates a slow-motion experience: four tall panels dominate the page and draw the audience's attention, which only returns to the top panel's set-up after registering the fall. The narrator's dramatic, somewhat disparaging account of his characters' actions highlights his own vivid memories: "So off I went, no speed checks, balls to the walls, without even checking the takeoff first. I remember a kid walking up the hill as I was going into the takeoff" ("Always" 6). Below, in a series of moment-to-moment transitions, the smiling stick figure leaves the jump, launches into the air, hangs there long enough to think "Oh shit, this is gonna hurt," before the fearful descent (6). Axel's storytelling here relies on spatial and gestural cues: "As I am going through the air, one will note the definite change in my facial expression from happy to extreme worry. The following panels also show this tactic by way of the pinwheel eyes and crooked mouth that I have to show my state of pain and daze" ("Analysis" 2). In a similar way, the jagged break in his stick leg and his yelling, represented in a speech balloon, evoke shock and pain as the child waits for help and is rushed to the hospital. Here the gaps set up by the title page are closed when the nurse remarks, "Without that helmet you wouldn't be here," and the audience is faced with the x-ray images of Axel's leg before and after those metal rods are inserted ("Always" 8). That sudden shift in medium, and the lack of narration surrounding it, requires the audience to fill in the gaps between a stick figure and the real child it represents. Unlike the rest of the memoir, this page employs a static, balanced layout that pauses the momentum. Axel silently invites the reader to pause and imagine the physical pain and psychological distress that cannot, it is implied, be verbalized.

Fig. 2. The climax of "Always Wear Your Helmet!"

After this climax, the narrative seems to wrap up neatly, as promised. In the final pages of the comic, however, Axel opens up a whole new gap; he appears as his grown-up self on a beach to explain that, in fact, the comic's ending was "really only the start of the most painful and trying experience of my life" (see fig. 3). The long process of recuperation and physical therapy was "all fruitless" because a cleft in the repaired bone caused it to break again the following summer. Squeezed into the bottom of an oversized speech bubble is Axel's final farewell, the lesson he takes from the experience: "Look before you leap and life's tough. Always wear a helmet, literally and figuratively" ("Always" 10).

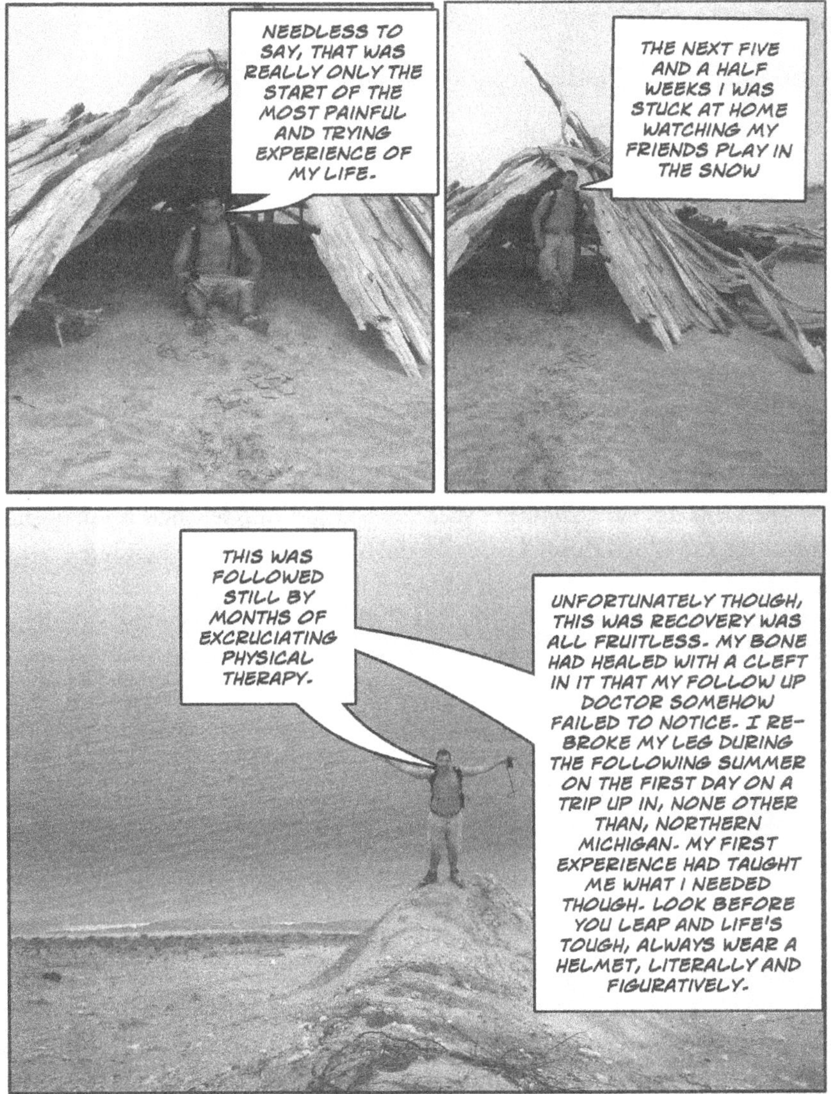

Fig.3. The conclusion of "Always Wear Your Helmet!"

In his analytic reflection, Axel commented on those crowded final moments: "I felt like I had too much to tell, and the fact was I really did." He had written and excised "several other pages on recovery and therapy" only to cut anything that detracted from "the moral of the story" ("Analysis" 3). But that tension remains apparent in the final panel, which acknowledges that the real story continues even as this constructed narrative is concluded.[9] Axel finally leaves the audience to provide their own closure of the new gaps he's just opened.

Narration: Visible Guidance

Axel's memoir relies on a conventional distinction between his present perspective and past experiences: for most of the text, the narrator's voice appears in text boxes above the panels in which his childhood self speaks and acts. However, he also frames that story within a present-tense representation, letting the audience see and relate to his narrating-I rather than including only his verbal voice in text boxes. In the introduction and conclusion, Axel exploits the rhetorical effect of "an author appearing amid the panels of his narrative, looking us in the eye, and delivering heartfelt testimony about him- or herself" (Versaci 39). He "speaks" to the audience while performing characterizing actions that establish a casual, fun-loving persona, one interested in sharing the wisdom earned through his own trials.

The clear differentiation between Axel-now and Axel-then is established early and maintained throughout. On the opening page, the narrator directly addresses his audience in speech balloons over pictures of his grown-up self playing Frisbee on a lawn (see fig. 4).[10] His verbal commentary highlights the contrast between his current self-awareness and his former feelings of invincibility: "I vividly remember the fateful day I finally learned the truth" ("Always" 2). This introduction is designed to invite the audience to "relax and trust" the narrating Axel, who then is heard in text boxes but not seen until the last page ("Proposal" 2). The performed informality—and the commonplace that young people think they are invincible—with which the comic begins initiates a friendly relationship with the audience that is maintained through these text boxes. The rest of the memoir consists of child-like crayon drawings with the distinctive voices of young Axel, his friend, and his father. This visual distinction between the narrating-I and experiencing-I is reinforced by their linguistic differences. Throughout, Axel sprinkles his narration with references to his characters' youth and his own perspective on "back then." This distancing move insistently highlights the author-narrator's maturity and suggests the perspective gained through not just age and experience but also the reflection and self-representation demanded by the graphic memoir genre.

Fig. 4. The introduction of "Always Wear Your Helmet!"

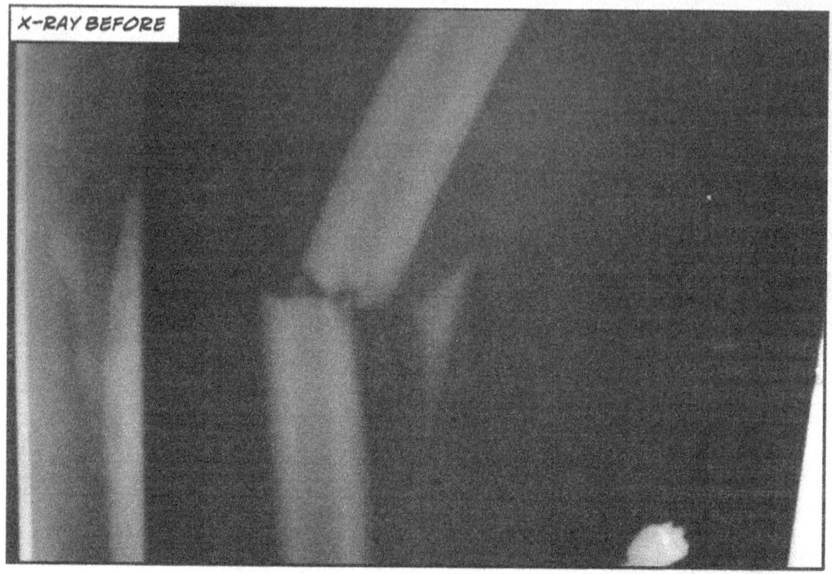

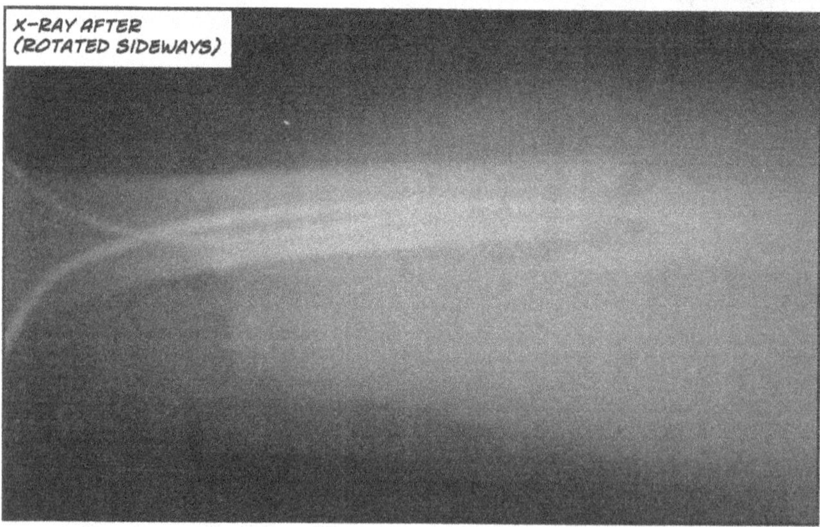

Fig. 5. The reality check of "Always Wear Your Helmet!"

The conclusion of the comic not only reinforces this distinction between past and present self, but it also brings those selves closer together. As Jerome Bruner explains, this move is central to the memoir genre, in which "the protagonist and the narrator eventually fuse and become one person with a shared consciousness" (27). For Axel, this fusion begins on "that fateful day I finally learned the truth" ("Always" 2). In the last hand-drawn panel, the young Axel learns of his broken femur and thinks, "Shit, shit, shit. Why wasn't I more careful?" ("Always" 8). He's already looking back on his risk-taking from a new perspective. That reality check is driven home by the page that follows, which features only two stark x-ray images of his broken and repaired bone (see fig. 5). As indicated above, the uncharacteristic lack of narration on this page forces the reader to supply their own commentary and interpretation: This jarring transition marks the end of Axel's cartoonish childhood and begins his growth into the narrating-I who reappears on the following, final page. Again, the narrator appears as an active, positive presence, this time hiking on a beach. With his arms raised in a gesture of accomplishment, he clarifies the lessons he learned and their relevance for the audience. With this advice, Axel leaves the audience to reflect on the tension between self-preservation and perseverance that characterizes his current perspective.

Focalization: The View from Now

Much as the narration makes a clear distinction between the narrating- and experiencing-I's, the focalization in this memoir highlights Axel's and the audience's shifting perspectives throughout. In the opening and closing panels, the audience sees Axel as he wishes to be seen: healthy and happy and living life well. These bright images present carefully constructed carefree moments in the life of a typical college-aged American male. The visual style of the illustrations, meanwhile, distinguishes between present clarity and past childishness; it also highlights the impressionistic nature of Axel's memories. Having no pictures other than his x-rays, Axel created simple illustrations of the events, with characters represented as different-colored stick figures; buildings and cars are basic blocks; snowflakes are scattered asterisks; and shading is deliberately messy. This drawing style contributes to the audience's interpretive experience: "My lack of artistic skill was actually somewhat handy though as it was able to clearly show these images were from the past, as noted by the elementary level look" ("Analysis" 3).

From the point of view of narrator and reader, these images reinforce the distinction between past and present; we see the literal childishness of young Axel's worldview. Notably, that perspective changes dramatically after the nurse remarks that the helmet saved his life and the doctor confirms the severity of the injury. The next page features the real x-rays: one of the cracked femur and one of the rods pulling the bone's pieces back together (see fig. 5). This dramatic page, with labels but no narrative commentary, aligns the perspective of the experiencing-I, narrating-I, and audience—all faced with a harsh reality. On the final page, the visuals go back to photographs, returning Axel and the audience to the present with a clearer understanding of the past and its continuing influence. The audience is also back on the outside, looking *at* Axel rather than *with* him. The adult narrator appears on the page to wrap up his story and drive home its moral. The audience is presented with a clearly confident and strong young man in a posture of victory—a view that is only somewhat belied by the verbal acknowledgement of the struggles that followed. As discussed above, however, that tension remains visible on the page and complicates the audience's final perspective on the story and its teller.

Negotiating the Unnarratable: Untitled

The next, untitled memoir engaged core themes in autobiographical theory and personal narrative in composition studies—memory, self-construction, self-disclosure, and agency—through one momentous day in Kayan G.'s childhood:

> When I was ten years old, my father, whom I had not seen in months, arrived at my home with his sisters and new wife, put me in a car without any explanation and drove us away. I did not understand what was going on. . . . All I remember was feeling really confused and angry at everyone around me. From that day forward, my life dramatically changed. The events that followed helped to shape me as the person that I am today. ("Proposal" 1)

The decision to tell this story was not an easy one. On more than one occasion, she considered switching topics to something more comfortable: "I was tempted to take the easy way out and simply retell a recent trip that I had taken. I was really scared that I wouldn't be able to tell an important story in a way that really captures what I was going through" ("Analytic" 1). Kayan persevered in this task in large part because she felt that the graphic memoir form would allow her to communicate something she found difficult to verbalize: "It is a lot easier to show what you were experiencing at a particular time than trying to explain it in words" ("Proposal" 1). Though telling this particular story was not necessarily easy, the resources afforded by the comic form offered Kayan new ways to understand and share her experience.

In a strategically limited self-presentation, Kayan controlled her self-disclosure while forcing the audience to fill in the gaps on their own. Her original intention was to provide a neat moral: "I will show how my early life has been about myself overcoming obstacles . . . . The audience will respond to the rags-to-riches aspect of my story and the hope that the future will be a good one" ("Proposal" 1). These plans changed as she struggled not just to craft the narrative but to understand the events and their lasting impression. The resulting ambiguity was a deliberate choice, one linked to Kayan's decision to narrow her focus from childhood in general to just that one fateful day: "At first I thought that I would lose my purpose, but I didn't. I felt like it might be more mysterious and have a greater impact with a shorter comic" ("Comment"). That sense of mystery, and its emotional effect, was made possible by Kayan's manipulation of conventional comics narration for her particular authorial purposes. Writing, in the end, primarily for her own understanding and healing, Kayan constructed deliberately wide gaps that maintain her privacy while enabling audience participation.

Narrative Gaps: The Unexplained and Inexplicable

Fig. 6. The opening page of "Untitled"

Kayan's memoir both invites and avoids interpretation. It begins abruptly, leaves much unexplained, and ends on an ambivalent note. Unlike Axel, she provides neither title nor moral and offers only the bare minimum of narration. Instead, the memoir relies on the audience to decode the subtleties of the text, which is in many ways a series of gaps in need of closure. It begins conventionally enough, though without a title page: A single image of a young woman playing with a dog on a lawn, with a text box at the top of the page in which the narrator declares, "There wasn't anything different about that day…" (see fig. 6) ("Untitled" 1). The solitary panel and introduction launches the narrative slowly and somewhat ominously. This foreshadowing is heightened on the next page by a mysterious arrival. Again, the scene unfolds slowly, with two images of a black car and a close-up image of her wary face wondering, "Who is that?"—one of the few questions actually answered ("Untitled" 2).

Subsequent pages conceal as much as they reveal; the audience is directly informed of only the bare outline of events, such as the young woman's father arriving to take her away from "home" to join a family she'd never known existed. There are hints of family drama: Janice (the woman she lived with) "had a lot to hide" ("Untitled" 4); a birth certificate has vanished; the car is full of women who "acted like they knew me" (7); her father had been married to a woman for two years "before I even knew her name" (8). But instead of delving into these fascinating dynamics, the memoir simply notes these revelations as they arise. Like the young protagonist, the reader struggles to keep up, let alone achieve closure. The resulting shared confusion involves the audience in the story, creating an "intimacy… a silent, secret contract between creator and audience" (McCloud, *Understanding* 69). One gets the sense that the preferred audience would be discrete and respectful enough not to ask impertinent questions.

In the final pages, though, the audience discovers a different kind of gap: that between the represented characters and their real-life counterparts. Without a family archive or confidence in her drawing ability, Kayan decided to recreate key events with actors, casting college-aged friends in the role of herself, her father, and her father's girlfriend. For the first-time reader, there is no way to know how old the protagonist is, nor a reason to question it. For six of the memoir's nine pages, the audience witnesses and sympathizes with a young woman. This physical and psychological set-up results in a moment of visual shock when Kayan finally reveals a picture of herself with her father that day (see fig. 7). The narrator does not acknowledge the disclosure, leaving the audience to make the connection through a single visual clue: the yellow shirts worn by both the young woman actor and the small child. The quietly dramatic moment reveals just how young the memoirist was when these events transpired, disrupting the reader's experience and interpretation. The resulting disorientation forces the audience back, to review what they have seen and to reconcile it with this new information.

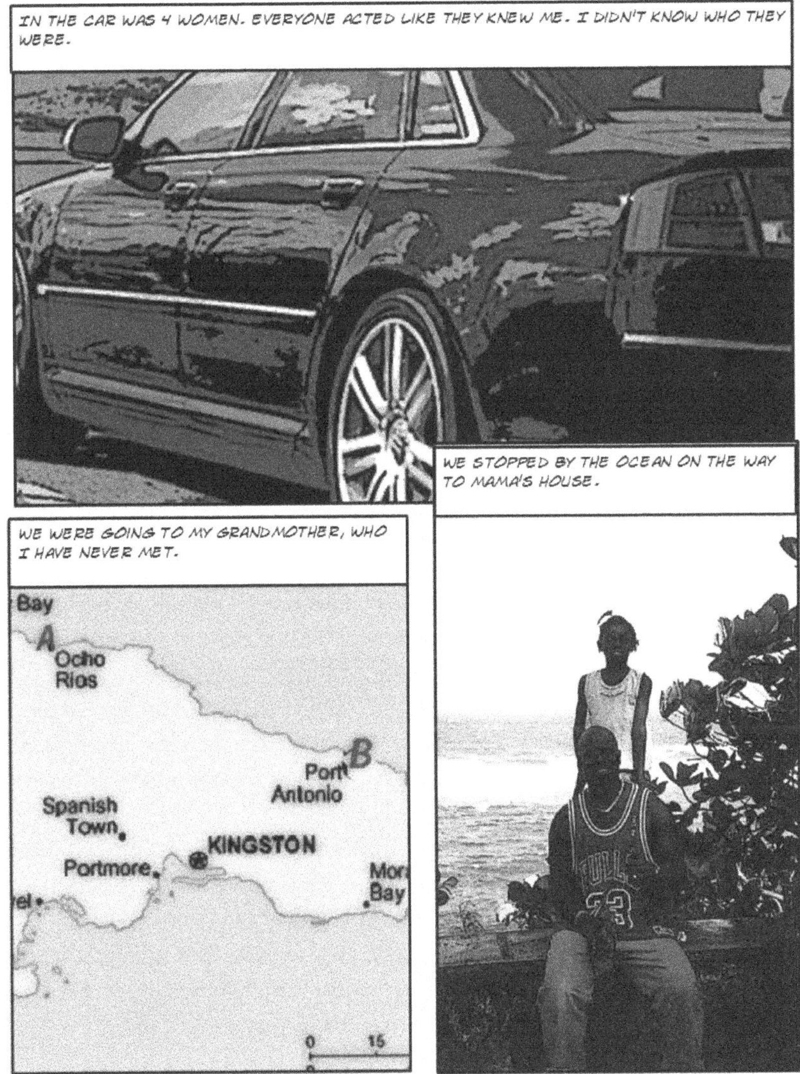

Fig. 7. The reveal in "Untitled"

Even as the audience is reeling from this recognition and the reconfigurations it demands, the memoir moves quickly to its conclusion. For two pages, the audience glimpses the real players in the family drama, though their motives and feelings remain mysterious. An unlabeled map sets the story in Jamaica, while the narrator's comment that the "American drink" made her feel "special" suggests the child's awareness of some kind of cultural power differential—layers upon layers of unspoken complexities ("Untitled" 8). In the penultimate panel, the child is surrounded by her new family. That potential resolution is immediately withdrawn on the final, single-panel page, on which appears the comics' one hand-drawn image: a soda bottle knocked over, its last drops spilling on the ground (see fig. 8). The last comment from the narration suggests but does not elaborate on lingering traces of regret and miscommunication. As the comic concludes, the final gap opens wide, leaving the audience "wondering what happens after this" ("Analytic"). Like perhaps the author herself, the reader remains in the gutter—McCloud's "limbo" (*Understanding* 66)—trying to achieve some kind of closure that may never be possible.

Narration: Minimalist Pathos

The preceding analysis of Kayan's gap-riddled composition highlights her strategic choices regarding how much (and how little) narrative guidance to provide. Following dominant conventions, the present-tense narrator's voice is contained in the text boxes at the top of most panels. Although Kayan planned to "use narration of the adult me to show the effects" of her past events on her current life, her narrating-I is succinct, even terse ("Proposal" 1); the final version contains only spare exposition without reflection until the very last page. Short, direct sentences provide basic information and straightforward descriptions of the protagonist's response: "I didn't know what was going on… I left my home with nothing" ("Untitled" 6). This minimal narration allows the audience to experience only the same amount of knowledge available to the young protagonist: confusion in the face of adults' inscrutable behavior. The experiencing-I within the panels is similarly quiet. The character of Kayan communicates only one thought and three lines of speech, almost all of which are the questions of an anxious child: "Are you mad?" (3). She voices one (unanswered) objection, as she is pulled out the door: "But I haven't packed my stuff yet" (6). That is the last time she speaks. Over the remaining pages, a single speech balloon reads: "Nice to finally be with your family, isn't it Kayan?" (8). The child offers no response.

Fig. 8. The conclusion of "Untitled"

In this panel and the striking last page, the narrator reveals a bit more of both her past and present selves' feelings. The young protagonist appears surrounded by this new family as the narrator explains that her initial shyness is overcome by a foreign treat that makes her "feel special"; her father teases her about how easily she became someone's "best friend" ("Untitled" 8). Only on the final page does the narrator refer to the present, with a conclusion that is both blunt and oblique: "I didn't think much about that joke then. But now my father still jokes about it… I should never had [sic] drank it" (see fig. 8) ("Untitled" 9). The adult acknowledges that she should have resisted the temptation—but true to form, she does not explain why. Instead, she leaves the reader to contemplate the combination of her regret and the image of a spilled soda. The reticence of the verbal narration ensures that the audience is both excluded from the author's personal reflections and invited to fill in the interpretive gaps.

Focalization: The Presence of the Past

Kayan's visual representation of events factors in the revisions of memory. Unlike Axel's approach, however, this present-day vantage point is not clearly distinguished from past experiences. Whereas most students used the visible distinction between the experiencing-I and narrating-I to prove how different, how much more mature, their present selves were, Kayan resisted that neat dividing line. Instead, she deliberately plays with time and identity, manipulating her visual focalization and restricting her verbal narration to match the child's limited knowledge—at least until that final page and her retrospective judgment. Kayan's strategy emphasizes the ever-present nature of that past; her decision to represent her childhood self as a college-aged woman highlights "how certain things still affect me today" ("Analytic" 1). The revelation of her true age therefore serves both to emphasize the vulnerability of the child and the damage to the adult.

Throughout most of Kayan's memoir, the perspective offered to the audience invites them to sympathize with the young woman. The mysterious car looms threateningly, as do the fighting adults. As she packs, the camera is positioned above her, emphasizing her vulnerability while the gesture of wiping a tear away illustrates the emotional stress she's under. When she is pulled out the door, the young woman looks back over her shoulder, directly at the reader who is positioned as a (witnessed) witness to her sadness (see fig. 9). This scene solidifies the connection between reader and character—immediately before Kayan pulls back the curtain to reveal her "true" younger self. Suddenly, the relationship between narrator and audience is destabilized as the audience must revise their perception of the story and its teller. The effect demonstrates the persistence of this past in the present, the author's own focalization. From her current vantage point, those childhood scenes merge past and present selves, the narrating-I and experiencing-I both still living this experience. It's a powerful move made possible through a sophisticated negotiation of available resources.

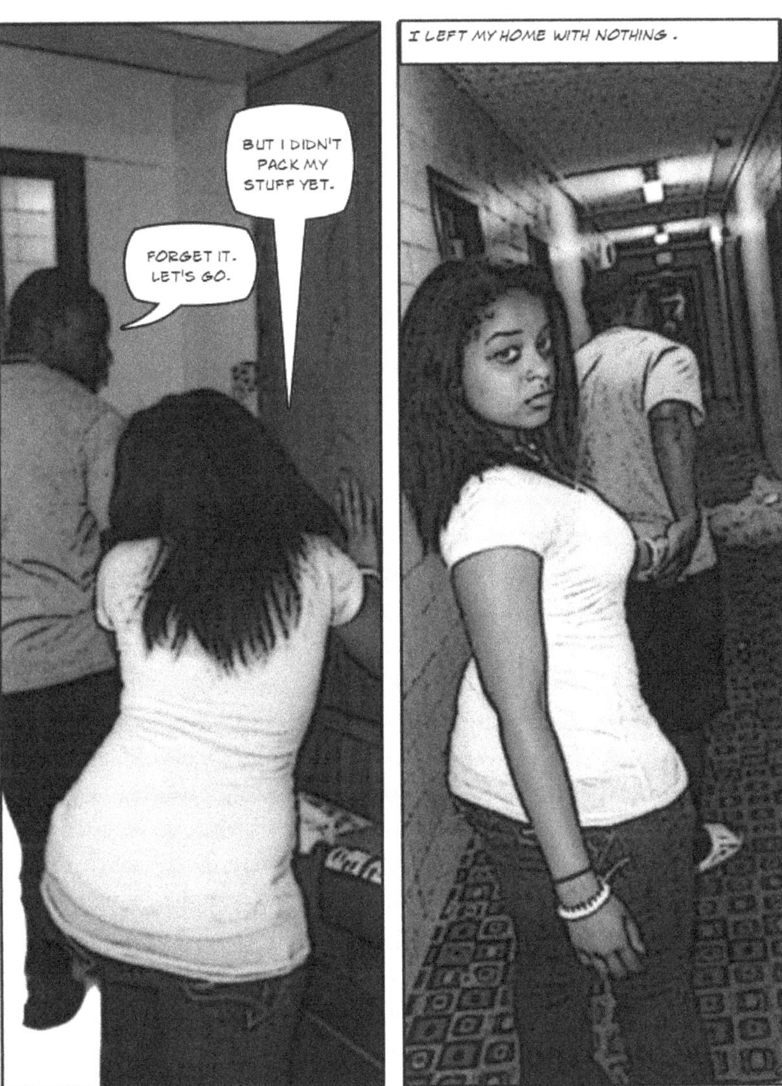

Fig. 9. The protagonist's gaze in "Untitled"

The Redesigned: Rhetorical Multiliteracies

The value of reading comics in the classroom has been well argued; these two students, like others from the class, make a compelling case for the potential of composing comics—and, in particular, graphic memoirs—to help students achieve the core outcomes of critical literacy pedagogies, which include the following:

1. understanding that a text is not a transparent window on reality, but is constructed;
2. developing and demonstrating rhetorical awareness both as a composer of text and as a reader of text; and
3. developing agency as a communicator and as a reader, rather than opting for the passivity that our popular media environment makes so easy. (Duffelmeyer and Ellertson, n.p.)

According to my own observations and students' reflections, their investment in this course easily surpassed typical student engagement in (required) composition courses, resulting in high attendance, active participation, and a positive workshop dynamic. Even as they struggled with technical and conceptual frustrations, students expressed relief at finding a course that they "actually" (a telling and frequently used adverb) enjoyed and found intellectually stimulating. The theory-driven study of comics in this course expanded students' understanding of what "counts" as rhetoric, while the critical perspectives on identity and self-representation prompted by graphic memoir highlighted rhetoric's stakes in their own lives. These results exceeded all of our expectations and extended beyond a single semester. Of course, I am neither suggesting that all composition courses should incorporate comics, nor that they should replace other valuable assignments, nor that this course indelibly affected students' worldviews or communication styles. But with a critical framework and creative practices, comic narratives offer students and teachers opportunities for serious play with significant rewards.

Notes

1. Comics master Will Eisner highlights the centrality of the gestural mode: "In comics, body posture and gesture occupy a position of primacy over text. The manner in which these images are employed modifies and defines the intended meaning of the words" (103). Spatial literacy comes into play, as Scott McCloud highlights in *Understanding Comics* and *Making Comics*, in the layout of panels on the page; their relation to each other, and the gutters between them, reflects crucial nuances of time, tension, and progression. In terms of audio communication, other resources combine to enable the representation of volume and tone, including what Catherine Khordoc calls "visual sound effects." As such claims suggest, comics demonstrate and demand multimodal literacies that are more than the sum of their parts.

2. Composition scholars and teachers draw extensively upon critical, social, and cultural theories as well as the social sciences to understand and validate "personal" or "life" writing. For recent work, see Cook-Sather; Higgins and Brush; Jackson; Kill; LeCourt; Park; Robillard; and Weiser, Horak, and Monroe. Informed and inspired by these approaches, my own draws heavily upon rhetorical theories of narrative from within literary studies, whose analytic tools I find particularly valuable for a rhetorical approach to autobiographical narratives.

3. Students' point of entry into this class was a university-wide advanced/upper-division writing requirement; almost all would have previously taken the first-year writing course, which emphasized rhetorical analysis and academic inquiry. The setting was a large public midwestern university populated by a predominantly white, middle-class, traditional-age student body, in 2010. This case study formed part of an IRB-approved classroom-based research project in which the vast majority of students enrolled in the course consented to participate. Data collected includes anonymous surveys distributed at the beginning and end of the semester as well as the course assignments: an informal blog, verbal- and visual-only micro memoirs (building on *SMITH Magazine*'s "Six Words" memoir project), an analytic essay, and a graphic memoir composition, with reflections on each. Course readings included Art Spiegelman's *Maus*, Marjane Satrapi's *Persepolis*, an assortment of short autobiographical comics, and secondary readings from comics and narrative scholars like Scott McCloud, Rocco Versaci, Jerome Bruner, and James Phelan. All student quotations are used with IRB consent. Because some wished to remain anonymous, I cite student authors using pseudonym initials only.

4. This selection of theoretical informants, like the secondary readings assigned in class, was by no means exhaustive. As a relative newcomer to comics studies, I was not yet familiar with Thierry Groensteen's *System of Comics*; his *Comics and Narration* and Barbara Postema's *Narrative Structure in Comics* were not yet published. Future work in narrative and comics studies would benefit from consideration of these and other contributions. However, because my goal here is to examine students' conscious rhetorical praxis, the analyses refer to those theoretical concepts and readings I introduced to them at the time.

5. Groensteen's notion of arthrology—the sequential or networked relations among comic images through which meaning is made—would complement examinations of narrative gaps and closure in a more advanced comics studies course than the level I discuss here.

6. For the sake of clarity, the discussion of narration in this course focused specifically on *verbal* narration, the voice of the storyteller, and therefore deemphasized the role of visuals in supplying descriptions of the setting and action within comics. Postema's chapter "Show and Tell: The Process of Narration" productively complicates this convenient distinction between the verbal and visual and would be useful for more advanced pedagogical applications.

7. A complementary concept from narratology, that of the implied author, can be a useful extension of this distinction to prevent students from conflating the author as evident in the text with his/her "real" flesh-and-blood self. The debates surrounding the implied author are extensive; for an overview, see Kindt and Muller; Lanser; and Phelan.

8. Students used the affordable and user-friendly software ComicLife, which provides page templates, text boxes, speech and thought balloons, visual effects, and other design details. An expanding assortment of free comics-creation tools can also be found online.

9. The relative weight of words and images on this page is an example of what Postema calls verbal overdetermination, or a departure from conventional balance

that may be either flawed design or deliberate creation of tension (91). Because this text and concept were not part of the course conversation, I cannot directly speak to Axel's decision-making process for this page. The crowded results, however, seem to communicate the "too much" quality of the story that he edited out.

10. Whitlock's expression, "auto-biographic avatar," would offer students a helpful label for these visual self-portraits, whether drawn or photographed (971).

Works Cited

A.B. "Comment on 'Composition 4 Story'." *Illustrating Lives*. Private course blog. N.p., 29 May 2010. Web. 3 Feb. 2014.

Bruner, Jerome. "Self-Making and World-Making." *Narrative and Identity: Studies in Autobiography, Self and Culture.* Eds. Jens Brockmeier and Donal Carbaugh. Philadelphia: John Benjamins, 2001. 25-37. Print.

Case, Alison A. *Plotting Women: Gender and Narration in the Eighteenth- and Nineteenth-Century British Novel.* Charlottesville: UP of Virginia, 1999. Print.

Chute, Hillary. "Comics as Literature? Reading Graphic Narrative." *Publications of the Modern Language Association* 123.2 (2008): 452-65. Print.

---. *Graphic Women: Life Narrative and Contemporary Comics.* New York: Columbia UP, 2010. Print.

Cook-Sather, Alison. "Students Transforming Notions of Narrative and Self." *CCC* 55.1 (2003): 91-114. Print.

Crilley, Mark. "Getting Students to Write Using Comics." *Teacher Librarian* 37.1 (2009): 28-31. Print.

Duffelmeyer, Barb Blakely, and Anthony Ellertson. "Critical Visual Literacy: Multimodal Communication Across the Curriculum." *Across the Disciplines: A Journal of Language, Learning, and Academic Writing* 3 (2005): n. pag. Web. 13 Apr. 2014. <http://wac.colostate.edu/atd/visual/dufflemeyer_ellerston.cfm>.

Eisner, Will. *Comics as Sequential Art.* Tamarac: Poorhouse, 1985. Print.

G., Kayan. "Untitled." 2010. TS. Collection of Kathryn Comer.

---. "Comment on 'Narrowing the Topic'." *Illustrating Lives.* Private course blog. N.p., 8 June 2010. Web. 10 Jan. 2014.

---. "Analytic Refection." 2010. TS. Collection of Kathryn Comer.

---. "Proposal." 2010. TS. Collection of Kathryn Comer.

Gardner, Jared. "Autography's Biography, 1972-2007." *Biography* 31.1 (2008): 1-26. Print.

Genette, Gerard. *Narrative Discourse: An Essay in Method.* Ithaca: Cornell UP, 1983. Print.

Groensteen, Thierry. *Comics and Narration.* Trans. Ann Miller. Jackson: UP of Mississippi, 2013. Print.

---. *The System of Comics*. Trans. Bart Beaty and Nick Nguyen. Jackson: UP of Mississippi, 2007. Print.

Handsfield, Lara J., Tami R. Dean, and Kristin M. Cielocha. "Becoming Critical Consumers and Producers of Text: Teaching with Web 1.0 and Web 2.0." *The Reading Teacher* 63.1 (2009): 40-50. Print.

Hatfield, Charles. *Alternative Comics: An Emerging Literature.* Jackson: UP of Mississippi, 2005. Print.

Higgins, Lorraine D., and Lisa D. Brush. "Personal Experience Narrative and Public Debate: Writing the Wrong of Welfare." *CCC* 57.4 (2006): 694-729. Print.

I.M. "Trouble with Preaching the Word." 2010. TS. Collection of Kathryn Comer.

Iser, Wolfgang. *Prospecting: From Reader Response to Literary Anthropology.* Baltimore: Johns Hopkins UP, 1989. Print.

---. "The Reading Process: A Phenomenological Approach." *New Literary Studies* 3.2 (1972): 279-99. Print.

Jackson, Zoevera Ann. "Connecting Video Games and Storytelling to Teach Narratives in First-Year Composition." *Kairos* 7.3 (2002): n. pag. Web. 15 May 2013. <http://kairos.technorhetoric.net/7.3/coverweb/jackson/>.

Jacobs, Dale. "Marveling at *The Man Called Nova*: Comics as Sponsors of Multimodal Literacy." *CCC* 59.2 (2007): 180-205. Print.

---. "More than Words: Comics as a Means of Teaching Multiple Literacies." *English Journal* 96.3 (2007): 9-25. Print.

---. "Multimodal Constructions of Self: Autobiographical Comics and the Case of Joe Matt's *Peepshow*." *Biography* 31.1 (2008): 59-84. Print.

K., Axel. "Always Wear Your Helmet!" 2010. TS. Collection of Kathryn Comer.

---. "Analysis and Reflection on 'Always Wear Your Helmet!'" 2010. TS. Collection of Kathryn Comer.

---. "Illustration for Comp 4." *Illustrating Lives.* Private course blog. N.p., 23 May 2010. Web. 10 Jan. 2014.

---. "Proposal for 'Always Wear Your Helmet!'" 2010. TS. Collection of Kathryn Comer.

K.S. "Images in Persepolis." *Illustrating Lives.* Private course blog. N.p., 2 May 2010. Web. 3 Feb. 2014.

Khordoc, Catherine. "The Comic Book's Soundtrack: Visual Sound Effects in Asterix." *The Language of Comics: Word and Image.* Ed. Robin Varnum and Christina T. Gibbons. Jackson: UP of Mississippi, 2001. 156-73. Print.

Kill, Melanie. "Acknowledging the Rough Edges of Resistance: Negotiation of Identities for First-Year Writing Composition." *CCC* 58.2 (2006): 213-35. Print.

Kindt, Tom, and Hans-Harald Müller. *The Implied Author: Concept and Controversy.* New York: Walter de Gruyter, 2006. Print.

Lanser, Susan S. "(Im)plying the Author." *Narrative* 9.2 (2009): 153-60. Print.

LeCourt, Donna. "Performing Working-Class Identity in Composition: Toward a Pedagogy of Textual Practice." *College English* 69.1 (2006): 30-51. Print.

Lejeune, Philippe. "The Autobiographical Pact." *On Autobiography.* Trans. Katherine Leary. Ed. John Paul Eakin. Minneapolis: U of Minnesota P, 1989. 3-30. Print.

M.S. "Illustrating Composition 4." *Illustrating Lives.* Private course blog. N.p., 24 May 2010. Web. 7 Feb. 2014.

McCloud, Scott. *Making Comics: Storytelling Secrets of Comics, Manga, and Graphic Novels.* New York: Harper Collins, 2006. Print.

---. *Understanding Comics: The Invisible Art.* New York: Harper Perrenial, 1993. Print.

Micciche, Laura R. "Seeing and Reading Incest: A Study of Debbie Drechsler's *Daddy's Girl*." *Rhetoric Review* 23.1 (2004): 5-20. Print.

Morrison, Timothy G., Gregory Bryan, and George W. Chilcoat. "Using Student-Generated Comic Books in the Classroom." *Journal of Adolescent & Adult Literacy* 45.8 (2002): 758-67. Print.

New London Group. "A Pedagogy of Multiliteracies: Designing Social Futures." *Harvard Education Review* 66.1 (1996): 60-92. Web.

Olney, James. "Autobiography and the Cultural Moment: A Thematic, Historical, and Bibliographical Introduction." *Autobiography: Essays Theoretical and Critical.* Ed. James Olney. Princeton: Princeton UP, 1980. 3-27. Print.

Park, Jeff. *Writing at the Edge: Narrative and Writing Process Theory.* New York: Peter Lang, 2004. Print.

Phelan, James. *Experiencing Fiction: Judgments, Progressions, and the Rhetorical Theory of Narrative.* Columbus: Ohio State UP, 2007. Print.

Postema, Barbara. *Narrative Structure in Comics: Making Sense of Fragments.* Rochester: RIT P, 2013. Print.

Q.K. "Comment on 'Comp 4'." *Illustrating Lives.* Private course blog. N.p., 18 May 2010. Web. 10 Feb. 2014.

Robillard, Amy E. "It's Time for Class: Toward a More Complex Pedagogy of Narrative." *College English* 66.1 (2003): 74-92. Print.

Satrapi, Marjane. *The Complete Persepolis.* New York: Pantheon, 2004. Print.

Schwartz, Adam, and Elaine Rubinstein-Avila. "Understanding the Manga Hype: Uncovering the Multimodality of Comic-book Literacies." *Journal of Adolescent & Adult Literacy* 50.1 (2006): 40-49. Print.

"Six Words." *SMITH Magazine*, 2015. Web. 5 Jan. 2015. <http://www.sixwordmemoirs.com/>

Spiegelman, Art. *Maus, Volumes 1 & 2.* 1973; 1986. New York: Pantheon, 1991. Print.

V.A. "What Is There to Be Afraid of?" 2010. TS. Collection of Kathryn Comer.

Versaci, Rocco. *This Book Contains Graphic Language: Comics as Literature.* New York: Continuum, 2007. Print.

Weiser, M. Elizabeth, Joseph J. Horak, and Debra Monroe. "Beyond Shame: The Dialogic Narrative and Comic Cognition." *JAC* 27.3/4 (2007): 563-89. Print.

Whitlock, Gillian. "Autographics: The Seeing 'I' of the Comics." *Modern Fiction Studies* 54.4 (2006): 965-79. Print.

Witek, Joseph. "Seven Ways I Don't Teach Comics." Ed. Stephen E. Tabachnick. *Teaching the Graphic Novel.* New York: MLA, 2009. 217-22. Print.

The Work of Comics Collaborations: Considerations of Multimodal Composition for Writing Scholarship and Pedagogy

Molly J. Scanlon

Though multimodality is increasingly incorporated into our pedagogies and scholarship, explorations of collaborative multimodal composition are lacking. Existing literature on collaborative writing focuses predominately on texts either composed in singular modes or by a single author, neglecting the ways in which multimodal texts are composed collaboratively. Likewise, scholarship of multimodality largely leans toward digital texts/contexts in its examinations of such work. As a field, we need a more comprehensive grasp on the work of collaborative multimodal composing. This essay uses case studies about comics writers and artists to complicate our understanding of collaborative multimodal composition and to generate considerations for writing scholarship and pedagogy. Multimodal composers should (1) understand the audience as co-collaborators; (2) identify the genre of the deliverable; (3) develop custom production and feedback loops; and (4) foreground the *work* of multimodal composing. Understanding these four factors enriches our understanding of the disorienting phenomena experienced by those composing multimodal texts collaboratively.

Multimodal composition is always already a result of collaboration between modes, challenging the work of composition as much as enriching its rhetorical potential. In the case studies presented here, collaboration between authors becomes a complicating force in multimodal composition processes. I extend phenomena observed in two case studies toward considerations for scholarship and pedagogy.

The existing scholarship on multimodal composition engages several metaphors: frameworks, hybrids, convergences, amorphous genres, tireless knotwork, elusive ecologies, and new labor.[1] Collectively the literature communicates how composing collaboratively in multiple modes can be a disorienting process. Henry Jenkins writes that convergence is a mechanism to navigate such a "moment of disorienting change. Convergence is, in a sense, an old concept taking on new meanings" (6). This article asks readers to acknowledge two different types of disorientation related to collaborative multimodal composing: first, how old concepts in collaborative writing scholarship and pedagogy take on new meanings in the context of multimodal composition, and second, how old concepts in multimodality scholarship and pedagogy take on new meanings in the context of collaboration.

While collaborative writing has been defined in relation to the social nature of meaning-making practices, discussion of collaborative multimodal composition has been sparse in recent publications. I address this absence by focusing on two texts that have helped me understand how teams of comics writers and authors work together: Liz Losh, Jonathan Alexander, Zander Cannon and Kevin Cannon's *Understanding Rhetoric*, as well as the Cheo Comics series by Maria Brunette, Carlos Evia, and Nick Thorkelson.

Of course, studying teams of multimodal composers is not unprecedented. Barbara Mirel, Susan Feinberg, and Leif Allmendinger—two writers and a graphic designer—cooperatively composed a software manual and recorded conflicts that arose throughout the process. Mirel, Feinberg, and Allmendinger found that identifying and overcoming conflict together could be effective and "involved negotiating about principles from our respective fields, which—not surprisingly—fell into three broad areas: writing issues, graphic design issues, and issues common to both practices" (265-6). The collaboration eventually resulted in a shared identity: "[D]espite concrete differences between our disciplinary perspectives, in a more global sense we all belonged to the discourse community of information designers" (268). Mirel, Feinberg, and Allmendinger conclude with reflections on how the work of collaboration has the potential to enrich multimodal texts: "[N]ew arrangements characterized by increased dialogue, codevelopment, and coproduction will generate innovative textual choices and improve the quality of documentation" (262).

Writing in 2010, nearly twenty years after Mirel, Feinberg, and Allmendinger, Geoffrey Cross conducted a study of writers and artists at an advertising agency. Cross's study focused on how visual and verbal skills were enacted during brainstorming sessions for the development of a multi-genre advertising campaign. He concludes: "[W]hen we investigated a verbal-visual variety of collaboration, not only does the concept of authorship change from that of the romantic writer working alone in the garret, but also *our very concept of writer and artist change as these roles overlap and to a degree merge*" (149-50, emphasis in original). Cross, like Mirel, Feinberg, and Allmendinger, not only describes the dynamic nature of author identity and roles in visual/verbal collaboration but also identifies the ways in which dialogue can facilitate collaborative acts by merging multiliteracies.

When a text is multimodal, the collaborative composing process becomes increasingly complex. Comics are especially rich for exploring multimodal composition because they combine image and text interdependently.[2] According to Mirel, Feinberg, and Allmendinger as well as Cross, the work of collaboration becomes an issue not of *either* artist *or* writer, but of *both* writer *and* artist. As an extension of these prior studies, this article seeks to redefine specific aspects of the work of collaboration—audience, genre, and recursivity—by focusing on two cases: the Cheo comics (a comics tutorial for construction safety) and *Understanding Rhetoric* (a first-year writing textbook in comics form). I use findings from my analysis of these comics collaborations to argue that collaborative work in this context is more complicated than what is depicted in existing collaborative composing and multimodality scholarship. While analyzing interview data and collaborative documentation from the teams, I found it difficult—if not impossible—to ignore the disorientation collaborators experienced as they composed multimodally. Such disorientation became productive for authors and for this study. Their collective ability to navigate disorientation became a marker of success for authors. Observing the difficult work of multimodal collaboration forced me to consider how familiar concepts like audience, genre, and recursivity take on new meaning in dynamic composing scenes.

To some extent, the nature of multimodal collaboration extends work we already do in the classroom, such as teaching conceptions of audience and genre. These collaborations, however, also emphasize long-overlooked aspects regarding the genres and materiality of multimedia, such as composing in hybrid genres and developing structures for feedback and revision. This essay uses case studies about comics writers and artists to complicate our understanding of collaborative multimodal composition and to generate considerations for writing scholarship and pedagogy: (1) understand the audience as co-collaborators; (2) identify the genre of the deliverable; (3) develop custom production and feedback loops; and (4) foreground the *work* of multimodal composing. Findings from these case studies are presented as descriptive, not generalizable understandings of collaborative multimodal composition. Similarly, the resulting considerations I offer here are intended to be generative, not definitive suggestions for multimodal composers as they collaborate. It is my hope that sharing the results of my research can stimulate conversations about the work of collaborative multimodal composition.

Understand the Audience as Co-Collaborators

An initial finding from research on comics teams regards the pervasiveness of the audience in helping authors articulate and achieve project goals in ways productive to the collaboration. An examination of the Cheo comics reveals how the authors included their audience as co-collaborators in an effort to produce the most effective comic tutorial for Latino construction workers, who are more likely to incur workplace injuries than any other group. Maria Brunette articulates the additional exigence to reach this particular audience:

> Besides agriculture, the construction industry is the top employer for these immigrant workers who usually lack trade related skills and, more significantly, language skills (approximately one third of Hispanic construction workers speak only Spanish). These workers also bring with them a unique sociocultural background that deserves to be taken into account. (244)

Brunette and colleague Carlos Evia are both scholars of workplace communication in addition to being authors of the Cheo comics. Together with Nick Thorkelson, long-time cartoonist and illustrator, they composed a series of three comics. One of three comics produced by the collaborative group, "Cheo and his Uncle," focuses on safety practices when using stationary and mobile scaffolds. In this comic, the authors recreate vicarious learning, a common practice in workplace communication and safety training. More often than not, workers learn more effectively from the experiences of their co-workers than from traditional formats like training presentations and handouts. In "Cheo and his Uncle," Cheo visits his uncle, who was injured in a fall from a scaffold while on the job, in the hospital before going to work. After the visit, Cheo arrives at work and begins building a scaffold. As he works, he can't help but hear his uncle's voice reminding him of the do's and don'ts of scaffold safety (see fig. 1).

Fig 1. Example page from "Cheo and His Uncle." Used with permission of Carlos Evia and Nick Thorkelson.

Cheo's Uncle: "This thing I told you is for stationed scaffolds; that means, those that do not move; mobile scaffolds have their own risks."
Always secure the wheels of a mobile scaffold when it is being used.
--

It's never a good idea to move the scaffold from the elevated nest.

--

You can miss some obstacles invisible from above. "Yikes!"Flying like a catapult!

The Cheo comics present tutorials using concepts with which workers identify—like the nod to vicarious learning in "Cheo and his Uncle." The success of the comics is due to the collaborators' inclusion of the target audience—Latino construction workers—in the composition of safety materials. The authors' collaborative multimodal composition was highly informed by feedback from the workers themselves.

Cheo Comics as Intercultural Communication

The Cheo comics have to serve a complex set of needs for its audience. Latino workers populate much of the construction workforce in the United States, and yet Occupational Safety and Health Association (OSHA) standards and regulations rarely address their language and literacy needs. Occupational culture is an aspect of technical communication that functions as a significant constraint for collaborators. For safety tutorials like the Cheo comics, workers' literacies and workplace culture[3] inform the tutorial's effectiveness to catalyze behavioral change in workers' safety practices. Construction is an industry marked by competitive contractors and subcontractors, as well as bottom-line managerial priorities that conflict with the personal safety priorities of workers (Evia and Patriarca 2). Working within the constraints of this culture is crucial. Brunette and Evia engage workers in the collaboration through participatory design, a technical communication best practice that enables authors to create more effective materials for their audience.[4] In order to address audience needs, the authors had to center the workers in the collaborative composing process and position the Cheo comics as intercultural communication that addresses the influence of both Mexican-American culture and workplace culture on the text.

Evia's childhood in Mexico was spent poring over the pages of any comic book he could find. His Mexican culture informed the collaborators' use of comics in workplace communication, because in Mexico comics are not just for entertainment; comics can reaffirm or challenge issues of national identity, regional cultural values, family structure, gender roles, and workplace responsibility. Throughout the twentieth century comics became helpful resources, particularly for Mexicans who emigrated to the U.S. and found themselves employed at construction sites with extensive government regulation and industry standardization, both of which were often communicated in a language and/or delivered in genres unfamiliar to them.

The comics' main character, Cheo, is always thinking about his family while he is making decisions. Since many Mexican comics center on work, there is an implicit focus on family and financial support (Rubenstein). Cheo's commitment to family became a cornerstone appeal toward persuading workers to make safer choices in the workplace. The team focused on familial responsibility and financial support to counteract some workers' tendencies to take risks, which the authors aligned with Latino machismo culture. The first comic in the series, "Lucky Cheo," builds on the commitment to family while engaging workplace expectations in occupational culture as it tells the story of a young worker pressed by management to take risks when using ladders so that the labor can be more profitable. Cheo's luck nearly runs out when he falls, but ultimately he suffers no injury. In the end, Cheo decides, "I've got a family that depends on me. From now on, I'm depending on smarts, not luck." "Cheo and His Uncle" demonstrates how family connections can inform workplace decision-making, especially after a family member is injured on the job. "Cheo and His Advisors" examines machismo culture through a story in which Cheo is visited by an angel, Mr. Use-Your-Head," and a devil, Mr. Know-It-All. Cheo must make good decisions despite the pressure to take risks (see fig. 2). He turns to each visitor for advice:

Fig. 2. Mr. Know-It-All and Mr. Use-Your-Head. From "Cheo and His Advisors." Used with permission of Carlos Evia and Nick Thorkelson.

Cheo: Mr. Know-It-All…
Mr. Know-It-All: Take a few risks.
Mr. Know-It-All: Time is money, Old-Timer!
Mr. Know-It-All: Show them what you're made of.
--

Cheo: And Mr. Use-Your-Head.
Mr. Use-Your-Head: Better safe than sorry.
Mr. Use-Your-Head: Your crew is depending on you,
Mr. Use-Your-Head: not to mention your family.

Evia's ability to identify with Latino culture forms the basis of "Cheo and His Advisors." Mr. Know-It-All eggs Cheo on through narrow definitions of masculinity in Latino culture (i.e., by saying "Show them what you're made of."). But constructs of masculinity are only one piece of the puzzle. Mr. Know-It-All uses a two-pronged approach, pressuring Cheo through the bottom line as well as job insecurity ("Time is money, Old-Timer!").

Workers as Co-Collaborators

In addition to the influences of workers' ethnic culture, workplace microculture can sway worker decision-making. Elaine Cullen and Albert Fein argue that "[f]or any training to be truly effective, it is necessary to choose the theoretical framework that best fits the trainees themselves as well as the organization's training objectives and its occupational culture" (13). In order to more fully comprehend the influences of culture on their audience, Thorkelson and Evia had to take into account factors that largely influence how workers interpret and comprehend workplace communication—be it visual, textual, or otherwise. Understanding the constraints that influence workplace communication better equipped Evia and Thorkelson to compose the Cheo comics *with* their audience of Latino construction workers, thus positioning audience members as co-collaborators.

Brunette and Evia were largely responsible for involving the workers in the collaborative process in order to produce comics tutorials that were equipped to articulate why/how workers should change their behaviors to be safer at work. It was Brunette who first engaged workers through a series of focus groups on the first phase of training flyers and presentations (see fig. 3). This feedback was then passed on to Thorkelson for an early prototype of Cheo: "I did a cartoon of a worker with his family and someone said, 'He wouldn't be wearing a hard hat' with his family." While the intention was to show Cheo with his family before leaving for work, Thorkelson had denoted Cheo's identity primarily as a worker in his early representation, even in the context of Cheo's life at home with his family, which confused workers in a focus group study.

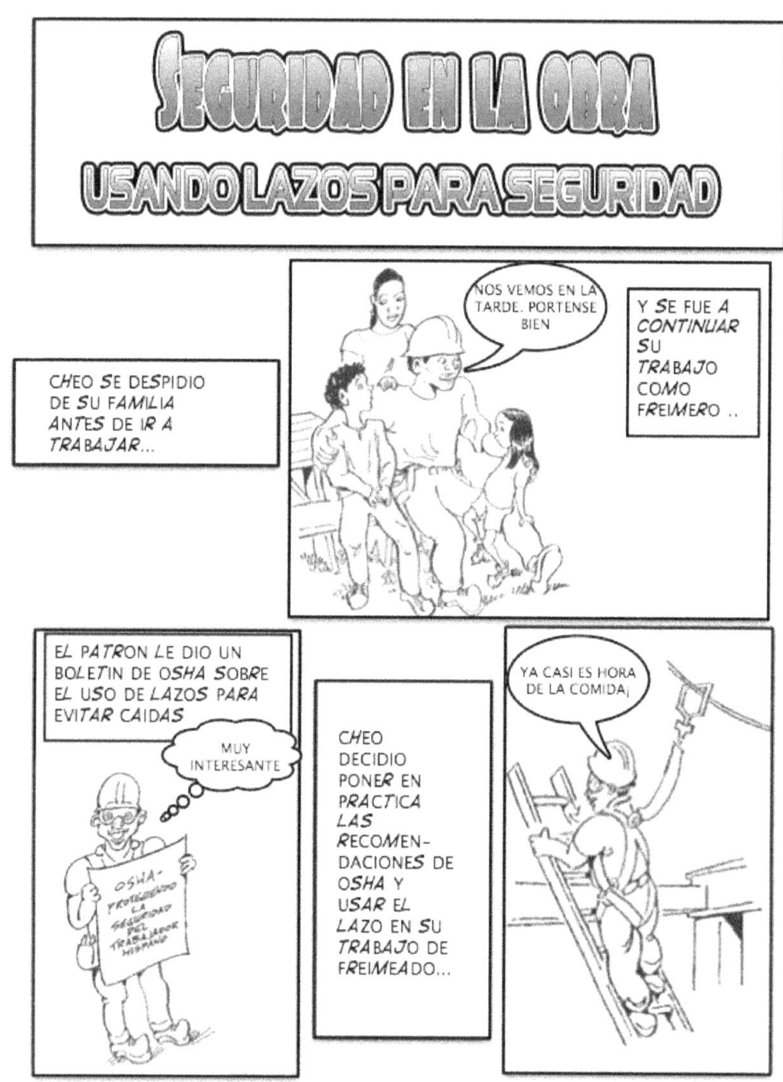

Fig. 3. From "Seguridad en la Obra." Used with permission of Nick Thorkelson.

"Safety on the Job: Using restraints for safety."
Cheo said goodbye to his family before going to work…
Cheo: "See you in the afternoon. Be Good."
…and continued to his job as a framer.

--

The boss gave him an OSHA newsletter on the use of restraints to prevent falls.
Cheo: *Very Interesting.*

--
Cheo decided to follow the OSHA recommendations to use the restraint when working as a framer.
--
Cheo: "It's almost dinner time."

Evia elicite feedback on the "Seguridad en la Obra" flyer from another group of workers and shared their responses with Thorkelson in an email:

> In previous experiments, I have seen workers who develop their own context for the comic books based on their experiences. I showed them one of the images of Cheo [Brunette] created before (the one where he is with his family) and of course the context was that Cheo was still at home and going to work. However, they didn't/couldn't read the whole text and assumed Cheo was with his family at work, and said it was a bad thing because "you are not supposed to bring your family to the jobsite." (Evia, "Ladder Safety Comic")

Instead of interpreting Cheo and his family as being at home, workers skipped the dialogue and assumed Cheo had brought his family to the jobsite without hard hats, a serious risk to their safety. Thorkelson incorporated the feedback. In this revised excerpt from "Cheo and His Advisors," he depicted Cheo as leaving for work in his everyday clothing, without his hardhat or safety vest, but donning the safety gear as soon as he is on the worksite (see fig. 4).

Fig. 4. From "Cheo and His Advisors." Used with permission of Carlos Evia and Nick Thorkelson.

Cheo: "Every morning I leave for work by myself."

--

Cheo: "But when I get to the job, I have these two with me."

The Cheo comics resulted from a growing interest in workplace communication research that uses multiple modes in order to create more effective training materials for the 2.7 million Latino construction workers in the U.S. (Brown; Brunette; Canales; Evia and Patriarca; Jaselskis et al.). In a recent article, Evia and co-writer Ashley Patriarca discuss how technical communicators engage the audience as co-collaborators in order to work toward a more effective learner-centered, participatory design process. Evia and Patriarca conclude that "Latino construction workers provided us with direct creative input, helping us create safety and risk communication products that not only complied with OSHA regulations but were evaluated as effective and culturally relevant for these workers and their peers" (3). Only by their exhaustive investigations of and collaborations with their audience did the authors understand the workers' literacy needs and cultural constraints and use this expertise to create successful tutorials about construction safety that would keep workers safe.

Audience inclusivity is not necessarily a new concept, even to those who don't teach or study technical communication. In various areas of writing studies—public rhetoric, genre studies, feminist research methodology, and community engagement—scholars have long called for more inclusive practices in teaching, research, and service.[5] In "Rhetorician as Agent of Social Change," for example, Ellen Cushman urges readers to engage "a deeper consideration of the civic purpose of our positions in the academy, of what we do with our knowledge, for whom, and by what means. . ." (12). The Cheo comics serve as evidence of the quality of multimodal compositions that can be produced through inclusive collaborative efforts. The authors understood the capacity of rhetoric to effect change and utilize inclusive participatory design, making their audience co-collaborators.

Identify the Genre of the Deliverable

During the process of composing any text, identifying the genre becomes an opportunity to articulate the formal and rhetorical qualities of the final product. Rhetorical genre studies (RGS) is proving especially effective in writing pedagogy because of its understanding of writing as performative, rhetoric as an agent of social change, and texts as entities that *do* things. Cheryl Ball argues for the ways in which purpose, form, and context must be considered simultaneously during the multimodal composing process. She recommends students compose using RGS to "choose their technology depending upon what arguments they want to make" (70). Ball conveys the significance of having students identify and analyze the desired genre in order to articulate the purpose of the argument, comprehend the interdependent relationship between form and content, and inform the text's design from the beginning stages of composing. In the case of Cheo comics, technical communication scholars and writers have long touted the multimodal affordances of the comics medium. An examination of the genre of technical communication comics—or techcommix—explains why.

Technical communication has shifted its audience focus to account first for the literacies of the workers/managers for whom the authors are writing. Literacy levels must be addressed for every training medium chosen, whether print, personal instruction, film and video, or computer-based training programs (Dholakiya 10). For genres like instructions and tutorials, the common training medium is often a combined visual/textual approach using comics and other visual narrative forms. The efficacy of the visual is invaluable to a genre like the tutorial and can include, "[p]ictures of tools, especially unfamiliar ones, needed for the construction of something; wiring diagrams or process flow diagrams; concept drawings, perhaps showing inputs, processes, and outputs; [and] sequence drawings that intentionally avoid words so that all audiences (and languages) can follow the development" (Penrose 412). Visuals can—and, arguably, should—be used for effective persuasion and increased audience engagement. The team behind the "Cheo Comics" exploits the affordances of visual communication through the hybrid genre techcommix. Techcommix effectively address workplace expectations as well as audience literacies, multilingual competencies, and the influence of culture.

For technical communicators, there are three primary strengths of comics: they can (1) increase accessibility to complex concepts; (2) engage multiple cognitive meaning-making processes; and (3) aid memory through improved retention of concepts learned. Brian Boyd argues that the most advantageous affordance of comics becomes the cognitive efficiency for readers, achieved through the interdependent combination of images and text that convey complex concepts in widely accessible ways. Mico Tatalovic argues that comics are especially suited to task-based activities because "the performance of technical tasks that such comics address is sequential in nature, just as comics are. . . ." (12). Comics also engage diverse cognitive meaning-making processes by asking readers to engage "multiple learning modalities (visual-spatial, kinesthetic-tactile, and auditory-sequential)" (Afrilyasanti and Basthomi 553) so that during the process of meaning-making, "both halves of the brain are involved in the interpretation of image contents" (Petterson 52-53). Active engagement is the basis of numerous contemporary learning theories according to Afrilyasanti and Basthomi, and Petterson, and one which improves not only learners' comprehension, but also their ability to retain and recall information long after. And when potential readers work in high-risk occupations, like construction, there is a very real exigence to make complex concepts accessible.

Brunette, Evia and Thorkelson were looking to engage a medium and a genre that best served its audience. The deliberate manner in which the Cheo comics' authors engaged techcommix starkly contrasts with the disorientation experienced by the collaborators of *Understanding Rhetoric*. The Cheo comics resulted from a technical communication tradition that long ago touted the potential of comics to increase audience comprehension. The authors of *Understanding Rhetoric* also sought the accessibility of comics, but for a different audience, purpose, and instructional tradition. The absence of educational comics genres in composition led to disorientation as authors formed a hybrid genre.

"We don't know what to call it": The Genre of Understanding Rhetoric

While comic textbooks in other disciplines have been in circulation for decades, the publication of *Understanding Rhetoric*[6] is a first for writing students, teachers, and scholars.[7] Writers Elizabeth Losh and Jonathan Alexander—with the help of Big Time Attic comics creators Zander Cannon and Kevin Cannon (no relation)—composed a first-year rhetoric textbook entirely in comics form. *Understanding Rhetoric* includes content typical of an instructional college writing textbook. For example, the page below presents Plato's argument that rhetoric was inferior to philosophy because, at best, it would become a hindrance to truth seeking and could, at worst, corrupt audiences through "ambiguous moral messages" (see fig. 5). In this example, Plato's fears about rhetoric—recorded more than 2,300 years ago—are illustrated through contemporary debates about video game violence and self-representation via the Internet. In *Understanding Rhetoric*, the medium was part of the text's earliest conception; the objective was to produce a print textbook in comics form. The genre, on the other hand, became less clear as the composing process unfolded.

In composition textbook publishing, there are three major genres: readers, handbooks, and rhetorics. *Understanding Rhetoric* is a rhetoric, the primary instructional text for a writing course. Outside of the textbook publishing industry, however, naming *Understanding Rhetoric*'s genre was not so easy. Writers, publishers, and artists alike struggled to name the genre, settling on a term only to abandon it and grasp at another. In interviews with Cannon and Cannon, as well as with Alexander and Bedford/St. Martin's development editor Carolyn Lengel, I asked, "What would you call this genre? How would you describe it?"

Fig 5. Page from *Understanding Rhetoric*, Issue 1: Why Rhetoric? Page 6. Permission from Bedford St. Martin's/Macmillan Higher Ed.

ZC This book? The rhetoric book? The genre? I don't know… [*Zander turns toward Kevin with an inquisitive look on his face. At the same moment Kevin turns toward him, looking equally thoughtful but puzzled*]…educational comics? textbook? [*Laughter*]

KC Sure, textbook. [*Kevin throws his arms up as he shrugs his shoulders*]

[. . .] I think this is above our pay grade. [*Laughter*]

ZC What it's trying to do, that it has in common with comics, is sort of leverage comics' accessibility and say, "Rhetoric seems to be this ill-understood word. [L]et's use comics' accessibility to make that story [. . .] or this concept a little bit more accessible." So, in that way, I think that it wants to make it as much like other comics as it can, but I think by its very nature—and the fact that it's this sort of educational, pedagogical narrative means that it's going to be different from Spider-man [*Laughter*] and all of that stuff, obviously, but even than other nonfiction comics.

JA I am working on a comic with my colleague Elizabeth Losh, called *Understanding Rhetoric*. And, it is a graphic book—we kind of actually don't know what to call it—I think a lot of people who work in this form don't necessarily know what to call what they produce. It's not a graphic novel because it's not a work of fiction. But, it's not exactly a comic book because it's an instructional book, so it's a graphic comic. Comic instructional. Words don't really capture it. But we've settled pretty much on graphic book or graphic guide.

CL And there are an awful lot of people teaching with graphic texts now. I mean, people who are using that kind of text in their writing class as readings. People are teaching *Maus* all over the place, and *Persepolis* and things like that [. . .] there's the canonical graphic novel text or graphic memoir—graphic text comic—we're still playing around with terminology. [*Laughter*] Yeah, that's the thing that makes my head spin.

Authors' reflections regarding the text's genre—and the language they used while deliberating—allowed me to understand the phenomenon of disorientation that occurs when a hybrid genre is first formed by collaborating authors.

In order to reorient the project after this disorientation, authors and editors had to carefully reflect upon which rhetorical and formal features the textbook would retain/discard from each of its antecedent genres: the first-year writing rhetoric textbook, and the didactic, instructional comic book. In interviews,

I asked each author, "How does the text simultaneously challenge and affirm the genre tradition of the Rhetoric?" Their replies were organized by comments about form and content (see Table 1):

What was so interesting about this interview data was the agreement among writers, artists, and editors on the fundamental purpose and larger project goals of the textbook, particularly the formal and rhetorical properties, despite their inability to name the hybrid genre itself. While the collaborative team ultimately chose "graphic guide" to describe the genre, this discussion of *Understanding Rhetoric* led to the realization that disorientation was experienced both by producers (authors and publishers) and consumers (writing instructors and their students).

Research on these comics teams supports Ball's assertions that RGS offers a frame for understanding process in a way that can translate to the classroom. Identifying the genre is an important part of the composing process but is particularly crucial in collaborative multimodal composing because of the increased possibility that students may converge more than one existing genre and/or medium and interpret the formal and rhetorical qualities of these in divergent ways.

Develop Custom Production and Feedback Loops

Like hybrid genres, the complex materiality of multimodal texts can complicate composing processes and the lenses we apply to the resulting products. This consideration reminds us to acknowledge that altering the mode(s) of communication necessarily alters the process through which the text is composed. During the publication of *Understanding Rhetoric*, several negotiations occurred in order to revise the traditional textbook publishing process to accommodate the comics medium, perhaps the most compelling finding from this case. Forming a hybrid genre resulted in one type of disorientation for the authors; the work of collaboratively composing this multimodal text resulted in yet another.

In the traditional textbook production process the most time-consuming stage includes development of the manuscript. In the case of *Understanding Rhetoric*, the scripts went through at least eight revision cycles before they were drawn in pencil for the layouts stage. The initial process of developing the manuscript took four years, nearly twice as long as a traditional textbook manuscript.

Table 1. Interview Responses from *Understanding Rhetoric* authors about form and rhetorical purpose.

UR affirms the rhetoric genre tradition in that its form:	*UR* challenges the rhetoric genre tradition in that its form:
Is a print medium, albeit predominantly visual. Organizes pages into chapters. Organizes content via themed chapters. Includes questions at the conclusion of each chapter. Concludes each chapter with assignments. Differs from handbooks and readers.	Does not include textbook elements such as call-out boxes and other marginalia/ commenting. Resists the textbook design in order to take the comics medium seriously. Intentionally borrows tropes from the comics medium (visual, linear, imagetext), including movement outside of the panel in the gutter. Directly addresses readers via cartoon characters representing the authors. And content was produced through a collaboration with academic and non-academic (credited) authors. Becomes part of what is scrutinized rhetorically. It becomes an object of study in itself in the classroom. Is intended to draw potential readers from outside of the academic context.
***UR* affirms the rhetoric genre tradition in that its rhetorical purpose:**	***UR* challenges the rhetoric genre tradition in that its rhetorical purpose:**
Is intended to be read by students Serves as the primary instructional text for students in a lower division writing course Introduces students to traditional content of the course, reflective of contemporary composition research: rhetorical concepts (ethos, pathos, logos), the rhetorical situation, the writing process (its recursive nature), conducting research (finding and integrating sources, entering the conversation), multiliteracies, and visual rhetoric. Is to articulate the nature of how we make arguments in public spaces and how we see our own/develop our own voices as civic actors. Includes meta-awareness in that the authors refer back to a topic that readers were introduced to earlier. Is to problematize how writing is defined.	Is informed by writing studies scholars who acknowledge the value of diverse literate acts and model them in the form and content of the textbook itself. Is to serve as an example of visual rhetoric and multimodal composition. Resists some aspects of traditional course content: linear representation of the writing process, a full research paper example, etc. Includes content not traditional in the content tradition: e.g. an entire chapter focused on writer identity. Delivers narrative and didactic content through characters and stories in each chapter. Is to portray writing as public, social, and involves both embodiment and identification in the examination of written expression.

Understanding the importance of refining the manuscript before it entered the layouts stage was the collaborators' first struggle because the collaborators had to anticipate the eventual inclusion of visual elements in the next stage. In our interviews, authors and editors spoke about the difficulty of providing useful feedback to the artists during layouts. During this stage each page included panels complete with dialogue and loosely sketched artwork of setting and characters' actions.

This lack of visual nuance led the writers and editors to assume such sketches were as flexible as a rough draft and to suggest revisions on content. Lengel recalls that, during this stage, one of the comments asked for a revision that would have required adding/deleting/moving panels, an act that creates a ripple effect and requires changes to panels and pages that precede and follow. In response, Zander Cannon and Kevin Cannon drafted the checklist, "Checklist for Stage 1 (Layouts) from [Big Time Attic]," a document that offered guidelines to the writers and editors about which comments were most appropriate during this initial drafting stage.

Checklist for Stage 1 (Layouts) from BTA

1. Page Layout
Check panel sizes, arrangement of panels on pages, overall flow.

2. Backgrounds and Settings
Ensure character situations are clear and make sense for the narrative (where that's important).

3. Images
Make sure they work with text and convey appropriate message.

4. Dialogue and Captions
Note anything to add, change, cut.

5. New characters (if any)
Is the design OK? Note corrections to weight, race, clothing, general appearance.

6. Navigational content
Add cross-references to other content in the chapter or in other chapters?

Do we have any/enough quick-reference features? If not, consider placement and content of reference material.

The primary goal of this checklist was to communicate to the writers and editors that global revision at this stage should be avoided for labor efficiency purposes. Changing content in layouts means revising entire panels and sometimes pages. Feedback should be geared toward nuances within the images and the text, falling somewhere between global and local issues. These regional revision issues, as I will call them, related to narrative flow, literary devices, conceptual explanations, image conveyance, page order, speaking order, dialogue balloon/narration placement, cross-reference, and page design elements such as color, style consistency (gutter size, page numbers, etc.), or action that breaks the frame and extends into the margin.

Recursivity was utterly redefined by the materiality of the comic in the context of collaborative multimodal composing. The collaborators' confusion during the layouts stage proved to be a pivotal moment in redefining recursivity in collaborative multimodal composing. A rough draft in one medium may not allow the same level of revision—global, regional, or local—as it would in another medium. As writing teachers, we hear "rough" and most likely envision composing in word processing software. But "layouts" and "rough pencils" suggest multiple modes at play in the draft. Cooperatively developing a feedback loop that is unique to each multimodal composition is essential and should become another part of the collaborative process. Students resistant to preplanning before they write will be forced to reconsider when they realize how much labor is involved in global revisions of a multimodal text later on.

We know that multimodality fundamentally changes the materiality of a text, but research into how this materiality affects the composition process—collaborative or otherwise—is lacking. Observation of this phenomenon in a single case study is just a drop in the bucket. Until we have more conclusive evidence to guide our engagement in multimodal composition, multimodal assignments should allow for substantial dedication of class time to assisting students in establishing and carrying out several recursive stages of composing in unfamiliar and disorienting modes.

Foreground the Work of Multimodal Composition

Through survey results from a CCCC-supported research initiative conducted in 2005, Daniel Anderson and colleagues found that teachers of writing who integrated multimodal composition into their writing courses drew on a number of other disciplines to inform their own training, curricula development, and student assessments. One field not included in this list, however, was comics studies. Despite the fact that several of the surveyed specifically noted Scott McCloud's *Understanding Comics* as a text they used with both undergraduate and graduate students, the theories behind their pedagogies came instead from new media, web design, multimodality, graphic design, and film theory. The survey results also documented a consensus among instructors that textbooks were lacking in "[a]ctivities instruction (e.g., tutorials for conducting research, collaborating, or composing) in multimedia" (76). It would seem that, despite our field's historical considerations and reconsiderations of process pedagogy and the complex social situations in which texts are produced, our scholarship as well as our pedagogy has fallen short of its aim in understanding the processes behind multimodal texts, particularly collaborative ones.

In order to compose multimodal texts collaboratively, instructors and students of writing need resources appropriate to the task. Joddy Murray's scholarship on non-discursive rhetoric emphasizes the news ways in which we are asking students to engage in multimodality, engagement that requires access to new tools and material resources: "The only way these students could have the tools they need to do this work is if they understand [. . .] the importance of the emotional charge that accompanies these images, and the way these images are composed to affect a particular audience at a particular time and place (given the correct material resources)" (156-7). Beyond the valuable theoretical work our field has produced, there are few practical sources that introduce tools intended for multimodal composition.[8] One respondent of Anderson et al.'s survey noted a dire need for "prompts for creation of multimedia works, so students move from analysis of samples provided to producing their own work, which they can then analyze in similar frameworks" (76).

During an interview with Cannon and Cannon, I asked what tools the artists used in composing the textbook. Kevin Cannon began speaking first, "It's all mixed. We'll start off old school and so the original artwork is just pencil and ink on paper. Then we'll scan—" He then interrupted his explanation of their process to say, "I don't know how detailed you want it...." Kevin Cannon's hesitation to go into further detail about the comics composing process signals a larger neglect and lack of appreciation of the work of multimodal composition—not just by scholars of writing, but by the authors themselves. It was evident from Kevin Cannon's response that such questions, while well intentioned, perhaps do not sincerely call for a detailed understanding of the composing process.

Jenny Edbauer Rice argues that the mechanics of writing should garner more of our attention now that the materiality of writing itself is no longer so easy to define or execute in an era of ever-expanding modes. Calling writers "logomechanics," she advocates the analogy of writer/designer as mechanic—an imaginative improviser, designer, and builder of tools, objects, machines, and texts. Likewise, Rob Simon, Alisa Acosta, and Eveline Houtman discuss multimodal composition as "new forms of labor" with "less predictable structures, characterized gaps, and indeterminacies that afford readers with more choices" (66; 62). Consistent with the work identified here, scholarship on multimodality calls for a more deliberate examination of the work of multimodal composition as authors (writers, artists or designers) produce them, and as readers (civic or academic) consume them.

Just as our field critically engaged multiple lenses and methods/methodologies in its earliest investigations of students' writing processes (e.g., Emig; Flower and Hayes; Perl), it is time to reexamine and reapply these inquiries and methodologies to collaborative multimodal composition. When I reexamined Kevin Cannon's answer to questions about work, I identified a compelling pattern—his pronoun use: "*We*'ll start off old school." Despite his hesitation to detail the labor itself, the process is defined by collaboration. Scholarship on collaborative writing must continue to develop informed pedagogical resources for multimodal consumption and production.[9]

The Work of Collaboration

This study of collaborations focuses on comics texts in order to better understand the impact of multimodal meaning-making—on our field, our classrooms, our institutions, our workplaces and our broader cultures. Edbauer Rice warns that, "[i]f we dismiss this technical work as rote mechanics, we risk calcifying the distinction between the production work of texts (including the operations of buttons, cords, and wires that cut and record texts) and the produced texts themselves" (367-8). As Steven Fraiberg echoes, only recently has scholarship focused on the *work* of multimodal composition, the "production, distribution, mediation, and reception of multimodal texts (beyond interpretive and hermeneutic analyses)" (103). Fraiberg's commendation—while noteworthy—excludes the fact that scholarship on multimodal composition continues to neglect collaboration as well.

Collaboration is a thread that runs through each of the four considerations presented here: collaboration between text and image, between writers, editors, and artists, and between authors and their audiences. This study hopes to broaden the domain of multimodality—beyond digital[10]—and to deepen our understanding of the work behind multimodal composition, by studying how such texts are produced collaboratively. In asking students to produce multimodal texts, teachers of writing must revise traditional scaffolding and assessment strategies to accommodate the ways in which multimodal composition is both similar and different from traditional composing in the singular textual mode. Instructors who choose to assign multimodal compositions in their classrooms may begin this accommodation by incorporating some of the considerations introduced here. Despite the disorienting phenomena we experience when composing collaboratively in new modes, the convergence that results is ultimately productive. Collaborative multimodal composition is a valuable practice not only because of *what* it is capable of producing but also because of *how* it reenergizes concepts of audience, genre, and recursivity. My hope is that scholars of writing studies will further enrich our disciplinary scholarship and expand our classroom praxis to include the work of collaborative multimodal composition.

Notes

1. While there is not space to review all literature on frameworks for addressing the significance of multimodality in meaning-making activities, there are a few salient works in each domain that are important to acknowledge: discourse and disciplinarity studies (Barton and Heiman; Berkenkotter; Horowitz and Newman); rhetorical genre studies (Ball; Blakeslee); media studies (Alexander, "Media Convergence"; Bolter and Grusin, Jenkins; Manovich; Selfe); literacy studies (Jacobs; Selfe and Haiwisher; Kress; Selber); visual rhetoric/design (George; Hocks; Shin and Cimasko); comics studies (Brooks; McCloud; Eisner); and professional and technical communication (Cross; Mirel, Feinberg, and Allmendinger; Winsor).

2. It has also been argued that comics utilize spatial and aural modes as well. Scott McCloud's *Understanding Comics* argues that the passing of time in a visual narrative is achieved through the spatial manipulation of the page. Additionally, Neil Cohn argues that linguistic/alphabetic text is often representing aurality (e.g., dialogue, monologue, internal thought).

3. Culture essentially defines what is and is not acceptable among members of a social group (Cullen and Fein 16). Marvin W. Peterson and Melinda G. Spencer study organizational culture using a theoretical framework of visible behaviors as informed by underlying invisible values (histories, heroes, rituals and symbols). They define organizational culture as "the dominant behavioral or belief pattern that reflects or holds the institution together—a kind of 'organizational glue'" (7).

4. In the case of the Cheo comics, the workers themselves defined the texts as successful or unsuccessful. Both Brunette's and Carlos's research involves participatory design and usability studies that place the evaluation of the texts firmly in the hands of the audience (Evia and Patriarca). Participatory design is common in technical communication to emphasize user-centered communication practices (Spinuzzi).

5. In addition to Cushman's call for a civic application of our work in rhetoric, others extend a similar call for inclusivity to subdisciplines of the field. For example, Jeff Grabill's work in public rhetoric aims "to explore the notion that the public work of rhetoric might be to support the work of others—to help other people write, speak, and make new media and other material objects effectively" (193). Katrina Powell and Pamela Takayoshi's "Accepting the Roles Created for Us" calls for "more reciprocal, collaborative, and mutually enriching relationships between researchers and their subjects" (394). Finally, Derek Barker concludes: "The scholarship of engagement constitutes a distinct, important, and growing movement in American higher education that serves to broaden and deepen the connection between scholars and the public realm" (124).

6. *Understanding Rhetoric* is a nod to a landmark text in comics scholarship, McCloud's *Understanding Comics*. In it, McCloud animates himself and his concepts in a didactic, book-length treatise on reading and writing comics. Likewise, *Understanding Rhetoric* includes animations of all four of its authors—writers and artists—as well as concepts related to rhetoric, writing, and research presented in a didactic, conversational manner.

7. Larry Gonick is noted for his work in creating comics textbooks on statistics, physics, genetics, and history. A 2008 article in *ImageTexT* by Sol Davidson presents a fairly thorough discussion of educational comics.

8. Theoretical texts include: *Writing New Media* (Wysocki, Johnson-Eilola, Selfe, and Sirc); *Literacy in a New Media Age* (Kress); *Multimodal Discourse* and *Reading Images* (Kress and van Leeuwen); *Language of New Media* (Manovich); *Remediation* (Bolter and Grusin) and *Multiliteracies* (Cope and Kalantzis). In terms of pedagogical applications, several rhetorics fill this gap: *Compose, Design, Advocate* by Anne Wysocki and Dennis Lynch, and *Writer/Designer* by Kristin Arola, Jennifer Sheppard and Cheryl Ball. Arola, Sheppard, and Ball's textbook features a section entitled "Collaborating Effectively" in their fifth chapter, "Assembling Your Technologies and Your Team." The section discusses guidelines for success, strategies for composing, organizing/sharing assets, file naming conventions, and style guide development/use. This is by far the most comprehensive coverage of collaborative multimodal composing I have seen in a composition textbook.

9. I acknowledge that consumption versus production can sometimes be a false dichotomy, particularly in light of the work of scholars like Henry Jenkins who argue, quite persuasively, that text consumption can feed into fan production and remixes of original texts. In this essay, however, emphasizing the distinction allows me to highlight the existing gap in our literature on collaborative multimodal text production.

10. Of the works reviewed for this research, the following dealt exclusively with digital or web-based texts: Ball; Barton and Heiman; Shin and Cimasko; and Simon, Acosta, and Houtman.

Works Cited

Afrilyasanti, Rida, and Yazid Basthomi. "Adapting Comics and Cartoons to Develop 21st Century Learners." *Language in India* 11.11 (2011): 552–68. Print.

Alexander, Jonathan. "Media Convergence: Creating Content, Questioning Relationships." *Computers and Composition* 25.1 (2008): 1-8. Web. 23 Aug. 2014. < http://www2.bgsu.edu/departments/english/cconline/print/march2008.html>.

---. Personal Interview. 16 Feb. 2012.

Anderson, Daniel, Anthony Atkins, Cheryl Ball, Krista Homicz, Cynthia Selfe, and Richard Selfe. "Integrating Multimodality into Composition Curricula: Survey Methodology and Results from a CCCC Research Grant." *Composition Studies* 34.2 (2006): 59-84. Print.

Arola, Kristin L., Cheryl E. Ball, and Jennifer Sheppard. *Writer/Designer: A Guide to Making Multimodal Projects*. Boston: Macmillan Higher Education, 2014. Print.

Ball, Cheryl E. "Assessing Scholarly Multimedia: A Rhetorical Genre Studies Approach." *TCQ* 21.1 (2012): 61-77. Print.

Barker, Derek. "The Scholarship of Engagement: A Taxonomy of Five Emerging Practices." *Journal of Higher Education Outreach and Engagement* 9.2 (2004): 123-37. Print.

Barton, Matthew D., and James R. Heiman. "Process, Product, and Potential: The Archaeological Assessment of Collaborative, Wiki-Based Student Projects in the Technical Communication Classroom." *TCQ* 21.1 (2012): 46-60. Print.

Berkenkotter, Carol. "Paradigm Debates, Turf Wars, and the Conduct of Sociocognitive Inquiry in Composition." *CCC* (1991): 151-69. Print.

Blakeslee, Ann M. "Bridging the Workplace and the Academy: Teaching Professional Genres through Classroom-Workplace Collaborations." *TCQ* 10.2 (2001): 169-92. Print.

Bolter, J. David, and Richard A. Grusin. *Remediation: Understanding New Media.* Boston: MIT Press, 2000. Print.

Boyd, Brian. "On the Origin of Comics: New York Double-Take." *The Evolutionary Review* 1.1 (2009): 97–111. Print.

Brooks, Kevin. "More 'Seriously Visible' Reading: McCloud, McLuhan, and the Visual Language of *The Medium Is the Massage.*" *CCC* 61.1 (2009): W217-37. Web. 4 Mar. 2013. <http://www.ncte.org/library/NCTEFiles/Resources/Journals/CCC/0611-sep09/CCC0611More.pdf>.

Brown, Marianne P., and UCLA-LOSH Director. "An Examination of Occupational Safety and Health Materials Currently available in Spanish for Workers as of 1999." National Research Council. *Safety is Seguridad: A Workshop Summary.* Washington: National Academies Press, 2003. Print.

Brunette, Maria. "Construction Safety and Health Research and the Hispanic Workforce in the U.S.: The Need for a Research Agenda." *Injury Prevention* 10.4 (2004), 244-248. Web. 14 Dec. 2014. < http://injuryprevention.bmj.com/content/10/4/244.short>.

Brunette, Maria, and Nick Thorkelson. "Seguridad en la Obra." *Hispanics Work Safe.* n.d. n.p. Print.

Brunette, Maria, Carlos Evia, and Nick Thorkelson. "Lucky Cheo." *Hispanics Work Safe.* n.d. 1–10. Print.

---. "Cheo and His Advisors." *Hispanics Work Safe.* n.d. 1–10. Print.

---. "Cheo's Uncle." *Hispanics Work Safe.* n.d. 1–10. Print.

Burton, Leasa . "Checklist for Stage 1 (Layouts)." Email to the author. 24 Jan. 2013. PDF file.

Canales, Augusto R., Maurico Arbelaez, Edna Vasquez, Fernando Aveiga, Kelly Strong, Russell Walters, Edward J. Jaselskis, Charles T. Jahren. "Exploring Training Needs and Development of Construction Language Courses for American Supervisors and Hispanic Craft Workers." *Journal of Construction Engineering and Management* 135.5 (2009): 387-96. Web. 14 Dec. 2014. < http://ascelibrary.org/doi/abs/10.1061/(ASCE)0733-9364(2009)135:5(387)>.

Cannon, Zander, and Kevin Cannon. Personal Interview. 8 May 2012.

Cohn, Neil. "'Un-Defining' Comics: Separating the Cultural from the Structural in 'Comics.'" *International Journal of Comic Art* 7.2 (2005): 236-48. Print.

Cope, Bill, and Mary Kalantzis, eds. *Multiliteracies: Literacy Learning and the Design of Social Futures*. New York: Routledge, 2000. Print.

Cross, Geoffrey A. *Envisioning Collaboration: Group Verbal Visual Composing in a System of Creativity (Technical Writing and Communication)*. Amityville: Baywood Pub Co, 2010. Print.

Cullen, Elaine T., and Albert H. Fein. Department of Health and Human Services, Public Health Service, Centers for Disease Control and Prevention, National Institute for Occupational Safety and Health. *Tell Me a Story: Why Stories Are Essential to Effective Safety Training*. Cincinnati: NIOSH Publications Dissemination, 2005. Web. 20 Feb. 2013. <http://www.cdc.gov/niosh/mining/UserFiles/works/pdfs/2005-152.pdf>.

Cushman, Ellen. "The Rhetorician as an Agent of Social Change." *CCC* 47.1 (1996): 7–28. Print.

Davidson, Sol. "Educational Comics: A Family Tree." *ImageTexT: Interdisciplinary Comics Studies*. 4.2 (2008): n.p. Web. 12 Dec 2012. <http://www.english.ufl.edu/imagetext/archives/v4_2/davidson/>.

Dholakiya, Nishaben S. "Design and Development of Visual Learning Technologies to Construct Chemical Engineering Safety Knowledge." *Perspective* (2008): n.p. Print.

Edbauer Rice, Jenny. "Rhetoric's Mechanics: Retooling the Equipment of Writing Production." *CCC* 60.2 (2008): 366-87. Print.

Eisner, Will. *Comics and Sequential Art: Principles and Practices from the Legendary Cartoonist*. New York: W. W. Norton & Company, 1985. Print.

Emig, Janet. *The Composing Process of Twelfth Graders, NCTE Research Report, No. 13*. Urbana: NCTE, 1971. Print.

Evia, Carlos. Personal Interview. 14 Feb. 2012.

---. "Ladder Falls Comic." To Nick Thorkelson. 31 Aug 2009. Email.

Evia, Carlos, and Ashley Patriarca. "Beyond Compliance: Participatory Translation of Safety Communication for Latino Construction Workers." *JBTC* 26.3 (2012): 340-67. Web. 22 Apr. 2012. <http://jbt.sagepub.com/content/26/3/340.full.pdf>.

Flower, Linda, and John R. Hayes. "A Cognitive Process Theory of Writing." *CCC* 32.4 (1981): 365–87. Print.

Fraiberg, Steven. "Composition 2.0: Toward a Multilingual and Multimodal Framework." *CCC* 62.1 (2010): 100-26. Print.

George, Diana. "From Analysis to Design: Visual Communication in the Teaching of Writing." *CCC* (2002): 11–39. Print.

Grabill, Jeffrey T. "On Being Useful: Rhetoric and the Work of Engagement." *The Public Work of Rhetoric*. Ed. John M. Ackerman and David J. Coogan. Columbia: U of South Carolina P, 2010. 193-208. Print.

Hocks, Mary E. "Understanding Visual Rhetoric in Digital Writing Environments." *CCC* 54.4 (2003): 629-56. Print.

Horowitz, Milton W., and John B. Newman. "Spoken and Written Expression: An Experimental Analysis." *The Journal of Abnormal and Social Psychology* 68.6 (1964): 640. Print.

Jacobs, Dale. "Marveling at The Man Called Nova: Comics as Sponsors Of Multimodal Literacy." *CCC* 59.2 (2007): 180–205. Print.

Jaselskis, Edward, Thomas E. Cackler, Thomas Stout, Oscar Valverde-Barrantes, and Fernando Aveiga. "Developing an Effective Construction Training Program for Hispanic and American Craft Workers and Supervisors." NCTRE Project 04-133, 2007. Web. 14 December 2014. < http://www.ctre.iastate.edu/reports/hispanic-workforce4.pdf>.

Jenkins, Henry. *Convergence Culture: Where Old and New Media Collide*. New York: NYU P, 2006. Print.

Kress, Gunther. *Literacy in the New Media Age*. London: Routledge, 2003. Print.

Kress, Gunther R., and Theo V. Van Leeuwen. *Multimodal Discourse: The Modes and Media of Contemporary Communication*. New York: Oxford UP, 2001. Print.

---. *Reading Images: The Grammar of Visual Design*. New York: Routledge, 1996. Print.

Lengel, Carolyn. Personal Interview. 23 March 2012.

Losh, Elizabeth. Personal Interview. 24 March 2012.

Losh, Elizabeth, Jonathan Alexander, Zander Cannon, and Kevin Cannon. *Understanding Rhetoric: A Graphic Guide to Writing*. Boston: Bedford/St. Martin's, 2013. Print.

Manovich, Lev. *The Language of New Media*. Boston: MIT, 2001. Print.

McCloud, Scott. *Understanding Comics: The Invisible Art*. New York: Harper Paperbacks, 1994. Print.

Mirel, Barbara, Susan Feinberg, and Leif Allmendinger. "Collaboration Between Writers and Graphic Designers in Documentation Projects." *JBTC* 9.3 (1995): 259–88. Print.

Murray, Joddy. *Non-discursive Rhetoric: Image and Affect in Multimodal Composition*. New York: SUNY, 2009. Print.

Penrose, John M. "Teaching the Essential Role of Visualization in Preparing Instructions." *Business Communication Quarterly* 69.4 (2006): 411–18. Print.

Perl, Sondra. "The Composing Process of Unskilled College Writers." *Cross-Talk in Comp Theory*. Ed. Victor Villanueva. Urbana: NCTE, 1997. 17–42. Print.

Peterson, Marvin W., and Melinda G. Spencer. "Understanding Academic Culture and Climate." *New Directions for Institutional Research* 68 (1990): 3-18. Print.

Petterson, Rune. "Interpretation of Image Content." *Educational Communication and Technology* 36.1 (1988): 45–55. Print.

Powell, Katrina M., and Pamela Takayoshi. "Accepting Roles Created for Us: The Ethics of Reciprocity." *CCC* 54.3 (2003): 394-422. Print.

Rubenstein, Anne. *Bad Language, Naked Ladies, & Other Threats to the Nation: A Political History of Comic Books in Mexico*. Durham: Duke UP, 1998. Print.

Selber, Stuart. *Multiliteracies for a Digital Age*. Carbondale: SIUP, 2004. Print.

Selfe, Cynthia. *Multimodal Composition*. Cresskill: Hampton, 2007. Print.

Selfe, Cynthia L., and Gail E. Hawisher, eds. *Passions, Pedagogies, and 21st Century Technologies*. Logan: Utah State UP, 1999. Print.

Shin, Dong-shin, and Tony Cimasko. "Multimodal Composition in a College ESL Class: New Tools, Traditional Norms." *Computers and Composition* 25.4 (2008):

376-95. Web. 2 July 2014. <http://www2.bgsu.edu/departments/english/cconline/print/december2008.html>.

Simon, Rob, Alisa Acosta, and Eveline Houtman. "'Memeration': Exploring Academic Authorship in Online Spaces." *Exploring Multimodal Composition and Digital Writing*. Ed. Richard Eugene Ferdig and Kristen Pytash. Hershey: Information Science Reference, 2014. Print.

Spinuzzi, Clay. "The Methodology of Participatory Design." *Technical Communication* 52.2 (2005): 163–74. Print.

Tatalovic, Mico. "Science Comics as Tools for Science Education and Communication: a Brief, Exploratory Study." *Journal of Science Communication*. 8.4 (December 2009): A02. Web. 3 Mar. 2013. <http://jcom.sissa.it/archive/08/04/Jcom0804%282009%29A02/Jcom0804%282009%29A02.pdf>.

Thorkelson, Nick. Personal Interview. 28 Feb. 2012.

Winsor, Dorothy A. "Engineering Writing/Writing Engineering." *CCC* 41.1 (1990): 58. Print.

Wysocki, Anne Frances, Johndan Johnson-Eilola, Cynthia Selfe, and Geoffrey Sirc. *Writing New Media*. Logan: Utah State UP, 2004. Print.

Wysocki, Anne Frances, and Dennis A. Lynch. *Compose, Design, Advocate: A Rhetoric for Integrating Written, Visual, and Oral Communication*. Boston: Pearson, 2013. Print.

Course Design

English 177: Literature and Popular Culture, The Graphic Novel

Leah Misemer

Course Description

This section of English 177: Literature and Popular Culture, The Graphic Novel was designed to teach students to "make compelling arguments about and in various media" and to produce a "professional-like final product that represents their work to the world at large." While twice weekly lectures by Professor Robin Valenza explored the development of the graphic novel as a genre, my section meetings focused on multimodal composition, helping students hone analytical skills and guiding them to create multimodal texts. After analyzing comics as multimodal texts, students worked in teams to interview members of the comics community—cartoonists, librarians, comics store owners, researchers, etc.—and craft documentary videos. The course mobilized the analytic potential of the comics form and its multimodal nature to encourage production of authentic texts that students viewed as having value beyond the classroom.

Institutional Context

The Graphic Novel class was taught at University of Wisconsin-Madison, a large land grant university that pulls the majority of its 30,000 undergraduates from Wisconsin and Minnesota, while the rest are increasingly international students, with a small number of students from elsewhere in the US. The students in the course were from the Letters and Sciences division of the university, which, like many liberal arts programs, has breadth requirements that students must fulfill to obtain a degree. Many of the 250 students enrolled in this course were aiming to satisfy three of their twelve Humanities credits required for graduation. I had very few English majors in the three sections of twenty students I taught. Like many literature courses at UW-Madison, this course was structured as a literature lecture running parallel to a composition focused section. Consistent with the English department's stated goals, my section taught students how to write original papers that demonstrate analytical thinking, persuasiveness, significance, and organization.

However, unlike other literature courses, The Graphic Novel required students to create multimodal products, such as online library catalogues, documentary videos, and original graphic novels, rather than assessing student learning through essays and exams. Instructors wanted students to use the comics form as a model to move beyond the traditional literature paper into the realm of multimodal composition. As students encounter numerous multimodal texts in their everyday lives, and as they are frequently presented with the opportunity to choose between modes when communicating in various contexts, it is important for students to practice analyzing and producing texts that convey meaning using multiple modes. The instructors' goal was to help students apply the analytical skills of the literature classroom to multimodal texts in order to move from analysis to production. To fulfill this goal, section instructors chose from various multimedia assignments, and then designed their sections in a way that positioned comics as texts students could analyze in the process of making their own multimodal products.

My students produced documentaries about members of the comics community in Madison, an outgrowth of my commitment to the Wisconsin Idea. The Wisconsin Idea is a social action based philosophy that connects the university to communities in Madison and elsewhere in Wisconsin. Introduced by Charles McCarthy in 1912, the Wisconsin idea originally referred to the university's involvement in legislation, but the idea has evolved over time to encompass the many ways that, as stated on *The Wisconsin Idea* website, "the boundaries of campus are the boundaries of the state," resulting in initiatives through which the university can serve the public. Disciplines employ different practices in line with the Wisconsin Idea, from university members educating the surrounding communities about environmental and public health issues, to building businesses that help improve the Wisconsin economy, to conducting medical research. Many composition teachers interpret the Wisconsin idea as an opportunity for students to explore the different rhetorical practices and situations of communities outside the university. In my experience, the Wisconsin Idea is a useful teaching concept because community connections foster curiosity in students and position research as alive and authentic. Comics lend themselves to community research particularly well because of their popular appeal and the enthusiasm of comics community members, who are eager to talk about the texts they are passionate about. People who love comics are used to proselytizing about their favorite medium, which they often see as misunderstood or undervalued. The desire to discuss comics makes those involved in the comics community eager to speak with students investigating the medium for a class. Moreover, the documentary assignment, for which students interviewed members of the comics community in Madison and then crafted documentary films about those people, creates the opportunity for students to engage with communities outside the university, even when teachers are not guided by something as specific as the Wisconsin Idea.

When students interviewed those involved with comics in the community, they served as ambassadors for the class. Consequently, this course marked some of the first stirrings of comics studies as a collective enterprise at UW-Madison, which has culminated in an interdisciplinary workshop on comics supported by the A.W. Mellon Foundation and the current discussion of a PhD minor in comics studies. While this course speaks specifically to the coalescence of the comics studies community, the community research methods students used could be applied to help build communities for other emerging fields of study: in any field, teachers can integrate community networking with course preparation, while student ambassadors can help bring community members together through ethnographic research. When students serve as the vanguard for a program or initiative, they experience their research as authentic and consequential, rather than as an activity confined to the classroom.

Theoretical Framework

The course operated on the premise that comics serve as exemplary multimodal texts with discrete parts that lend themselves to analysis and as models for practice with multimodal composition. The sequence of assignments moved from analysis to production. More specifically, students analyzed comics, developed comic screenplays, and then created documentaries that integrated images and interviews. Each assignment encouraged students to think through inter-media translation, which highlights the affordances of each medium as well as the gaps of meaning that emerge during acts of translation.

At least since the formation of the New London Group, there has been a push towards multimodal instruction in composition classrooms, emphasizing the dynamic nature of multimodal literacy, the interplay between analysis and practice. The New London Group stresses a focus on "Design, in which we are both inheritors of patterns and conventions of meaning while at the same time active designers of meaning" (Cope and Kalantzis 7). Cynthia Selfe put the stakes of this argument best in 2004 when she warned that "if our profession continues to focus solely on the teaching of alphabetic composition—either online or in print—we run the risk of making composition studies increasingly irrelevant to students engaging in contemporary practices of communicating" (72). More recently, Frank Serafini claims that "multiliteracies" encompass "visual literacy, media literacy, critical literacy, computer literacy, and other types of literacies" as "a multidimensional set of competencies and social practices in response to the increasing complexity and multimodal nature of texts" (26). Selfe, with her emphasis on "practices of communicating," Serafini, with his emphasis on literacies as "social practices," and the New London Group highlight the active process of design (Cope and Kalantzis 7). Together, these positions suggest that teaching multimodal composition should increase students' rhetorical flexibility by providing options for how best to communicate in any given social context. Additionally, Serafini's call to teach multiliteracies emphasizes the importance of examining modes (semiotic systems of meaning) and media (technologies of transmission) as part of multimodal composition instruction (13-15).

In keeping with an emphasis on both analysis and practice, The Graphic Novel employed Serafini's suggested order of assignments, starting with exposure, moving to exploration, and then providing opportunities for engagement (92). "Exposure," in my course, meant practicing summary, while "exploration" (which Serafini defines as "exploring the designs, features, and structures of... particular multimodal ensembles") meant analysis, and "engagement" meant practice, as it does for Serafini (92). The course included four major assignments: an interview summary with a visual counterpart, a traditional analytical paper about one of the texts we were reading, a screenplay in comic form, and a final documentary film.

For the first assignment, students interviewed someone they knew about a typical day, wrote a summary of that interview, and then created a visual (e.g., comic, collage, drawing, painting, etc.) to accompany the summary. I chose this as the first assignment because I wanted students to think through questions of mode from the beginning of the course. Carl Whithaus stresses that "viewing multimedia literacy as a set of skills acquired after print-based literacy skills is detrimental to students' learning" (131), and John G. Nichols suggests that teaching with comics helps to keep alphabetic texts from becoming primary in the classroom (231). Beginning with this assignment helped keep the focus on the rhetorical choices involved in producing multimodal texts, already established by our reading and analysis of comics. The assignment also gave students an opportunity to practice the interview skills they would need as they researched for their documentaries and allowed me to assess student skill in drawing and writing, which I considered as I formed students into groups for their documentary assignment.

The ethnographic methodology of interviews helped to foster curiosity and allowed students time to practice verbal communication and listening skills, while also increasing student engagement. As Suzanne Blum Malley and Ames Hawkins state in the introduction to *Engaging Communities*, their online open-source textbook on ethnographic research, "[e]thnographic research provides a hands-on method for critical inquiry, through which students learn how to evaluate, question, synthesize, and apply what they are learning." Additionally, as Jennifer Arias states, "when we allow [students] latitude to explore, question, and create" as ethnographic research methods do, "engagement is increased" (93). In my class, evidence of student engagement came in the form of students doing extra research on their subjects and coming to office hours eager to talk about their projects. Barbara A. Morris argues that the specific research method of interviewing helps students recognize the importance "of prioritizing and organizing information," as they create a narrative out of what they learned from their subjects (287). Together these authors highlight the engagement, critical thinking, and analysis I expected from students as they interviewed two separate subjects and made decisions about how to present the information they learned in a multimodal format. In the first assignment, students had to analyze and summarize the information they acquired from their interviews. In the documentary assignment, student groups had to move beyond summary to craft a narrative based on the information they learned from their interview subjects.

Moving from interviews, the second assignment was an analytical essay, which gave students practice with a more traditional form within the context of our multimodal composition class. As Lisa Ede and Andrea Lunsford argue, "we must help our students to learn to conceive and produce a repertoire of texts," including the "convincing academic argument" (59). To that end, students analyzed multimodal texts and made arguments about how the various modes worked together for a particular purpose. In the process, they gained practice and feedback on the kind of traditional academic writing that remains prevalent in the university context, while also honing analytical skills that would help them in everyday life.

As a medium, comics, with their combination of text and image, provide unique opportunities for analysis. Both Scott McCloud (*Understanding Comics*) and Thierry Groensteen (*The System of Comics*) emphasize how the comics reader must actively weave together the various elements of a comic in order to make sense of the story: McCloud calls this "closure," while Groensteen calls it "braiding." Regardless of the name, this emphasis on the reader weaving elements together highlights the many discrete parts of comics—panels, pages, spreads, text boxes, word balloons, line, color, etc. This discreteness, particular to comics, means that comics more easily offer themselves up for analysis—which comes from the root for "to pick apart"—than other kinds of multimodal texts. Medium-specific analytical vocabulary, such as that discussed by McCloud in *Understanding Comics* or the more film-oriented vocabulary that Jessica Abel and Matt Madden use in *Drawing Words and Writing Pictures*, calls attention to the various parts of the comics page and provides students with the language to talk about those different parts. Once students can see these different parts and talk about them, they are more likely to think of the many choices comics authors must make in creating their texts and to consider the kinds of choices they will have to make in creating their own multimodal texts. Students can then use this analysis of mode when they create comics, where they must decide which information to include in each discrete element of the assemblage.

The Abel and Madden text, as well as McCloud's *Making Comics*, demonstrate that analyzing comics as models is one step toward crafting comics, which my students did in their third assignment for this course. In the comic screenplay assignment, students combined visual and written modes to produce a comics version of the documentary they planned to film, a task that involved making decisions about how to tell a story in what McCloud refers to as "a medium of fragments" (129). Abel and Madden and McCloud stress how drawing a comic involves discerning the most important parts of the story you want to tell, and focusing on those particular pieces of the story in the panels, leaving the reader to fill in what might happen between each panel. Abel and Madden refer to panel choices as guided by "rhythm and pacing," aligning the effect with music (26-30), while McCloud refers to panel choices as "choices of moment" (11-18). Similarly, creating these comic screenplays drawn from interview material involved analyzing and making choices. Students had to analyze the information they got from their interviews, decide what story that information told, and then depict that story using panels.

In depicting their stories, the students didn't just have to make choices regarding which pieces of the story were most salient, they also had to make choices about which mode would best represent each piece of information they wanted to convey. In *Making Comics*, McCloud stresses how cartoonists' choices are choices of mode because they involve "choice of moment, choice of frame, choice of image, choice of word, and choice of flow," where moment, frame, image, and flow are focused on visual presentation, and word choice involves thinking about how words and images work together to make meaning (10). When students crafted their comic screenplays, they had to think through what parts of the story they should tell in words (and which sets of words—speech bubbles, sound effects, or narration boxes—would work best) and what would be most effectively conveyed via image. Assembling comics thus provided students with an opportunity to practice design using multiple modes.

Comics provided ideal models for the assembly of information into a narrative, documentary format. As scholars have recognized, the fragmented, multimodal form of comics calls attention to the process of its construction, making the medium ideal for autobiographical and documentary material. Hillary Chute has discussed how the comics form allows for a layering of women's experience, from the secret and tragic to the mundane (2-6), while Jared Gardner has argued that the comics form uniquely represents the complex relationships between the past and present evident in the archive (802). Both of these authors position comics as calling attention to their own making, as Art Spiegelman does in *Maus* by including panels of him interviewing his father.

Documentary comics like *Maus* served as models for student documentaries because, by analyzing comics, students could see not just a complete narrative, but glimpse how the author put that narrative together. Seeing this assemblage then helped students think through how they would assemble their own research into a coherent narrative, organizing and analyzing as they put their stories together and wrote their screenplays.

In their fourth and final assignment, students translated their comic screenplays into films, mobilizing the potential for what Fiona Doloughan refers to as "intermedial translation," or translation across media, a process that highlighted the affordances of each medium, comics and film. Comics' connection to film allows students to hone their media literacy by thinking through how the affordances of print comics differ from the affordances of film as they translate one medium into the other. John G. Nichols has discussed how studying film adaptations of superhero comics helps students see the affordances of each medium (231). Like Nichols's students, my students compared a comic to a film during class discussion and then adapted a comic into a film, though they created original comics as screenplays for their films, rather than using a published text. This act of intermedial translation helped "[bring] to the fore a focus on process, as well as production" because the "cultural and linguistic topographies" of print and film, "while they may overlap, do not map directly onto one another and cannot be reduced to a set of one-to-one correspondences" (47). Thus, translation across media highlights the gaps in each medium, while also showing what each does well. For example, students learned that comics portray fantasy better than films because you can draw anything, but translating your drawings into film, which relies on real actors, is difficult without access to expensive special effects. Intermedial translation highlighted the affordances of hand drawn comics that were not available in films. Seeing the gaps across media allowed students to learn more about the available means of design in both film and print comics through active practice with that design (Kress 6-7). Together, all of the assignments helped students hone their analytical and production skills in regards to multimodal texts.

Critical Reflection

The course accomplished its primary goal of helping students hone their multiliteracies. From the first assignment, the visual component of the interview summary, accompanied by our in class analysis of comics, encouraged students to make deliberate choices about visual design based on what they had learned about their subject. For example, one student interviewed a family friend who worked as a freelance photographer. In his interview, the friend had talked a lot about how his job had changed as digital technology became more prevalent, so that he had to master many kinds of skills, such as writing emails and keeping a website, that he hadn't had to think about before the Internet. The student's visual for the assignment depicted the man with his camera on a computer desktop background surrounded by folder icons with titles like "Website," "Work Photos," and "Scanned Photos." Another student created a McCloud-style comic about the professor she had interviewed, astutely asserting that McCloud's instructional style fit the subject matter.

The analytical papers engaged with details in the comics in a way that assumed each detail was an authorial choice made in service of some larger argument. I have found it difficult to draw out this kind of response when talking about alphabetic literature, potentially because analyses of alphabetic literature involve no translation across modes. Moreover, students also tend to view alphabetic literature, particularly novels, as a cohesive whole. By contrast, analysis of comics requires students to translate the discrete fragments on the page—the panels, the speech bubbles, the narrative boxes, etc.—into alphabetic text. Because students can see how a comic is constructed, they are more likely to think of each detail as purposeful. One student discussed Frank Miller's assertion that the media was a pervasive influence by looking at a page of *The Dark Knight* that included many talking heads pictured on televisions. He ended his essay by highlighting that comics themselves were also a form of media, but that their print nature made them less all-encompassing than the television, which employed sound and moving images to get its message across. This assignment shows medium specific analysis that engages with the multiple modes of comics.

While both of these assignments demonstrated enhanced student ability to analyze and create multimodal texts, their understanding of how various modes worked became most apparent during the intermedial translation from comic to film. In their evaluations, students cited this transition as one of the most difficult and most rewarding. Whether because our class had spent so much time looking at static print comics as opposed to moving pictures on film or television, or because assignment parameters were unclear, students created interesting and imaginative comics that they had difficulty translating to film. One group used photographs of posed Lego figurines for their comic with the intention of doing a stop-motion film, but eventually abandoned that project due to time constraints. Another group used interesting color technique in their comic to depict the fantastical elements of their story, which used superhero iconography to show their subject serving as an ambassador for comics in academic settings. The comics included one panel of the subject discovering comics for the first time. The panel is half black and white, and half in vivid color. They found it difficult to film this fantastical narrative, and particularly this panel, because, while they could draw anything, they had to rely on real actors and settings—plus deal with their technical limitations—for the film. As a result, the project changed entirely during the translation.

Part of this difficulty with translation across media may have stemmed from the choice of compared film and comic. I chose *The Dark Knight* as our study of adaptation because the movie had recently come out on DVD and I hoped to tap into student interest surrounding that film. However, Christopher Nolan's adaptation of the comic is more in the spirit of the comic than an actual translation; he captures the gritty feel Miller used for Batman without pulling visuals from specific panels of the comic. While the comparison helped show creative ways to accomplish adaptation, it focused too much on the gaps between media without addressing their similarities. In the future, I might use Marjane Satrapi's comic *Persepolis* and the film of the same title to ensure that students can see both the gaps and the similarities between print and film.

More generally, my enthusiasm for the material meant the course sometimes felt unfocused as I tried to cover too much ground in terms of genre. Because this was the first course on comics taught in the English department, we tried to provide a broad overview of the medium with little attention to genre. When I teach this again, I might limit our exploration of comics to documentary and autobiographical comics, of which there are many. While this might cause students to lose some of the exciting superhero-inspired imagery they decided to use in their final documentaries—one group cast their documentary as a superhero story with the subject, a librarian in Madison who stocks the comics titles, as the superhero—being exposed to more documentary-style comics could help with student frustration stemming from having to translate fantastic comics to the more reality-oriented medium of film. In the new syllabus, I would replace "Heartburst" with one of Phoebe Gloeckner's shorter stories, *The Dark Knight* comic and film with the *Persepolis* comic and film, and add Joe Sacco's *Palestine* early in the term, which shows him interviewing people to put together his comic.

Despite some of these drawbacks, this documentary project helped students realize the value of multimodal literacy beyond the classroom. A year after I taught the course, I received an email from one of my students letting me know she had gotten into graduate school for journalism. In the email, she thanked me for assigning the documentary group project because, in her personal statement, she had talked about her experience interviewing a community member and working as a group to create a professional looking documentary about that community member. When she had her interview with the graduate school, she impressed them by talking more about her experience in my class, particularly about the process of editing footage to craft an interesting story, first by using the comic and then by editing the film. My students often come to appreciate the rhetorical choices at their disposal, choices related to mode and medium, not to mention being able to think critically about the different multimedia texts that surround them. Starting with comics, multimodal in nature, and making the transition to film helps students become thoughtful designers.

Works Cited

Arias, Jennifer. "Teaching Ethnography: Reading the World and Developing Student Agency." *The English Journal* 97.6 (2008): 92-97. Print.

Chute, Hillary. *Graphic Women: Life Narrative and Contemporary Comics.* New York: Columbia UP, 2010. Print.

Cope, Bill, and Mary Kalantzis, eds. *Multiliteracies: Literacy Learning and the Design of Social Futures.* New York: Routledge, 2000. Print.

Doloughan, Fiona. *Contemporary Narrative.* New York: Continuum, 2011. Print.

Gardner, Jared. "Archives, Collectors, and the New Media Work of Comics." *Modern Fiction Studies* 52.4 (2006): 787-806. Print.

Gloeckner, Phoebe. *A Child's Life and Other Stories.* Berkeley: Frog Books, 2000. Print.

Groensteen, Thierry. *The System of Comics.* Trans. Bart Beaty and Nick Nguyen. Jackson: U of Mississippi P, 2007. Print.

Kress, Gunther. *Literacy in the New Media Age.* New York: Routledge, 2003. Print.

Lunsford, Andrea L., and Lisa Ede. "Among the Audience: On Audience in an Age of New Literacies." *Engaging Audience: Writing in an Age of New Literacies.* Ed. M. Elizabeth Weiser, Brian M. Fehler, and Angela M. Gonzalez. Urbana: NCTE, 2009. 42-68. Print.

Malley, Suzanne Blum, and Ames Hawkins. "Introduction." *Engaging Communities: Writing Ethnographic Research.* Wordpress. Web. 27 July. 2014. <http://www.engagingcommunities.org>.

McCloud, Scott. *Making Comics.* New York: Harper Collins, 2006. Print.

Morris, Barbara A. "Use of the Personal Interview as a Teaching Tool in English Composition." *Teaching English in the Two-Year College* 34.3 (2007): 287-93. Print.

Nichols, John G. "Violent Encounters: Graphic Novels and Film in the Classroom." *Teaching the Graphic Novel.* Ed. Stephen E. Tabachnick. New York: MLA, 2009. 230-37. Print.

Persepolis. Dir. Vincent Paronnaud and Marjane Satrapi. Sony, 2008. Film.

Sacco, Joe. *Palestine.* Seattle: Fantagraphics, 1993. Print.

Satrapi, Marjane. *Persepolis: The Story of a Childhood.* New York: Pantheon, 2004. Print.

Selfe, Cynthia L. *Multimodal Composition: Resources for Teachers.* Cresskill: Hampton P, 2007. Print.

Serafini, Frank. *Reading the Visual: An Introduction to Teaching Multimodal Literacy.* New York: Teachers College P, 2014. Print.

Whithaus, Carl. *Teaching and Evaluating Writing in the Age of Computers and High-Stakes Testing.* Mahwah: Lawrence-Erlbaum, 2005. Print.

The Wisconsin Idea. Board of Regents of the University of Wisconsin, 2014. Web. 7 Dec. 2014. <http://wisconsinidea.wisc.edu>.

English 177: Literature and Popular Culture, The Graphic Novel

<u>Course Overview</u>

We are surrounded by multimodal texts: television, webpages, print advertisements, billboards, and movies are just some of the examples of the many multimodal texts you have to "read" every day. This class is designed to help you read those multimodal texts more critically. In service of that goal, we will analyze comics and, in a more limited way, films, both of which are multimodal texts. You will craft multiple multimodal texts of your own. In your quest for knowledge, you will be engaging with both your peers and with members of the non-University community in Madison. By the end of the course, you will be able to make arguments in and about various media and will have produced a documentary in collaboration with your group members that you can share with the world beyond our classroom.

<u>Course Objectives</u>

At the end of this course, students will be able to:

- Read images
- Listen actively
- Analyze how multiple modes work together to convey a message
- Compare and contrast how comics differ from other forms of media that use language and images (e.g. film, webpages, television)
- Use multiple modes thoughtfully to convey information
- Make movies using iMovie

<u>Required Texts</u>

Abel, Jessica, and Matt Madden. *Drawing Words and Writing Pictures: Making Comics, Manga, Graphic Novels, And Beyond.* New York: First Second, 2008. Print.

Veitch, Rick. "Heartburst." *Heartburst and Other Pleasures.* West Townshend: King Hell Press, 2008. Print.

McCloud, Scott. *Understanding Comics: The Invisible Art.* New York: HarperPerennial, 1993. Print.

Madden, Matt. *99 Ways to Tell a Story.* New York: Chamberlain Bros, 2005. Print.

Spiegelman, Art. *Maus: A Survivor's Tale.* 2 vols. New York: Pantheon; Random, 1986-91. Print.

Miller, Frank. *Batman: The Dark Knight Returns.* New York: DC Comics, 1986. Print.

The Dark Knight. Dir. Christopher Nolan. Warner Bros, 2008. DVD.

Course Requirements

Interview (15%): This assignment is designed to help you practice interviewing before you have to do so for your documentary. You will film yourself (or have someone film you) interviewing someone from the Madison community. This can be someone at the university (a professor, a student, a staff member) or someone from outside the university (waiter at a restaurant, store manager at the mall, leader of a community organization). Using the information you gather from the interview, you will write a summary of what you learned about that person, painting a clear picture, in other words, of that person for your audience and providing a visual accompaniment. 750-1000 words (3-4 pages double spaced, not including the illustration).

Comics Visual Analysis (CVA) (20%): This assignment will allow you to practice reading images and analyzing how text and images work together in comics and other media. You will discuss one of the texts for this course by analyzing the visual and textual elements of two pages of the book (we will practice this in class). This is not a summary, but a paper that pays attention to details in the book that enhance the author's message. This assignment will help you write your reflection for your screenplay, where you will be making choices about how to communicate in multiple modes. 1000-1250 words (4-5 pages double spaced).

Comic Screenplay (25%): This assignment will be done in groups as a sort of rough draft for your documentary. As a group, you will write a screenplay including images for your documentary. **As individuals**, you will write reflections about the screenplay explaining why you chose to present the material in the way you did. We will talk more in depth about elements of filming as this assignment approaches. 500 words (2 pages double spaced).

Documentary (25%): As a group, you will film a documentary about comics culture in the Madison area and at UW. This documentary will include an interview with either

- A librarian
- A store manager
- A comics artist
- A professor who teaches a course on comics

In order to spread out the interviews, you will hand in preferences to me and I will make assignments based on those preference sheets. We will do this early on because the **interview must be completed two weeks prior to the due date.** The final movie should use the tools in Adobe Premiere Pro thoughtfully to make a professional looking product. We will talk more about the documentary genre of film in class. As part of this assignment, you will turn in a one-page reflection on how your group worked together. This allows me to see who did what and to assign grades accordingly.

Participation (10%): Much of class time is spent discussing course materials and working in groups to share and respond to each other's writing. You cannot learn from them and they cannot learn from you if you aren't there. Similarly, if you do not participate in group discussions or activities, you are not learning and no one is learning from you. Class activities give you multiple ways to engage with others, formulate and express your ideas, and ultimately help you improve your ability to write, think, and communicate. Hence, attendance to section is required and you are only counted as present if you participate.

Discussion Board Postings (5%): Before some class periods, each class member will post a question about the text we are reading in order to spark discussion. These questions should not be about facts in the text (characters' names or events), but inquire into the text in a way that sparks analysis. "Why" questions are always good for this purpose, and "how" questions (when thinking about authorial technique) can spark discussion as well. The discussion board allows for posting of both images and text, and I encourage you to practice multimodal communication by including both in your posts. **These postings are due no later than 11am the day before class.**

Course Schedule

Week 1:

In class:

- Introduction to multimodality and media specificity
- Tips for interviewing
- Interview a classmate

Homework:

- Read first two chapters of Abel & Madden and "Heartburst"
- Discussion board post on "Heartburst"

Week 2:

In class:

- Discuss "Heartburst" using Abel & Madden's language
- Summary vs. Analysis

Homework:

- Read McCloud
- Discussion board post on McCloud
- Set up interviews

Week 3:

In class:

- Discuss how McCloud's text performs his theories
- Gleaning information from interviews: read McCloud interview and work in pairs to write a summary
- Project groups assigned
- Fill out preference forms for interview subjects

Homework:

- Brainstorm interview questions
- Read Matt Madden *99 Ways to Tell a Story*
- Discussion board post making connections between Abel & Madden and McCloud

Week 4:

In class:

- Speed workshop interview questions: work with a partner for five minutes, then switch and work with someone else. Repeat three times.
- Quick group summary of Madden
- Analyze Madden as a whole group

Homework:

- Work on interviews
- Read *Maus I*
- Discussion board post analyzing a page from *Maus I*

Week 5:

In class:

- **Interview Assignment Due**
- Interview gallery
- Introduction to iMovie
- Introduce CVA
- Documentary subjects assigned

Homework:

- Read *Maus II*
- Discussion board post summarizing and analyzing a page from *Maus II*

(Between Week 6 and Week 9, all students meet with me for individual conferences about the Comics Visual Analysis (CVA): students should come prepared with their idea and any questions)

Week 6:

In class:

- iMovie Training (continued)
- Analyze *Maus I* and *II* using discussion board posts in pairs then share with group
- Identify pages you want to discuss in CVA by talking in pairs

Homework:

- Discussion board post about chosen pages (brainstorm)
- Bring chosen comic with you to class next week

Week 7:

In class:

- Speed workshop on CVA brainstorm
- Paired activity: write a one sentence summary of a page; switch books with your partner and see if he or she can find that page; discuss and modify accordingly
- Draft email to documentary subject in groups
- Brainstorm interview questions in groups

Homework:

- Email documentary subject immediately
- Read *The Dark Knight*
- Rough draft of CVA due next week
- Email rough draft to group members the day before class

Week 8:

In class:

- Introduction to peer workshops
- Peer workshop of CVA in project groups

Homework:

- Revise CVA based on peer workshop and individual conference

Week 9:

In class:

- **CVA Due**
- Group work time

Homework:

- Watch *The Dark Knight*
- Discussion board post on a scene from *The Dark Knight*
- Bring the comic version of *The Dark Knight* with you next week

Week 10:

In class:

- Discuss *The Dark Knight* film
- Discuss film and comic together—adaptation and translation

Homework:

- Work with group to complete interview and summarize it
- **Interview must be completed by the end of this week**

Week 11:

In class:

- Group workshop: brainstorm ideas for comic (sketch, write, talk)

Homework:

- Comic due next week

Week 12:

In class:

- **Comic Screenplay due**
- Comics gallery and presentations
- Those not presenting provide written feedback on the presentation

Homework:

- As a group, plan how you want to film your documentary

Week 13:

In class:

- Individual group meetings with me (during class time)

Homework:

- Work on your documentary as a group

Week 14:

In class:

- Share ideas with another group and get feedback
- Group work time

Homework:

- Implement feedback from individual meeting and from share session
- Documentary due next week

Week 15:

In class:

- **Documentaries due**
- Screen documentaries
- Semester wrap up: review what we did and what we learned in a class discussion

Course Design

ENGL 1102: Literature and Composition: Handwriting and Typography

Aaron Kashtan, Georgia Institute of Technology

I taught three sections of ENGL 1102, the second course in a mandatory first-year writing sequence with a heavy multimodal focus, during my first semester as a Marion L. Brittain Postdoctoral Fellow in the Department of Literature, Media and Communication at Georgia Tech. The specific subject matter for these sections was handwriting and typography. Assignments and readings required students to develop sensitivity to the rhetorical potential of font choice and typographic design and to produce multimodal texts that made significant use of typographic rhetoric. For example, the second essay asked students to compose a handwritten essay that analyzed their own handwriting. In keeping with this special issue's focus on comics, this course design explains how my lifelong interest in comics provided the theoretical rationale for this course, even though comics was not its explicit subject.

Institutional Context

The Brittain Fellowship is a teaching fellowship through which instructors teach a course in the mandatory first-year writing sequence, ENGL 1101 and 1102, or technical communication. When the Brittain Fellowship was created in the late 1980s, its primary focus was on written communication. During Jay Bolter's tenure as Brittain Fellowship coordinator and writing program director from 2000 to 2007, the program increased its focus on digital pedagogy. On being hired as the Director of the Writing and Communication Program (WCP) in 2007, Rebecca Burnett implemented the current WOVEN model ("The Brittain Fellowship"). Under this model, each ENGL 1101 and 1102 course must incorporate assignments covering five specific rhetorical modes: written, oral, visual, electronic, and nonverbal (summarized by the acronym WOVEN). In lieu of a final exam, each ENGL 1101 and 1102 course culminates in a reflective portfolio, for which students select artifacts published over the course of the semester that fit into each of the WOVEN categories and write reflective essays that analyze the process of composing each of these artifacts. So long as they meet these and other requirements, Brittain Fellows are encouraged to teach their ENGL 1101 and 1102 classes on any topic within their area of expertise. The GT WCP's emphasis on multimodality is further indicated in the program's common rubric, which "emphasizes *rhetorical awareness, stance and support, organization, conventions*, and *design*, categories that shape multimodal communication" (Burnett et al.). In particular, the rubric recognizes that one of the important tasks facing students as they engage in multimodal communication is to "design in ways that increase engagement, comprehensibility, and usability" (Burnett et al.). When I entered the program, the Design for Medium component of the rubric was as follows:

Table 1: Georgia Tech Writing and Communication rubric, section on Design for Medium (as of 2011-2012)

Scale	**Design for Medium** Features that use affordances of the genre to enhance factors such as usability and comprehensibility
Basic	Lacks features necessary or significant for the genre; uses features that conflict with or ignore the argument
Beginning	Omits some important features; distracting inconsistencies in features; uses features that don't support argument
Developing	Uses features that support the argument, but some match imprecisely with content; involves minor omissions or inconsistencies
Competent	Supports the argument with features that are generally suited to genre and content
Mature	Promotes engagement and supports the argument with features that efficiently use affordances
Exemplary	Persuades with careful, seamless integration of features and content and with innovative use of affordances

Thus, ENGL 1102 instructors are encouraged to teach writing not merely as a semiotic process, but also as a process of careful integration of form and content, in which the visual and material form of a written document are crucial tools for shaping its rhetorical appeal. Moreover, this view of writing applies not only to nonprint texts like videos or blogs but also to traditional text-based essays.

The WCP's emphasis on multimodality is appropriate given the multimodal focus of the department, which has evolved over the past three decades to focus heavily on science, technology, and media studies rather than traditional literary studies. Reflecting this shift in focus, the department name was changed from "Literature, Communication, and Culture" to "Literature, Media, and Communication" during my time there. Moreover, a multimodal focus was appropriate given the nature of Georgia Tech's students. As an engineering school, Georgia Tech's most popular majors include engineering (58%) and business administration (14%; "Georgia Institute of Technology"). Georgia Tech's students tend to be extremely technologically savvy and interested in visual media such as film and video games, which makes topics like comics and gaming particularly appropriate for 1102 courses. Thus, a multimodal approach to first-year writing was both more relevant to this student body and more useful to their future professional lives than was an approach that emphasized traditional written communication. According to former Writing & Communication Assistant Director L. Andrew Cooper, "the GT WCP serves a student body in particular need of preparation for communication in dynamic environments that involve information in multiple modes and media synchronously and asynchronously" (n.p.).

I came to the Brittain Fellowship in 2011 having just completed a PhD thesis focusing on comics and media studies, yet my previous teaching experience had given me only modest preparation to teach within a multimodal and digital framework. While teaching composition as an adjunct during graduate school, I had typically assigned only traditional written projects. (This was not an uncommon experience among new Brittain Fellows; Rebecca Weaver, for example, refers to the "steep tech learning curve of the Brittain program.") Therefore, this essay explores how I drew upon an intuitive understanding of multimodality that I had acquired through a lifetime of reading and studying comics in order to teach a course with a heavy focus on multimodality.

Theoretical Rationale

I chose handwriting and typography as the subject matter for this course because I wanted students to understand multimodal composition as a process of conscious design. I wanted students to understand texts not as abstract vehicles for meaning but as material and visual artifacts, whose form helps to shape the reader's perception of their content, and whose meaning would change if any visual element were altered. I arrived at this understanding of multimodality through comics theory, and I would suggest that the process of document design, as theorized by rhetoricians in professional writing, bears surprising similarities to the process of making comics.

My favorite definition of comics comes not from a standard source like Scott McCloud or Thierry Groensteen, but rather from Dylan Horrocks's graphic novel *Hicksville.* In this book, a character named after the author interviews a fictional cartoonist named Emil Kopen:

> HORROCKS: Okay, how are *piktorii* [comics] like maps?
> KOPEN: They are the same thing: using *all* of language—not only words or pictures.
> HORROCKS: But some *piktorii* have *no* words.
> KOPEN: And some have no pictures. When we speak, we do not always use our whole vocabulary. . . .
> [. . .]
> HORROCKS: So it's still a comic even with no pictures?
> KOPEN: Perhaps. It is still a map. Why not? I have seen maps made entirely of text.

Whereas standard definitions of comics emphasize the primacy of the image,[1] Horrocks's radical insight is that *everything* is a comic, from a painting to an unillustrated novel. According to Horrocks's definition, making comics is not a specific and clearly definable craft, but a way of thinking, a mentality that recognizes words and images on a continuum. For Horrocks[2], images can be semiotic and words can be visual, as well as vice versa. Even when we compose a text that seems not to include pictures, for example, pictures are still part of the vocabulary we draw upon. And composing such a text is a visual activity, in the same way that painting is a semiotic activity.

What might a comic (or map) "made entirely of text" look like? It might simply be a written composition in which the visual and other sensory properties of text serve as means of generating meaning and in which any change in the visual arrangement of text produces a corresponding change in meaning (see fig. 1). In that sense, *any* text that employs document design—any text at all, in other words—can be viewed as a comic, whether or not it uses pictures. Comics, in the narrow sense, are different from other types of texts, such as prose texts, only insofar as their use of document design is more visible and deliberate. Reading and making comics is a process of what Horrocks calls "using our whole vocabulary," where "whole" is understood in the same sense as in Kathleen Blake Yancey's phrase "a composition made whole."

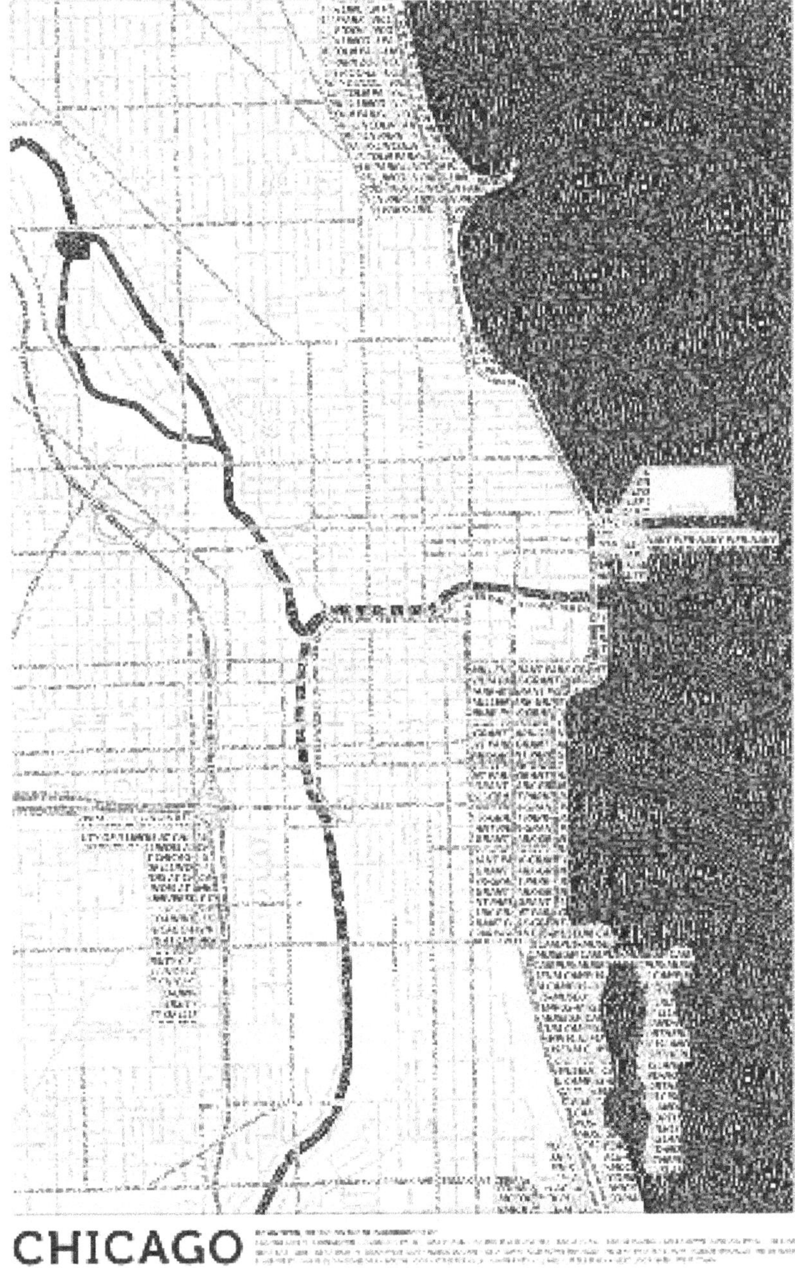

Fig. 1. Typographic map of Chicago. Copyright Axis Maps.

This understanding of comics bears a surprising resemblance to current theories of document design. The latter may be defined as a process of careful selection and arrangement of the visual elements of a text so as to achieve a desired rhetorical effect. In the introduction to her textbook *Dynamics in Document Design: Creating Texts for Readers*, Karen Schriver observes,

> Books on desktop publishing and professional communication have tended to treat design as mere formatting. This way of thinking relegates the designer to a support role—the one who squeezes content into girdles, who pours messages into templates for smoothing and shaping. This view wrongly separates form and content. (6)

Instead, successful document design is about thoughtful matching of form to content: "Document design is the field concerned with creating texts (broadly defined) that integrate words and pictures in ways that help people to achieve their specific goals for using texts at home, school or work" (10). Similarly, in the introduction to their textbook *Designing Visual Language: Strategies for Professional Communicators*, Charles Kostelnick and David Roberts write, "In each communication you design, you'll try to shape its visual language so that it fits the rhetorical situation—audience, purpose and context" (5).

The current importance of document design in the fields of professional communication and rhetoric and composition is partly attributable to technological changes:

> The reintroduction of design thinking to composition studies at least since 2002 has been driven by growing use of computers in first-year writing, an introduction of technology that has expanded understanding of first-year writing as document production requiring of students the integration of (minimally) textual and visual representations. (Marback 264)

Technological change has expanded the scope of design options available to communicators, while also giving individual writers responsibility for design choices, such as font choice, that were previously the purview of professional designers (Handa 225). Document design, however, is not specific to visual rhetoric but applies equally well even to alphabetic writing. As Stephen A. Bernhardt wrote in 1986, "The physical fact of the text, with its spatial appearance on the page, requires visual apprehension: a text can be seen, must be seen, in a process which is essentially different from the perception of speech" (66). Moreover, "outside the classroom visually informative prose is pervasive, and not just in scientific or technical fields" (67). Although the current emphasis on document design is at least partly attributable to the rise of digital technology, document design is not exclusive to digital or even to predominantly visual texts. And although document design is primarily taught in technical communication courses, it applies equally well to the kinds of texts students write in first-year composition courses—just as the thought processes involved in making comics also apply when making primarily verbal texts.

Based on my experience with comics, therefore, I want students to think about the design inherent in *everything* they write. For me, document design is about seeing texts not simply as abstract vehicles for meaning, but as material and visual artifacts whose form helps to shape the reader's perception of their content, and whose meaning would change if any visual element were altered. In other words, for me, document design is about seeing texts as comics in Horrocks's broad sense. In the course under discussion here, I sought to implement this theory not by having students make their own comics (though I did do that later in my time as a Brittain Fellow), but by having them create projects that required students to engage in the design-thinking characteristic of comics.

We began the semester by reading Tamara Plakins Thornton's *Handwriting in America: A Cultural History*, which analyzes handwriting as "one of the places where the self happened" (xiii), examining how changes in popular opinions about handwriting reflected changes in the prevalent understanding of selfhood. One of the topics Thornton covers is the pseudoscience of graphology, popular in the early twentieth century, which was based on the premise that handwriting is an index of the writer's personality. Graphologists claimed to be able to infer a writer's character traits from the graphic properties of their handwriting, such as size and slant (see fig. 2). While graphology itself has been discredited, the basic notion behind it—that handwriting has a more intimate connection to personality and selfhood than other writing technologies—is still central to the way handwriting is understood in twenty-first-century America. To show students the connections between handwriting and the self, we read Alison Bechdel's *Fun Home*. As I have argued elsewhere, *Fun Home* uses handwriting as a central metaphor for selfhood (Kashtan), and it graphically demonstrates the link between handwriting and selfhood through its accentuation of the idiosyncratic features of Bechdel's style of handwriting and drawing (see Chute for a similar argument). As a further demonstration of the rhetorical effects of document design, we read Jonathan Safran Foer's *Extremely Loud & Incredibly Close*. Though Foer's book is a prose novel, it arguably has more in common with comics than with most prose fiction in terms of its design because it violates the crystal-goblet principle and uses images and expressive typography as key components for creating meaning.

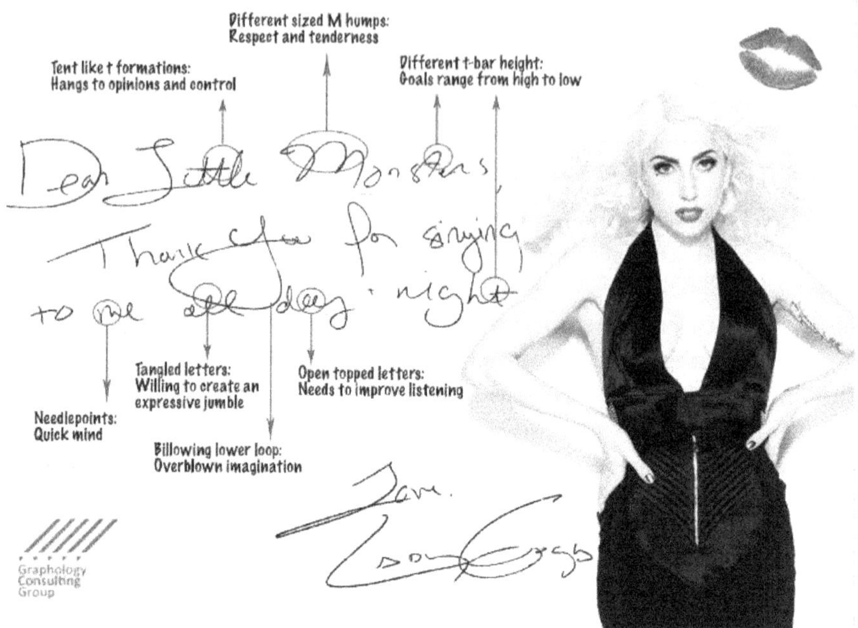

Fig. 2. Graphological analysis of Lady Gaga's handwriting. Copyright Sheila Kurtz.

All these readings, as well as the writing projects I am about to describe, introduced students to the notion that design features such as typography can serve as tools for creating meaning. For example, one of the early informal writing projects for this class asked students to do the following:

1. Write a story about yourself. It can be any story at all, but it should be about something that actually happened to you, and it should reveal something about you.
2. Prepare two versions of this story: a handwritten version and a typewritten or word-processed version. These versions do not necessarily have to be the same, but if they are different, then be prepared to explain why.

This assignment asked students to consider the rhetorical importance of design: would a typewritten essay have the same rhetorical effect as a handwritten version of the same essay?

The second formal assignment for this course asked students to confront the question of the relationship between design and content even more directly. In this assignment, I asked students to test graphological theories by discussing what, if anything, their handwriting revealed about them. Specifically, I asked students to write an essay analyzing their own handwriting and I specified that this essay had to be *handwritten*. This assignment required students to apply the understanding of design rhetoric that they drew from Thornton, Bechdel and Foer. It required them to think about writing as both semiotic process and visual and haptic process. Even more radically, this assignment required students to think about the semiotic and design components of their writing as integrated rather than separate. The arguments that students made about their handwriting had to be delivered through the visual appearance of the handwritten text itself. My goal in this assignment, in other words, was to create a feedback loop between document design and content. My hope was that as students wrote about their handwriting *in* handwriting, they would realize things about their handwriting that they might not have noticed otherwise and that they could then draw upon these insights as they continued to work on the essay. Like the informal writing project just described, this assignment asked students to produce an essay that primarily used the written mode of rhetoric, the "W" in WOVEN; students were not required to include other modes like images or videos (and thus, in a sense, this assignment exemplifies Shipka's claim that multimodality is not exclusive to digital composition). Yet the most successful essays produced in response to these assignments used document design in highly visible ways that enhanced meaning, and any changes in the design of these essays would have noticeably altered the rhetorical experience of reading the text.

Finally, in the last major assignment for this class, students chose a digital communication technology and explained its effects: "When you use your chosen communication technology, to what extent does it reveal, and to what extent does it conceal, your "self," "personality" or "identity"? Why is that? . . . When you use your chosen communication technology, how does it *change* the sort of person you are or appear to be? Are you (or do you appear to be) the *same* person when you use this technology, as when you use nondigital communications technologies?" This assignment challenged students to apply the design-thinking characteristic of comics to media that were produced by nonchirographic means. Furthermore, this assignment was motivated by my belief that despite common claims for handwriting and hand-drawing as uniquely personal and embodied technologies (see Kemp-Jackson for an example of such claims), the self-expression and attention to detail characteristic of handwriting are present, at least to some degree, in any writing technology. Neither comics-making nor document design, in other words, is medium-specific.

Critical Reflection

The assignments described above produced some spectacular results. For example, one student, Lauren "Rook" Jarrett[3], responded to the first informal assignment by producing an essay that detailed a Pokémon card game she had played in third grade (see fig. 3). This essay took full advantage of the affordances of handwriting, using multiple scripts and colors of ink for dramatic effect. In addition, the essay incorporated marginal illustrations depicting scenes from the story. Simply by looking at an essay like this, one can clearly see its resemblance to comics. Like the lettering in comics, the handwriting in this essay functions visually as well as semiotically; what it looks like matters as much as what it says. Like a comic, this essay uses document design as a tool for creating meaning, and if any graphic element of this essay were changed, it would offer an entirely different reading experience. Indeed, Rook Jarrett's typewritten version of this essay, while containing the same textual content, is comparatively visually impoverished, lacking the color or visual richness of the handwritten version (see fig. 4). (This should not be taken to imply that handwriting is superior to typewriting in terms of its visual richness. Students could also have responded to this assignment by producing a handwritten essay written in sober and boring handwriting, or a typed essay that used expressive typography and nonstandard font choices.)

Similarly, the same student's response to the second assignment is notable not only for the attractiveness of its handwriting but also for the ways in which her writing actually illustrates the argument of the text, visually documenting the changes that have occurred in her handwriting over time (see fig. 5). In terms of its deliberate, thoughtful use of design rhetoric, an essay like this has more in common with a comic book than with the 12-point, double-spaced papers in Times New Roman that we typically ask students to produce. Indeed, an essay like this one can be viewed as a comic "made entirely of text."

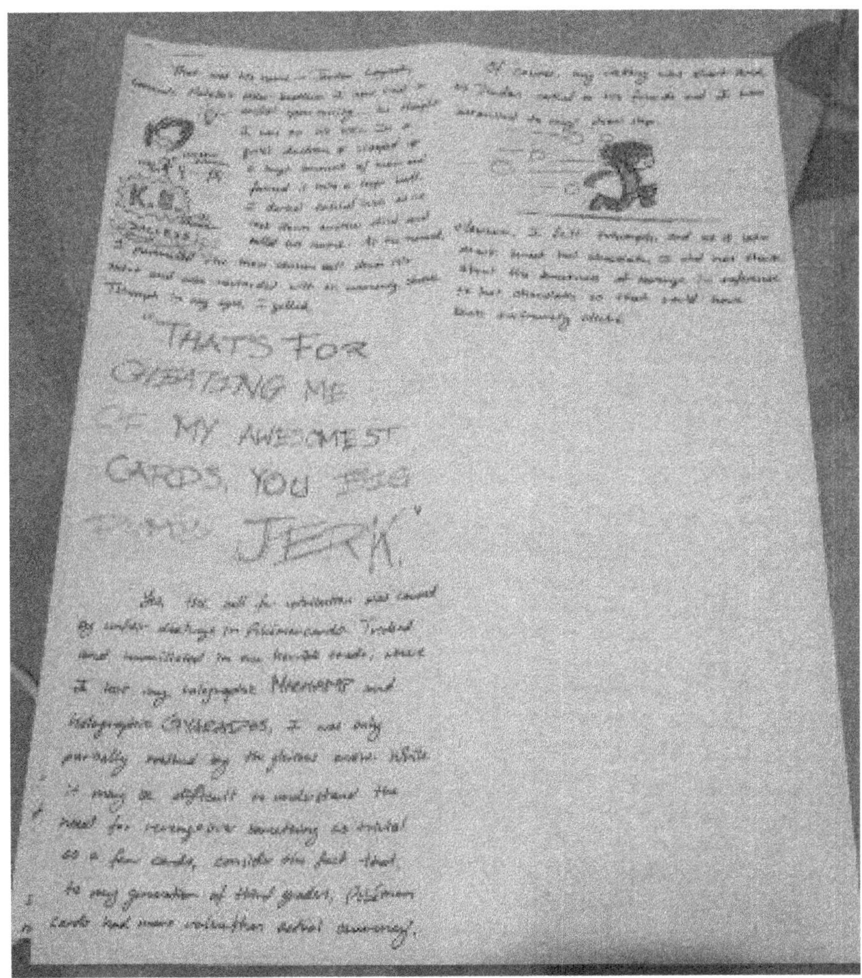
"THATS FOR CHEATING ME OF MY AWESOMEST CARDS, YOU BIG DUMB JERK."

Fig. 3. Rook Jarrett's handwritten response to the informal assignment described above.

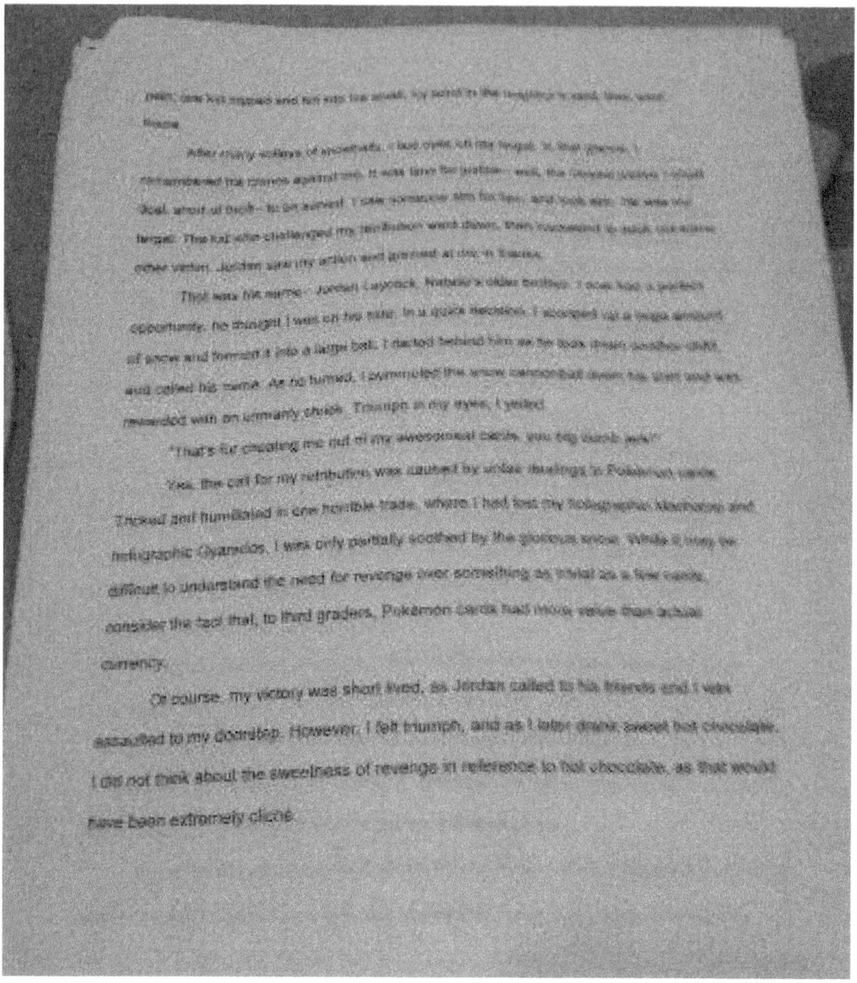

Fig. 4. Rook Jarrett's typed response to the informal assignment described above.

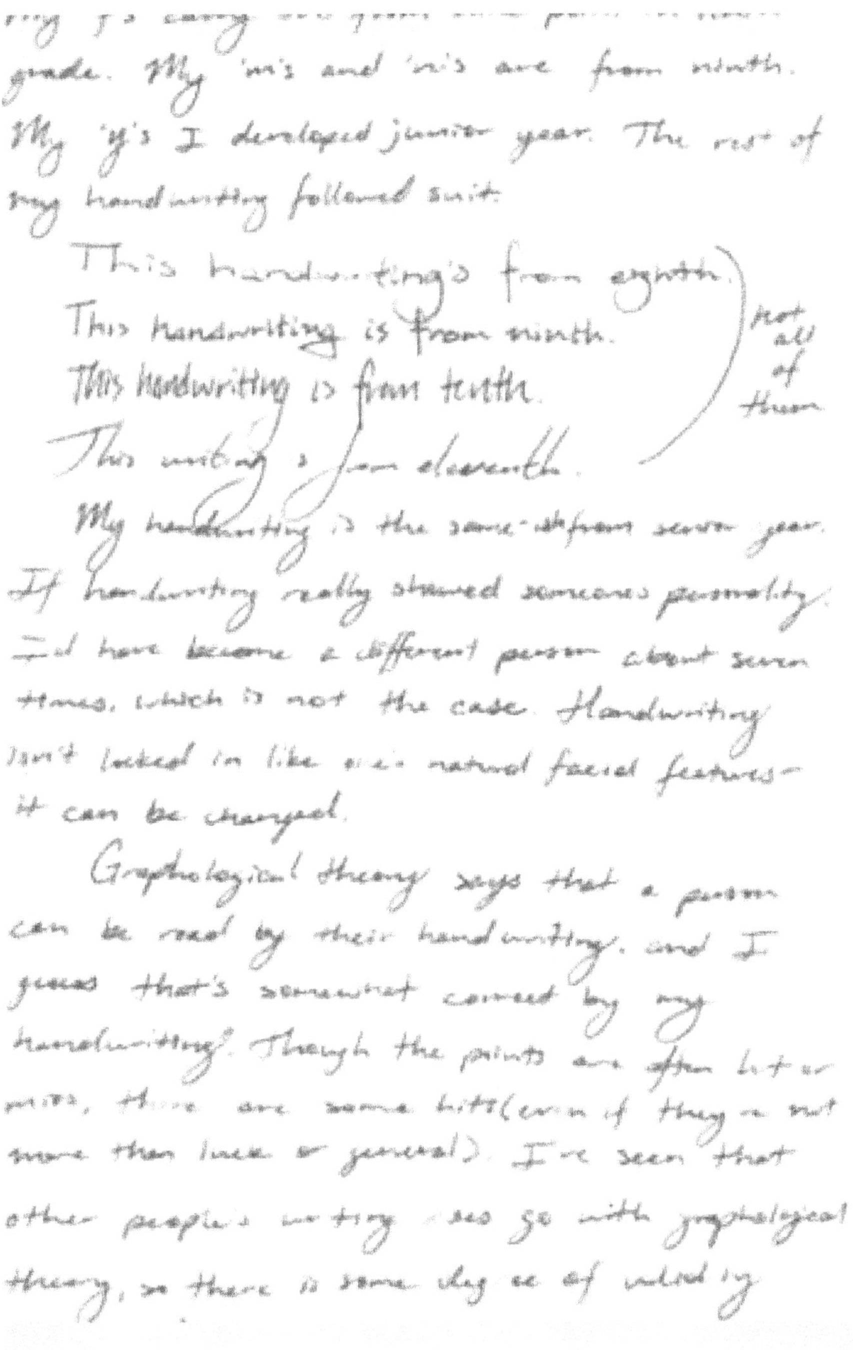

grade. My 'm's and 'n's are from ninth.
My 'y's I developed junior year. The rest of
my handwriting followed suit.

This handwriting's from eighth.
This handwriting is from ninth.
This handwriting is from tenth.
This writing's from eleventh.
not all of them

My handwriting is the same from seventh year. If handwriting really showed someones personality, I'd have become a different person about seven times, which is not the case. Handwriting isn't locked in like one's natural facial features—it can be changed.

Graphological theory says that a person can be read by their handwriting, and I guess that's somewhat correct by my handwriting. Though the points are often hit or miss, there are some hits (even if they're not more than luck or general). I've seen that other people's writing also go with graphological theory, so there is some degree of validity

Fig. 5. Rook Jarrett's response to the second formal assignment.

With the third assignment, students' essays moved far away from what one would normally think of as comics, yet continued to show careful attention to design and integration of form and content. Students took the third assignment and ran with it, producing essays that were formatted as Tumblr feeds, Facebook pages, text message conversations, or even more exotic objects of digital self-expression. For example, a computer science major chose to write about the way he expressed himself in comments on code. His final paper was submitted as a Java program that produced the text of the paper; however, he also included the source code of the Java program, which included commentary on his paper.

Despite my initial lack of experience with multimodal composition, I ended the semester feeling that this was one of the most successful composition courses I had taught, and tried to incorporate insights from this class into my future courses. I would speculate, however, that because I was teaching at an engineering school whose students tended to be extremely digitally savvy and competent with coding, they tended to be more willing to engage with the creative possibilities of multimodal design than other students may have been. At my current institutional home, a liberal arts university, I initially assumed a similar level of multimodal competency from my students and was surprised when some of them had trouble understanding what multimodality meant.

An additional benefit of teaching a course like this is personal, in that I was able to use my interest in comics to bridge the gap between my existing teaching experience and the multimodal approach that Georgia Tech demanded from me. The quality of the work I received from my students encouraged me to try to use similar practices in my own scholarly work. As I continued to assign projects like the ones described above, I felt increasingly embarrassed by the fact that my scholarly work tended to look exactly like my drafts of this essay—a series of gray pages of double-spaced 12-point font, with occasional images. When I accepted Roger Whitson's invitation to submit an article in comics form for his and Anastasia Salter's special issue of *Digital Humanities Quarterly* on the theme "Comics as Scholarship," I was initially terrified because of my lack of confidence in my own drawing and coding abilities. Without the experience of having had my students engage in similar projects, I might never have been willing to start that project at all.

Overall, the assignments discussed here suggest ways in which an understanding of comics can inform the way we teach not only multimodal assignments but also traditional alphabetic writing. My experience with comics informs everything I do when I teach composition, because I see comics not as a particular category of texts, but as a mode of design thinking that can potentially apply to any genre of texts. For Horrocks's fictional character Emil Kopen, the difference between comics and prose is a matter of degree rather than of kind: comics are simply texts that "use our whole vocabulary," including words and pictures. Thus, the design processes involved in comics are applicable to all texts, even texts in which we use only part of our vocabulary.

Notes

1. Familiar examples include McCloud's "juxtaposed pictorial and other images in deliberate sequence" (9) or Groensteen's "relational play of a plurality of independent images (128).

2. This definition is of course provided by the fictional character Emil Kopen, not by Horrocks the author. However, in his essay "Inventing Comics," Horrocks critiques McCloud's definition of comics in terms similar to those he places in Kopen's mouth.

3. Name used with permission.

Works Cited

Bechdel, Alison. *Fun Home: A Family Tragicomic*. Boston: Houghton Mifflin, 2006. Print.

Bernhardt, Stephen A. "Seeing the Text." *CCC* 37.1 (1986): 66–78. Print.

"The Brittain Fellowship: An Introduction." *DevLab*. Georgia Institute of Technology, n.d. Web. 31 Oct. 2014. <http://devlab.lmc.gatech.edu/wiki/index.php/The_Brittain_Fellowship:_An_Introduction>.

Burnett, Rebecca E. Sample syllabus for ENGL 1102, Georgia Institute of Technology, Atlanta, GA. August 2011.

Burnett, Rebecca E., Andy Frazee, Kathleen Hanggi, and Amanda Madden. "A Programmatic Ecology of Assessment: Using a Common Rubric to Evaluate Multimodal Processes and Artifacts." *Computers and Composition* 31 (2014): 53–66. Print.

Chute, Hillary. *Graphic Women: Life Narrative and Contemporary Comics*. New York: Columbia UP, 2010. Print.

Cooper, L. Andrew. "If you think about…" Facebook. 30 Oct. 2014. Web. 15 Jan. 2015.

Foer, Jonathan Safran. *Extremely Loud & Incredibly Close*. Boston: Mariner, 2005. Print.

"Georgia Institute of Technology." *U.S. News & World Report*. U.S. News & World Report, n.d. Web. 31 Oct. 2014. <http://colleges.usnews.rankingsandreviews.com/best-colleges/georgia-tech-1569>.

Groensteen, Thierry. *The System of Comics*. Jackson: UP of Mississippi, 2009. Print.

Handa, Carolyn. *Visual Rhetoric in a Digital World: A Critical Sourcebook*. Boston: Bedford/St. Martin's, 2004. Print.

Horrocks, Dylan. *Hicksville*. Montreal: Drawn & Quarterly, 2001. Print.

---. "Inventing Comics." *The Comics Journal* 234 (2001): 29–39. Print.

Kashtan, Aaron. "My Mother Was a Typewriter: *Fun Home* and the Importance of Materiality in Comics Studies." *Journal of Graphic Novels and Comics* 4.1 (2013): 92–116. Print.

Kemp-Jackson, Samantha. "We Should All Mourn the Death of Cursive Writing."*Huffpost Living.* The Huffington Post. 6 Aug. 2013. Web. 15 Jan. 2015. <http://www.huffingtonpost.ca/samantha-kempjackson/cursive-writing-in-schools_b_3707794.html>.

Kostelnick, Charles, and David D. Roberts. *Designing Visual Language: Strategies for Professional Communicators.* Boston: Longman, 2011. Print.

Marback, Richard. "Embracing Wicked Problems: The Turn to Design in Composition Studies." *CCC* 61.2 (2009): 397–419. Print.

McCloud, Scott. *Understanding Comics.* Northampton: Kitchen Sink, 1993. Print.

Schriver, Karen. *Dynamics in Document Design: Creating Texts for Readers.* New York: John Wiley, 1997. Print.

Shipka, Jody. *Toward a Composition Made Whole.* Pittsburgh: U of Pittsburgh P, 2011. Print.

Thornton, Tamara Plakins. *Handwriting in America: A Cultural History.* New Haven: Yale UP, 1996. Print.

Weaver, Rebecca. "Tech, No to Tech, Yes: How a Former Technophobe Becomes a Digital Teaching Fellow." *TECHstyle.* Georgia Institute of Technology, 13 Sept. 2012. Web. 31 Oct. 2014. < http://techstyle.lmc.gatech.edu/tech-no-to-tech-yes-how-a-former-technophobe-becomes-a-digital-teaching-fellow/>.

Yancey, Kathleen Blake. "Looking for Sources of Coherence in a Fragmented World: Notes Toward a New Assessment Design." *Computers and Composition* 21.1 (2004): 89–102. Print.

Syllabus

ENGL 1102

Course Description

We usually think of words and letters as simple containers or channels for communication. Yet words and letters, including the words and letters you are looking at now, are also things. Whether handwritten, printed, or electronically generated, words and letters are material and visual, and the material and visual properties of words can have a substantial impact on the way in which words and letters are understood by readers. In other words, the *look* of what we write influences the *content* of what we write. At a time when writing technology is changing rapidly and individual users have access to an unprecedented repertory of options for manipulating the appearance of their writing, sensitivity to the material and visual aspects of writing is more important than ever. In this class, you will examine works in various media that make use of the expressive potential of handwriting and typography; using these works as guidelines, you will create works of your own that take advantage of this same potential.

Textbooks

Bechdel, Alison. *Fun Home: A Family Tragicomic*. Boston: Houghton Mifflin, 2006. Print.

Foer, Jonathan Safran. *Extremely Loud & Incredibly Close*. Boston: Mariner, 2005. Print.

Hayles, Katherine. *Writing Machines*. Cambridge: MIT, 2002. Print.

Lupton, Ellen. *Thinking with Type: A Critical Guide for Designers, Writers, Editors, & Students*. New York: Princeton Architectural, 2004. Print.

Thornton, Tamara Plakins. *Handwriting in America: A Cultural History.* New Haven: Yale UP, 1996. Print.

In addition, you will be required to purchase *WOVENtext*, Georgia Tech's custom e-book for ENGL 1101 and 1102. Readings will also include various articles and handouts as specified on the syllabus.

Teaching philosophy

- My method in teaching is to train you to think nontransparently. That is, I want you to examine your own expectations and look critically at things you typically take for granted. In reading and writing about texts, I want you to be able to step outside the world of the text and examine the unstated assumptions and ideas behind the text.

- In grading student texts, I value creativity and innovation. I will be more impressed if you attempt something difficult, even if you do it less successfully, than if you try something easy.
- This class will be participatory in nature. I prefer to conduct discussions and ask leading questions, rather than lecturing. I feel that you will learn more effectively if you figure things out for yourself than if I tell you things.

Assignments

- *Rhetorical Analysis #1*: Choose a text of your choice and analyze its use of typography. Explain how the text communicates by means of its choice of typefaces, its arrangement of letters, and its distribution of letters relative to pictures. (10%)
- *Graphology*: Perform an informal graphological analysis of yourself. Explain why your handwriting looks the way it does, why you write the way you do, and what your handwriting reveals and/or conceals about you. This assignment must be handwritten. (20%)
- *Typographic History*: As a group, select a particular font or electronic typeface. Research the origin, history, uses, and associations of this typeface, and provide at least one example and analysis of a particularly effective use of it. Present this information to your classmates in the form of a group presentation with accompanying Prezi. (15%)
- *Rhetorical Analysis* #2: Select one of the pieces included in the Electronic Literature Collection. Prepare an oral presentation with accompanying Prezi in which you describe the way in which this piece makes use of typography, and assess whether its use of typography could be replicated in print or handwriting. (15%)
- *Electronic Graphology*: Perform a digital graphological analysis of yourself. Explain what your electronic writing looks like and why, and what it reveals or conceals about you. This assignment must incorporate features specific to digital writing. (20%)
- *Portfolio*: Select one assignment that fulfills each of the five WOVEN components (Written, Oral, Visual, Electronic, Nonverbal). For each assignment, write a short reflection essay. Prepare an attractively formatted and typeset document that incorporates each of the five assignments and the reflection essays. (10%)
- *Participation* (10%).

Grading: Essays will be graded on a rubric consisting of five components:

- Rhetorical Awareness (usually 25%)

- Stance and Support (25%)
- Organization (25%)
- Design for Medium (15%)
- Conventions (10%)

CLASS SCHEDULE

WEEK 1: Why letters matter

Day 1

- Course introduction
- Lecture: The crystal goblet theory of typography

Day 2

- In-class viewing of *Helvetica* (Gary Hustwit, 2007)

Day 3

- Finish in-class viewing of *Helvetica*
- Homework: Type design exercise; read Shaikh, A. Dawn, Barbara S. Chaparro, and Doug Fox, "Perception of Fonts: Perceived Personality Traits and Uses," *Usability News* 8.1 (2006): 1-6.

WEEK 2: How letters create meaning

Day 1

- Discussion: How does the design of letters affect meaning?
- Reading: Poems by Apollinaire and Marinetti to be announced

Day 2

- Discussion: How does the arrangement of text affect meaning?
- Homework: Read selected poems by Heaney, Blake and Keats
- Supplemental reading: WOVENtext 21, "Exploring, Planning, and Drafting"

Day 3

- Discuss Heaney, Blake and Keats poems
- Homework: Rhetorical Analysis, first draft

WEEK 3: Handwriting and the self

Day 1: NO CLASS—LABOR DAY HOLIDAY

Day 2

- Rhetorical Analysis first draft due
- Workshop: Rhetorical Analysis
- Homework: Begin *Fun Home*

Day 3

- Discuss *Fun Home*
- Homework: Continue *Fun Home*

WEEK 4: Cross-cultural theories of handwriting

Day 1

- Discuss *Fun Home*
- Homework: Read *Handwriting in America*, chapters 1-2

Day 2

- Discuss East Asian calligraphy
- Homework: Read *Handwriting in America*, chapters 3-4
- Rhetorical Analysis first draft will be returned

Day 3

- Discuss Thornton
- Homework: Read *Handwriting in America*, chapter 5 and epilogue

WEEK 5: Histories of handwriting

Day 1

- Rhetorical Analysis second draft due
- Homework: Read *Handwriting in America*

Day 2

- Discuss *Handwriting in America*
- Homework: Read Shmuel Yosef Agnon, "The Tale of the Scribe," *A Book That Was Lost and Other Stories*, eds. Alan L. Mintz, and Anne Golomb Hoffman (New York: Schocken, 1995), 167-183.

Day 3

- Discuss *Handwriting in America*
- Homework: Supplemental reading on East Asian calligraphy

WEEK 6: Rhetoric of typography

Day 1

- Discuss East Asian calligraphy
- Homework: Read *Thinking with Type*

Day 2

- Discuss *Thinking with Type*
- Homework: Read *Thinking with Type*

Day 3

- Discuss *Thinking with Type*
- Homework: Finish *Thinking with Type*

WEEK 7: Typography as expression

Day 1

- Discuss *Thinking with Type*
- Homework: Begin *Extremely Loud & Incredibly Close*
- Graphology first draft due

Day 2

- Discuss *Extremely Loud & Incredibly Close*
- Homework: Continue *Extremely Loud & Incredibly Close*

Day 3

- Discuss *Extremely Loud & Incredibly Close*
- Homework: Continue *Extremely Loud & Incredibly Close*

WEEK 8: Presentations

Day 1

- Homework: Finish *Extremely Loud & Incredibly Close*
- Supplemental reading: WOVENtext 83-84

Day 2

- Workshop: Oral/Nonverbal Presentations

Day 3

- Workshop: Oral/Nonverbal Presentations
- Supplemental reading: WOVENtext 80-82

UNIT III. LETTERING AND TECHNOLOGY

WEEK 9: Presentations

Day 1

- NO CLASS—FALL RECESS

Day 2

- Oral/Nonverbal Presentations

Day 3

- Oral/Nonverbal Presentations
- Homework: Begin *Writing Machines*

WEEK 10: Text as technology

Day 1

- Discuss *Writing Machines*
- Homework: Continue *Writing Machines*

Day 2

- Discuss *Writing Machines*
- Homework: Continue *Writing Machines*

Day 3

- Discuss *Writing Machines*
- Homework: Continue *Writing Machines*

WEEK 11

Day 1

- Discuss *Writing Machines*
- Homework: Begin reading Electronic Literature Collection

Day 2

- Discuss electronic literature
- Workshop: Rhetorical Analysis #2
- Supplemental reading: WOVENtext 106

Day 3

- Workshop: Rhetorical Analysis #2
- Supplemental reading: WOVENtext 97-99 and 101

WEEK 12: Presentations

Day 1

- Rhetorical Analysis #2 presentations

Day 2

- Rhetorical Analysis #2 presentations

Day 3

- Rhetorical Analysis #2 presentations
- Homework: Read Jessica Helfand, "Electronic Typography: The New Visual Language," *Print*, 48.3 (1994): 98-101.

WEEK 13: Electronic typography and the memory of handwriting

Day 1

- Discuss Helfand

Day 2

- In-class viewing: *Up*

Day 3

- In-class viewing: *Up*
- Discuss *Up*

WEEK 14

Day 1

- Discuss *Up*
- Electronic Graphology first draft due
- Homework: Read excerpts from Heller, Steven. *The Education of a Typographer*. New York: Allworth, 2004. Print.

Day 2

- Discuss Heller

Day 3

- NO CLASS—THANKSGIVING HOLIDAY

WEEK 15

Day 1

- Electronic Graphology first draft will be returned
- Peer review and conferences: Electronic Graphology

Day 2

- Peer review and conferences: Electronic Graphology

Day 3

- Peer review and conferences: Electronic Graphology and Portfolio

WEEK 16: Week Preceding Final Exams

Day 1

- In-class portfolio workshop
- Electronic Graphology final draft due

Day 2

- In-class portfolio workshop

Day 3

- In-class portfolio workshop
- Portfolios due at end of class

Where We Are: Intersections

"Where We Are" highlights where we are as a field on matters current and compelling. In these invited contributions, we bring together a small group of scholars at the forefront of a particular issue or practice, who together issue a progress report of sorts (in 800-1200 words). *–Editor's Note*

The Underdog Disciplines: Comics Studies and Composition and Rhetoric

Susan Kirtley, Portland State University

I have always been drawn to the underdog, the scrappy survivor, and much as composition and rhetoric scholars have had to (and continue to) fight for legitimacy, so, too, do comics scholars. In fact, as fairly recent additions to the academy, comics studies and composition and rhetoric share many commonalities. Yet what might comics studies learn from the slightly older field of composition and rhetoric? I ask this question as a member of both fields. I have been a devoted reader of comics ever since a particularly unpleasant fifth grade classmate coldly informed me, "Girls don't read comics." I took this statement as a challenge and set out to read every comic I could get my hands on. However, it has only been in the past few years that my obsession with comics has made its way into my academic career; for most of my scholarly life I have worked, quite happily, in composition.

In search of guidance for a fledgling field, I look to the self-narratives of composition, and the 2010 special issue of *College Composition and Communication* provides an excellent starting place, as the journal reflects on its 60th anniversary, studying the past and looking to the future. In the issue, editor Kathleen Blake Yancey notes that composition was an "*intimate* group in the early years, one with a short modern history and fairly singular focus" (6), but over time "we have *expanded* and diversified; we have recovered not one history but several histories and narratives" (6). Thus, composition and rhetoric already maintains numerous origin stories. Comics studies, an even newer field with "a general start-date of the early 2000s" (Steirer 265), is still formulating its foundational narratives.

It is clear that both disciplines struggle for legitimacy within the academy. While comics studies strives for respectability given the popular nature of its research subject, composition and rhetoric struggles with its service reputation. Still, each field looks to find authority, acceptance, and a place within the academy. Philip Troutman contends that comics studies

> sits somewhat uneasily within the academy, both because of the medium's image/text composition, which sets it outside traditional disciplinary purviews, and because of its popular nature, which has engendered both an ivory-tower skepticism on the one hand and an "anti-academic" response by some popular culture scholars on the other. (120)

Many compositionists similarly chafe at distinctions between high and low culture and reject the notion that only certain materials merit scholarly consideration, a perspective that may reinforce a feeling of being an outsider within the academy.

The two disciplines further share a focus on interdisciplinarity, which makes the fields exciting, innovative, and difficult to locate within institutions. Compositionists have long valued writing across the curriculum and writing in the disciplines movements, and comics studies, by nature, draws from numerous fields, including English, Art, History, American Studies, and many others. Unfortunately, while the benefits of interdisciplinarity are myriad, this multifaceted approach may cause challenges as the fields struggle to find an appropriate place within the academy. In 1970 Janice Lauer urged writing instructors to "break out of the ghetto" and "look beyond the field of English, beyond even the area of rhetorical studies for the solution" (396), and since that time many composition and rhetoric programs have split from English departments, forging a new path and a new place in the university. Nevertheless, in 2010 Greg Columb notes that composition and rhetoric still has "no optimal institutional home" (13). Some comics studies programs are developing within English departments, others in Art and additional areas, but as an interdisciplinary enterprise that challenges the structure of the university itself, comics studies may have trouble locating a firm footing within the academy. Gregory Steirer argues, "without the ability to position itself in relation to existing disciplinary formations, comics studies thus risks 'ghettoizing' itself within the academy" (263). Both areas, then, may find it difficult to lobby for resources without a stable foundation. Is the answer to cut ties with English or other sponsoring departments and establish a separate space as some composition and rhetoric departments have done? Or, alternately, is there a way to build an interdisciplinary space across boundaries? These will be key questions as comics studies continues to develop.

Comics studies and composition and rhetoric, as relatively new academic disciplines, share several important commonalities. Yet, as the somewhat more senior discipline, composition and rhetoric has the advantage of time and self-reflection in defining itself. In the article "Making the Case for Disciplinarity in Rhetoric, Composition, and Writing Studies: The Visibility Project," Louise Wetherbee Phelps and John M. Ackerman provide an exceptionally helpful account of "The Visibility Project," a focused effort to achieve validation for composition "by focusing on the ways that fields of instruction and research are identified, coded, and represented statistically and descriptively for the purposes of data collection, reports, records, comparison, analysis, and assessment of higher education" (184). The authors maintain that "external validation matters; disciplinary status can't be willed from within, nor can it be solely written into existence" (182) and that "it is important as a field to generate and control our own data" (206-7). If comics studies is to thrive, scholars in the field must also gather evidence to support our endeavors. If we are to grow and expand, we must be able to make the case for additional resources with solid data and evidence, drawing inspiration from efforts such as "The Visibility Project."

As comics studies develops it would be wise to remember that, as scholars Linda Adler-Kassner and Susanmarie Harrington note of composition and rhetoric, "if we want to change stories…we must *reframe* those stories with alternative ones that revolve around what we *want*, not what we *do not want*" (86). Comics studies has the opportunity to write its origin story, charting a course for the future, and I would encourage comics scholars to look not just at what we *are not* and *do not want*, but rather, consider what it is we *do well*, and what we *want* for our students, our discipline, and ourselves. Personally, in the days to come I hope to see more fruitful collaborations between the fields of composition and rhetoric and comics studies, such as the work represented in this special issue, as these projects remain scarce at this time. There is so much more work to be done in both fields separately and in concert, and frankly, we underdogs need to stick together.

Works Cited

Adler-Kassner, Linda, and Susanmarie Harrington. "Responsibility and Composition's Future in the Twenty-first Century: Reframing 'Accountability.'" *CCC* 62.1 (2010): 73-99. Print.

Columb, Greg. "Franchising the Future." *CCC* 62.1 (2010): 11-30. Print.

Lauer, Sister Janice. "Heuristics and Composition." *CCC* 21.5 (1970): 396-404. Print.

Phelps, Louise Wetherbee, and John M. Ackerman. "Making the Case for Disciplinarity in Rhetoric, Composition, and Writing Studies: The Visibility Project." *CCC* 62.1 (2010): 180-215. Print.

Steirer, Gregory. "The State of Comics Scholarship." *IJOCA* 13.2 (Fall 2011): 263-85. Print.

Troutman, Philip. "Interdisciplinary Teaching: Comics Studies and Research Writing Pedagogy." *Graphic Novels and Comics in the Classroom: Essays on the Educational Power of Sequential Art.* Ed. Carrye Kay Syma and Robert G. Weiner. Jefferson: Macfarland and Co., 2013. 120-32. Print.

Yancey, Kathleen Blake. "Designing the Future." *CCC* 62.1 (2010): 5-10. Print.

Graphic Disruptions: Comics, Disability and De-Canonizing Composition

Shannon Walters, Temple University

Composition can be a normative endeavor, unfriendly to composers who communicate outside of a narrow range of acceptable ways. The goal in a well-written essay is usually to convey a message clearly and efficiently using well-ordered discourse to make a persuasive argument. An effective speaker is assumed to be someone with a clear strong voice who communicates in accepted, neurotypical ways to a receptive audience. Multimodal approaches to composition, while heralded as innovative, can reinforce these normative assumptions. Gunther Kress, for example, describing a sign with separate written and pictorial elements, writes that each of these elements having "distinct potentials for meaning" typifies "the argument for taking 'multimodality' as the normal state of human communication" (1). Ascribing normative properties to multimodality, however, marginalizes the potential contributions of a wide range of composers, especially disabled ones.

Disability theorists have challenged assumptions underlying the concept of "normal," demonstrating that what we think of as normal is socially and culturally constructed (Davis). In rhetoric and composition, theorists interested in disability apply this analysis and related critiques to composing situations, questioning normative impulses and finding new spaces for valuing disabled composers (Brueggemann; Dolmage; Lewiecki-Wilson; McRuer; Price). Recently, composition theorists have applied critiques from disability studies to multimodality, interrogating normative assumptions circulating at the intersection of word, image, sound and space. The authors of the collaborative webtext "Multimodality in Motion," for example, explain that "multimodality as it is commonly used implies an ableist understanding of the human composer" (Yergeau et al.). They re-examine a normalized understanding of "*the* rhetorical situation" and explore ways to intervene in the ableist underpinnings of multimodality.

The study of comics is an important part of the project of critiquing normative assumptions underlying multimodality and composition. Extending the efforts of the authors of "Multimodality in Motion," and their focus on "the" rhetorical situation, I explore how multimodal comics can intervene in normalizing understandings of "the" rhetorical canons. Using examples from several comics that feature disability, I show how disability can productively disrupt normative expectations about the "typical" composition process. Marking these disruptions contributes to the project of destabilizing normative assumptions of composition and multimodal theories, while also revealing the generative possibilities that disability yields for multimodal composition.

De-Canonizing through Comics

Comics theorist Scott McCloud calls the first step of comics creation "idea/purpose," identifying this step as including the "content," "emotion," and "philosophies" of a work (170). This characterization aligns with the rhetorical process of invention. Traditionally, invention is the canon through which one finds the "available means of persuasion" through a logical process of knowledge creation (Aristotle). As Lisa Ede, Cheryl Glenn, and Andrea Lunsford argue, invention, "the heart and soul of inquiry," is closely linked to the rhetorical canon of memory, "the very substance of knowledge" (410). This linkage loosely aligns with the comics composition process. McCloud, for example, represents "idea/purpose" generation as the first step in the process, drawing a light bulb in the mind of the comics' creator, with a dotted line connecting the mind's content to the material result—the comic book. The comic book is the form the idea takes and constitutes McCloud's second step in the creative process (172).

Alison Bechdel, in her graphic memoir *Fun Home*, complicates the seamless linkage between invention and memory frequently assumed in both rhetorical theory and comics theory. Bechdel describes an occurrence when she was ten years old in which she experienced an episode of Obsessive Compulsive Disorder (OCD). Her compulsions revolve around certain literacy practices, including writing in her diary. Bechdel starts by recording the events of her days, but then begins questioning herself, using first the "minutely lettered phrase" and then a symbol for "I think" in between all her sentences, obscuring them (141). Bechdel sprinkles this symbol, a "curvy circumflex," throughout her journal until her writing becomes "fairly illegible," a way of documenting the "troubling gap between word and meaning" in her experience (143). She describes this gap as "a sort of epistemological crisis," doubting whether what she wrote was "objectively true" and wondering if her "simple, declarative sentences" were actually "utter lies" (141).

In rhetorical terms, Bechdel experiences disconnection between invention and memory—she questions her recollection of events and feels unable to record reliably any substance of her knowledge. In McCloud's terms, she is unable to transmit the ideas in her head to the physical form of the page. Rather than interpreting this disconnect as a failure, however, Bechdel positions it as integral to her narrative. The arc of the memoir, which deals with questions swirling around her father's possible suicide, negotiates similar instabilities regarding the relationship between knowledge and inquiry. Bechdel can never know absolutely the details of her father's death, an uncertainty that she productively reflects in her own literacy practices. In Ede, Glenn and Lunsford's terms, Bechdel's memoir assumes "the very substance of [her] knowledge" (410) by recording uncertainty that reflects rather than edits out confusion.

In the hybrid graphic-text memoir *The Ride Together*, a memoir of autism in the family, Judy and Paul Karasik also use comics to trouble an assumed seamless connection between invention, memory and delivery, particularly in the context of collaborative composition. Like Bechdel, rather than editing out the messy elements of their composition process, they include them, delivering a product that is not finished or polished but that documents the issues they faced while composing. This form of delivery leads readers to ask crucial questions about representation within the context of autism.

In the final pages of the memoir, Paul, who draws the graphic chapters of the memoir, depicts himself and his sister Judy sharing the latest version of the memoir with David, their brother with autism. Drawing attention to the process of revision, Paul tells David, "I know you saw an earlier version but we've changed parts" (196). After showing David several graphic scenes from the memoir and asking David if he remembers them, Paul asks David to help them finish the memoir with a concluding remark or an update on what he is up to. David demurs and strides away to perform one of his favorite Superman scenes, which he does everyday at 4:30, with Paul looking on. By including this exchange, Paul and Judy draw attention to the fact that they are delivering an incomplete product. Their recollections may differ from David's; their impetus to compose and interest in narrative closure may not be shared by David. By including this scene, they also show their awareness of their own inability to accurately represent David, at least by neurotypical standards. David's closing Superman scene gives him the last word; he is depicted as purposefully initiating his performance, yet readers may not know quite how to interpret this scene, again drawing attention to the challenges and ethics of representation, especially of someone else's cognitive status.

When a composer uses the multimodal format of comics to convey a sense of his or her experience of disability, he or she potentially delivers a new way of thinking about, expressing, and sharing that experience. The multimodal composition process reaches into every aspect of creation—invention, arrangement, style, memory, and delivery. When Bechdel reproduces on the page the words, symbols, and images of her experience with OCD, she delivers an approach to multimodality not as representative of a "normal" way of communicating by a "normal" composer, but instead explores alternative ways that disability enlivens her approach to composition. When the Karasiks draw attention to the representational challenges of depicting David, they ask crucial questions about how multimodality can or cannot communicate nonnormative expression. Bechdel and the Karasiks join a wide range of others who use multimodal comics to explore disability in new ways (B.; Forney; Leavitt; Small). This diverse use of comics by disabled people and those close to them reveals the possibilities that delivery and disability possess for destabilizing and transforming the entire composition experience

Works Cited

Aristotle. *On Rhetoric: A Theory of Civic Discourse.* Trans. George A. Kennedy. Oxford: Oxford UP, 1991. Print.

B., David. *Epileptic.* New York: Pantheon, 2006. Print.

Bechdel, Alison. *Fun Home: A Family Tragicomic.* Boston: Mariner Books, 2006. Print.

Brueggemann, Brenda Jo. *Lend Me Your Ear: Rhetorical Constructions of Deafness.* Washington: Gallaudet UP, 1999. Print.

Davis, Lennard. *Enforcing Normalcy: Disability, Deafness and the Body.* New York: Verso, 1995. Print.

Ede, Lisa, Cheryl Glenn, and Andrea Lunsford. "Border Crossings: Intersections of Rhetoric and Feminism." *Rhetorica* 13.4 (1995): 401-41. Print.

Forney, Ellen. *Marbles: Mania, Depression, Michelangelo, and Me.* New York: Gotham Books, 2012. Print.Karasik, Paul, and Judy Karasik. *The Ride Together: A Brother and Sister's Memoir of Autism in the Family.* New York: Washington Square P, 2003. Print.

Kress, Gunther. *Multimodality: A Social Semiotic Approach to Contemporary Communication.* New York: Routledge, 2010. Print.

Leavitt, Sarah. *Tangles: A Story about Alzheimer's, My Mother and Me.* New York: Skyhorse Publishing, 2012. Print.

Lewiecki-Wilson, Cynthia. "Rethinking Rhetoric through Mental Disabilities." *Rhetoric Review* 22.2 (2003): 154-202. Print.

McCloud. Scott. *Understanding Comics: The Invisible Art.* New York: Harper Perennial, 1993. Print.

McRuer, Robert. *Crip Theory: Cultural Signs of Queerness and Disability.* New York: NYU P, 2006. Print.

Price, Margaret. *Mad At School: Rhetorics of Mental Disability and Academic Life.* Ann Arbor: U of Michigan P, 2011. Print.

Small, David. *Stitches: A Memoir.* New York: W. W. Norton & Company, 2009. Print.

Yergeau, Melanie, Elizabeth Brewer, Stephanie L. Kerschbaum, Sushil K. Oswal, Margaret Price, Cynthia L. Selfe, Michael J. Salvo, and Franny Howes. "Multimodality in Motion: Disability and Kairotic Spaces." *Kairos* 18.1 (2013): n. pag. Web. 31. Oct. 2014. http://kairos.technorhetoric.net/18.1/coverweb/yergeau-et-al/index.html.

Comics and Scholarship: Sketching the Possibilities

Erin Kathleen Bahl, Ohio State University

Thus far, attention to comics in academia has been focused *on* comics as a subject of literary (Chute; Gardner; Hatfield), theoretical (Cohn; Groensteen, *The System of Comics* and *Comics and Narration*; Postema), or pedagogical studies (Bakis; Carter; Jacobs). There has been less emphasis on scholarly composing *with* comics (some notable exceptions include Scott McCloud's celebrated *Understanding Comics* and Nick Sousanis's recently published dissertation, *Unflattening*). If you'll excuse the irony of writing on such a topic in an alphabetic format, I suggest that fusions between comics and scholarship can (1) fruitfully challenge definitions of scholarly genres, (2) offer resources for designing arguments in digital environments, and (3) invite all who practice scholarly composing to reflect critically upon their mediating decisions.

Messy Genres

In discussing comics and scholarship, I include texts within academic discourse in which the words, images, and layout all contribute substantially to the argument (rather than, for example, a primarily alphabetic text accompanied secondarily by images as illustrations). In *The Visual Language of Comics*, Neil Cohn argues that comics are not a language, but rather that "comics *are written in* visual languages in the same way that magazines or novels *are written in* English" (2; emphasis original). Whereas some scholars compose comics in the widespread sense, complete with full-page panel layout, speech balloons, an illustration-heavy environment, etc. (Losh et al.; McCloud, *Understanding Comics, Reinventing Comics, Making Comics*; Parish; Selfe and Kurlinkus; Sousanis), others compose in word-image fusions that draw from a vocabulary similar to comics' verbal-visual language (Bono and McCorkle; Crisp et al.; Delagrange; McCloud, "Scott").

Although the latter texts bear little immediate resemblance to traditional comics, I include these more ambiguous examples to explore how elements of comics might gradually be adapted as resources for academic communication, which would necessarily involve some experimentation and genre messiness along the way. Comics take an incredible amount of work to compose, and regardless of interest, the majority of academics do not have the time, training, or resources to fully flesh out an argument as a thoroughly composed comic. Additionally, there is a professional risk in composing nonprint scholarship that might not be valued as a contribution to the field (Purdy and Walker). However, a series of what de Certeau calls "small, potent gestures" (qtd. in

Selfe 1164), consisting of texts that equally weight words, images, and layout, may go a long way towards welcoming comics more fully into the field as a knowledge-making modality.

Digital Environments

Because I write from a digital media studies perspective, the overlaps and possibilities I highlight for scholarly composition are (with some exceptions) largely centered on webtexts and digital composing. This is not to say by any means that there are no such possibilities for incorporating comics practices into print-based scholarly composing, as Scott McCloud (*Understanding Comics*), Jonathan Alexander and Elizabeth Losh (*Understanding Rhetoric*), and Nick Sousanis (*Unflattening*) have clearly demonstrated. However, digital environments have the benefit of rapid, comparatively inexpensive textual dissemination; screen-reader processing for broader accessibility; and image/text editing software for those with less training in (or time to complete) pen-and-paper rendering. These affordances suggest to me that digital spaces have the potential to become leading environments for the composition and communication of comics scholarship.

Some of the foremost online venues for publishing verbal-visual scholarship today include *Kairos: A Journal of Rhetoric, Technology, and Pedagogy*; *Computers and Composition Online (C&C Online)*; *Harlot: A Revealing Look at the Arts of Persuasion*; and Computers and Composition Digital Press (CCDP). *Kairos*, *C&C Online*, and *Harlot* all publish shorter, article-length webtexts, while CCDP focuses on longer projects and eBooks. Each of these publishers invites innovative, multimodal texts that take advantage of the communicative resources digital environments have to offer. It can be challenging to consider new ways of filling up an empty page as broad as an "infinite canvas" (McCloud, "The Infinite Canvas"). As scholars brainstorm new ways to organize and construct their arguments in these online spaces, comics' familiar visual-verbal vocabulary can offer one potential blueprint for composing and experiencing the architecture of a scholarly argument in digital environments.

Reflective Making

Though many scholars' preferred means of composing may seem distant from the works and venues mentioned above, there is value nevertheless in considering the intersections between comics and academic composing practices. Regardless of disciplines, contemporary academic discourse occurs within a "global order" marked by "the multiplicity of communications channels and media" (New London Group 63). Kress and van Leeuwen remark that "in the age of digitization, the different modes [...] can be operated by one multi-skilled person, using one interface, one mode of physical manipulation, so that he or she can ask, at every point: 'Shall I express this with sound or music', 'Shall I say this visually or verbally?'" (*Multimodal Discourse* 2). Such questions open up both greater abilities and responsibilities in critically considering how to communicate knowledge among peers within an academic community, and also invite an "ethics of making" (Hayles and Pressman), in which "conceptual understandings are deepened and enriched by practices of production, a conjunction that puts critique into dynamic interplay with productive knowledges" (xv). These practices are not opposed to print, but rather invite awareness of other possible ways of making and communicating knowledge and challenge composers to critically consider their expectations of what a scholarly text should be.

Final Thoughts

I believe that the comics form has much to offer contemporary scholarly composing practices: they invite attention to alternative ways of meaning-making, new spaces for thought and dialogue, new questions about what scholarship can and should do, and perhaps even a sense of fun. With recent technological developments' expansion of the available meaning-making resources in screen-based digital communication, I view the present moment as an exciting time to experiment with new forms of scholarly discourse that draw on interdisciplinary literacies in order to broaden, enrich, enliven, and challenge our ways of making and communicating knowledge. Though I fully support the need for formal alphabetic prose as a mode of communication in academic discourse, I suggest that comics give voice to an alternative mode of meaning-making that (echoing Delagrange) embraces a sense of wonder, discovery, and delight in the messy process of knowledge creation in and of itself.

Works Cited

Bakis, Maureen. *The Graphic Novel Classroom: Powerful Teaching and Learning with Images*. Thousand Oaks: Corwin, 2012. Print.

Bono, Jamie, and Ben McCorkle. "Ludic Literacies: Mapping the Links Between the Literacies at Play in the DALN." *Stories that Speak to Us*. Ed. H. Lewis Ulman, Scott Lloyd DeWitt, and Cynthia L. Selfe. Logan: Computers and Composition Digital Press/Utah State UP, 2013. Web. 25 Apr. 2014. <http://ccdigitalpress.org/stories/bono.html>.

Carter, James Bucky. *Building Literacy Connections with Graphic Novels: Page by Page, Panel by Panel.* Urbana: NCTE, 2007. Print.

Chute, Hillary. *Graphic Women: Life Narrative and Contemporary Comics*. New York: Columbia UP, 2010. Print.

Cohn, Neil. *The Visual Language of Comics*. London: Bloomsbury, 2013. Print.

Crisp, Huey, Sally Crisp, David Fisher, Greg Graham, and Joseph J. Williams. "Scaffolding Stories." *Stories that Speak to Us*. Ed. H. Lewis Ulman, Scott Lloyd De-

Witt, and Cynthia L. Selfe. Logan: Computers and Composition Digital Press/ Utah State UP, 2013. Web. 25 Apr. 2014. <http://ccdigitalpress.org/stories/crisp.html>.

Delagrange, Susan. "Wunderkammer, Cornell, and the Visual Canon of Arrangement." *Kairos: A Journal of Technology, Rhetoric, and Pedagogy* 13.2 (2009): n. pag. Web. 1 Mar. 2014. < http://technorhetoric.net/13.2/topoi/delagrange/>.

Gardner, Jared. *Projections: Comics and the History of Twenty-First Century Storytelling*. Stanford: Stanford UP, 2012. Print.

Groentsteen, Thierry. *Comics and Narration*. Jackson: UP of Mississippi, 2013. Print.

---. *The System of Comics*. Trans. Bart Beaty and Nick Nguyen. Jackson: UP of Mississippi, 2007. Print.

Hatfield, Charles. *Alternative Comics: An Emerging Literature*. Jackson: UP of Mississippi, 2005. Print.

Hayles, N. Katherine, and Jessica Pressman, eds. *Comparative Textual Media: Transforming the Humanities in the Postprint Era*. Minneapolis: U of Minnesota P, 2013. Print.

Jacobs, Dale. *Graphic Encounters: Comics and the Sponsorship of Multimodal Literacy*. London: Bloomsbury, 2013. Print.

Kress, Gunther R., and Theo van Leeuwen. *Multimodal Discourse: The Modes and Media of Contemporary Communication*. New York: Oxford UP, 2001. Print. Losh, Elizabeth, Jonathan Alexander, Kevin Cannon, and Zander Cannon. *Understanding Rhetoric: A Graphic Guide to Writing*. New York: Bedford/St. Martin's, 2013. Print.

McCloud, Scott. "The 'Infinite Canvas.'" *ScottMcCloud.com*. Feb. 2009. Web. 25 Apr. 2014. <http://scottmccloud.com/4-inventions/canvas/>.

---. *Making Comics: Storytelling Secrets of Comics, Manga, and Graphic Novels*. New York: HarperCollins, 2006. Print.

---. *Reinventing Comics: How Imagination and Technology are Revolutionizing an Art Form*. New York: Paradox, 2000. Print.

---. "Scott McCloud: A Comics-Format Interview." Interview by Scot Hanson. *Kairos: A Journal of Rhetoric, Technology, and Pedagogy* 14.1 (2009): n. pag. Web. 1 Mar. 2014. < http://technorhetoric.net/14.1/interviews/hanson/index.html>.

---. *Understanding Comics: The Invisible Art*. New York: HarperCollins, 1993. Print.

New London Group. "A Pedagogy of Multiliteracies: Designing Social Futures." *Harvard Educational Review* 66.1 (1996): 60-92. Print.

Parish, Rachel. "Sappho and Socrates: The Nature of Rhetoric." *Kairos: A Journal of Rhetoric, Technology, and Pedagogy* 17.1 (2012): n. pag. Web. 1 Mar. 2014. <http://kairos.technorhetoric.net/17.1/disputatio/parish/index.html>.

Postema, Barbara. *Narrative Structure in Comics: Making Sense of Fragments*. Rochester: RIT P, 2013. Print.

Purdy, James P., and Joyce R. Walker. "Valuing Digital Scholarship: Exploring the Changing Realities of Intellectual Work." *Profession (2010)*: 177-95. Print.

Selfe, Cynthia L. "Technology and Literacy: A Story About the Perils of Not Paying Attention." *The Norton Book of Composition Studies*. Ed. Susan Miller. New York: Norton, 2009. 1163-85. Print.

Selfe, Cynthia L., and Will Kurlinkus. "The Watson Symposium: What might we be missing . . . and why?" *Watson Response*. Blogger, n.d. Web. 1 Mar. 2014. <http://watsonresponse.blogspot.com/>.

Sousanis, Nick. *Unflattening*. Cambridge: Harvard UP, 2015. Print.

Book Reviews

Comics and Composition, Comics as Composition: Navigating Production and Consumption

Contemporary Comics Storytelling, by Karin Kukkonen. Lincoln: U of Nebraska P, 2013. 248 pp.

Linguistics and the Study of Comics, edited by Frank Bramlett. New York: Palgrave Macmillan, 2012. 328 pp.

Narrative Structure in Comics: Making Sense of Fragments, by Barbara Postema. Rochester: RIT Press, 2013. 172 pp.

Reviewed by Tammie M. Kennedy and Jessi Thomsen, University of Nebraska at Omaha, and Erica Trabold, Oregon State University

Composition has a vested interest in exploring how comics studies can inform our teaching of writing, multimodal literacies, and visual rhetoric. Composition and rhetoric has already demonstrated a growing interest in comics (including graphic literatures, graphic novels, graphic narratives, digital storytelling) as complex sites of literacy and as spaces to theorize and practice multimodal composing. Comics also provide opportunities to explore the rhetorical choices and transactions that must be negotiated between composers and readers. However, despite composition scholars' interest in multiliteracies, multimodal composing, and visual rhetoric, the interdependent and fluid connections between images and words remain largely disengaged.

Fig. 1. Consumption versus production of comics.

For example, in *Embodied Literacies,* Kristie Fleckenstein coined the term "imageword" to disrupt the binary that often exists between word and image and to revitalize the use of images in the composing process.

Despite such efforts, this disengagement also prevails in comics studies. More specifically, as we note in Figure 1, there remains a persistent divide between using graphic texts for interpretation, or as a means to understand something else (consuming), and composing graphic texts (producing). While composition instructors and textbooks are developing more multimodal and visual assignments, production-based pedagogical practices are slower to emerge, or they focus too heavily on what Diana George describes as the traditional uses of visuals, such as "image analysis, image-as-prompt, or image as dumbed-down language" (32). Steve Westbrook argues that the problem with the consumer-based paradigm that accompanies the use of visual texts such as comics is that "[t]his approach does not position students as genuine agents of change precisely because it places them outside of the discourses that they are examining" (465). The groundwork has been laid to incorporate comics studies into composition studies; it is now imperative that students compose *with* images instead of just write *about* their analyses of various images found in comics.

Our review of the books by Karin Kukkonen, Frank Bramlett, and Barbara Postema provides an opportunity to address more specifically the impetus for editor Dale Jacobs' special issue on comics, multimodality, and composition, and to answer a central question that undergirds this impetus: How can comics studies inform writing theories and practices, for both students and instructors? From a pedagogical perspective, the immediate concern that follows this question is *how* to deploy comics to help students read and write more effectively. Our focus on production-based comics pedagogies stems from three different but complementary perspectives (see fig. 2). Tammie is a rhetoric and writing professor who teaches students how to write comics, especially graphic memoir, and draws on comics as a way to teach writing and revision. Erica is an MFA student in creative nonfiction with no formal background in art. Jessi is a rhetoric and composition graduate student who also has a background in art and digital writing. Both Jessi and Erica compose comics in digital and non-digital forms, as well as teach writing using comics. We believe that students in composition classrooms can benefit from the tools required for analyzing and producing comics. In fact, we already ask composition students to make the leap between reception and production all the time: students read essays, articles, and samples, and then produce their own writing. Therefore, the composition classroom is already structured for the type of work comics studies invites.

Fig. 2. The reviewers.

The three texts reviewed here articulate varying arguments for comics to be analyzed and regarded as literature; however, none of these texts explicitly address *instruction* in the creation of comics. In addition, because these texts are heavily reception-oriented, they do not delve into the possibilities of using comics for the purposes of invention, composing, or revision. While these texts do much to advance comics studies, they also expose some of the gaps that remain in terms of how comics studies might be deployed more productively in composition. As we review the texts, we highlight specific chapters that might inform composition theory and provide richer, more production-based pedagogical practices. Although the authors do not make explicit production-based connections, we believe each book provides generative spaces within comics studies that can augment both composition theory and student writers' composing processes. We maintain that composition studies needs to embrace more production-based pedagogies associated with comics to bridge effectively the gaps between consumption and production that have stalled a more expansive approach to literacy and multimodality within composition studies' meaning-making practices.

Defining a Genre: Providing Comics Vocabulary for Composing

Regardless of whether the goal for writing students is the reception or production of comics, it is important to first define the elements unique to the genre. In order to fully capture the complexity of comics as a means of composing, those undertaking its study have used several terms. The Modern Language Association has proposed "graphic narratives" be used in place of "comics" to frame its discussions (qtd. in Postema xi). However, Kukkonen, Bramlett, and Postema all use the term "comics" to focus their studies, as does the title of this special issue of *Composition Studies*. In the introduction to *Narrative Structure in Comics,* Postema provides a rationale for this choice:

> There is danger inherent precisely in creating a separation and disassociation between different kinds of comics genres, especially when

> the labels are ill-defined or haphazardly applied. . . . The scope of what the comics form can represent or incorporate becomes limited, diminishing the form itself, at least for casual observers, and the graphic novel or narrative becomes a genre without precedent or tradition, as if it originated all of a sudden in a vacuum, thereby misrepresenting the genre. (xi)

Postema goes on to propose that the term "comics" should be used broadly, but it should not be all encompassing. A narrative sequence should only be considered a "comic" if it includes a combination of purposeful gaps, words, and images.

The issues surrounding this broad genre's terminology, however, remain quite complex (see fig. 3). Kukkonen, Bramlett, and Postema derive their analytical work in relation to comics rooted mostly in fiction. Based on the traditional literary divide between fiction and nonfiction texts, we began to wonder if nonfiction comics, like those composition students may be invited to compose, call for a term of their own. We considered adopting a term like "graphic narratives" or "graphic literatures" to broaden the scope of our inquiry. In the end, we decided that extending the use of the word "comics" in our review seemed best suited to advance the genre. Just as "creative nonfiction" is used as an umbrella term to signify the subgenres of autobiography, memoir, the personal essay, or any combination thereof, "comics" can function as a term that represents a variety of texts and subgenres, including the graphic novel and those based in nonfiction. As the body of work surrounding comics continues to grow, scholars will likely continue to refine these terms. At the moment we find ourselves entering the conversation, however, we feel that introducing a new term may do more harm than good in advancing the academic study of the genre.

Fig. 3. "Comics" as a term for genre.

Once students understand the genre features of comics, including the contested terminology, and how comics' attributes mirror and diverge from other kinds of texts, they need a language that helps them articulate what a text says and how it says it. Postema offers the most straightforward description of *how* comics function to build a narrative sequence, which provides students with not only an understanding of the complex function of panels—the lines separating images from one another in comics—and the gaps and spaces that generate meaning, but also a vocabulary for discussing how students interpret and produce comics. According to Postema, "the framed panels and the page on which they are laid out create their own gaps, namely the spaces that now separate the panels—the gutters" (xiii). Students, as savvy readers, may already recognize gutters as a visual representation of the passage of time between panels, which can then be read as a sequence (see fig. 4). What may be new to them, however, is the understanding that these sequences rely heavily on what is missing, "making the reading of comics an active, productive process" (Postema xiv). Whether composing comics or performing an analysis, students' attention should be drawn to the act of closure, or filling these gaps, which is an action essential for the reader to perform in order to decode a comics narrative.

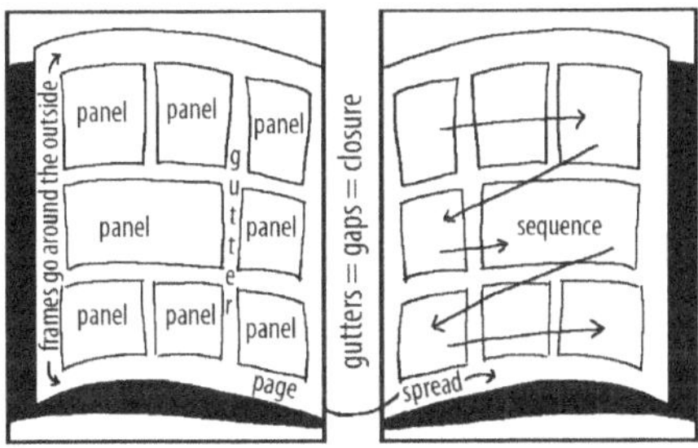

Fig. 4. Comics terminology.

Consuming Comics: Navigating the Gaps between Writer-Based and Reader-Based Texts

The three books under review demonstrate that comics has established itself as a genre fit for critical inquiry in English studies and that the production and consumption of comics involve complex processes of encoding and decoding. Arguably, the least helpful book for composition scholars interested in teaching students how to produce comics is Karin Kukkonen's *Contemporary Comics Storytelling*. Kukkonen promotes the analysis of comics, not because of their increasing popularity, but because of their narrative complexity that places them on equal footing with text-based literature. For example, in her chapter, "How to Analyze Comics Cognitively," Kukkonen provides a literary-based context for analyzing comics by defining a number of terms (inferences, clues, codes, gaps, closure) that connect the two genres. Overall, she proposes that comics must be viewed in terms of "the complex combinations of clues and gaps in the text that interface with the cognitive process our mind runs when reading fiction" (14). Her strategy to equate comics with literature is an important enterprise, but one that many composition scholars already embrace. Although Kukkonen asserts that the postmodern relationship between composer, text, and audience increases the complexity of the comic narrative and places it more solidly in the realm of literature (see fig. 5), this chapter can help composition scholars better articulate the complexities of the rhetorical triangle when reading and composing comics. Furthermore, Kukkonen uses postmodernism to interrogate comics, explaining that "postmodern texts take the identity- and empire-building narratives of modernism and subvert them with retellings from a different perspective" (3). Students are often asked to tackle various perspectives (cultural, ideological, political, etc.) within reading and writing. Comics provide a platform for teaching analyses of these differing viewpoints as well as tools for composing texts that navigate multiple perspectives.

Fig. 5. Kukkonen's argument for comics as literature.

The rest of the book's chapters feature case studies that perform literary analyses of comics and specifically address intertextuality, storyworlds, and fictional minds. More specifically, "Fictionality in Comics: *Tom Strong*, Storyworlds, and the Imagination," might be of interest to composition scholars. Here, Kukkonen focuses on layers within the comic, demonstrating how both image and text contribute to the reader's understanding of the multiple worlds or "multiverse" within the *Tom Strong* comic, increasing its narrative complexity. Moreover, this chapter demonstrates how the comic enters moments of metanarrative in which the fictional comic shows awareness of the reader and/or writer. This attention to the complexities of the reader/writer relationship illuminates how rhetorical choices shape reader/writer transactions in meaning-making processes. Overall, Kukkonen illustrates the potential for analyzing comics using literary tools and theory, as well as provides a postmodern lens, which helps readers consider the dynamics of closure, audience investment and participation, and narrative structure, and leaves space for addressing how comics might inform the production of complex narrative texts.

In *Linguistics and the Study of Comics,* editor Frank Bramlett compiles chapters that construct a generative space where the interdisciplinary nature of English studies and comics might better inform each other through linguistics (1). Drawing on the extant works of Scott McCloud and Will Eisner, Bramlett's collection advocates studying the language *in* comics versus the language *of* comics by applying linguistics to comics studies to explore both the visual and verbal in varying degrees (2). The first four chapters "peer into the minds of readers and artists, accessing linguistic and visual codes through cognitive linguistics" to better theorize how words and images shape the medium (8). The other seven chapters explore the "sociocultural landscape" of comics and characters in comics, focusing on how comics represent and provide a means to understand language issues, such as accents, dialects, jargon, and group identity (8). Furthermore, Bramlett assembles a wide range of expertise in comic studies, representing different background fields (linguistics, sociology, library science, media artist/designer, communication, English, and education) and home languages (e.g., Swedish, Spanish, and Hebrew).

Elisabeth Potsch and Robert F. Williams open the collection using concepts of image schemas and conceptual metaphors from cognitive linguistics to analyze how speed and direction are conveyed in comics so readers can conceptualize a sequence of events from still images such as in *Spider-Man* and *The Green Lantern.* These concepts are useful for teaching students the rhetorical nature of spatial cues. Neil Cohn's significant contribution draws on cognitive linguistics and psycholinguistics as he uses comics to articulate a theory of what he calls "visual language." Cohn argues that "while 'visual language' is the biological and cognitive capacity that humans have for conveying concepts in the visual-graphic modality, 'comics' are a sociocultural context in which this visual language appears (frequently in conjunction with writing)" (113). Cohn's work challenges the notion of the language *of* comics. From Cohn's perspective, "visual languages" have a vocabulary of patterned graphic representations and a specific grammar, just like spoken languages. For example, Cohn focuses on the translation process between visual and verbal and how this translation shapes representations of meaning. In composition courses, we often ask students to use description to support their arguments, embolden their narration, and illustrate results, concepts, and theories in their essays. Description, in essence, is a visual language, which requires the writer to translate mental images into words that create visual images in the minds of the readers.

The remaining seven chapters focus on the sociolinguistic elements in comics from a range of perspectives. These chapters are important for rhetoric and composition scholars because they demonstrate *how* representations of identity and difference are constructed through linguistic and visual systems and create meaning for the artist/creator and reader. For example, Miriam Ben-Rafael and Eliezer Ben-Rafael examine how French language comics incorporate English and other languages to reflect youth culture and vernacular, which appeals to a broad range of readers. Editor Frank Bramlett contributes to the study of manga in the collection by examining varieties of English in *Afro Samurai* and how linguistic differences mirror the politics of language and social struggles across various identity groups. Carla Breidenbach examines how bilingual code switching and other linguistic tools operate in the U.S. comic strip *La Cucaracha* as a way to create and critique political discussions about English as an official language. Kristy Beers Fägersten examines the effect of code switching from English to Swedish in the Swedish comic *Rocky,* revealing how English represents cultural appropriation and affinity within U.S. popular culture, especially African American culture. Overall, Bramlett's book provides an important treatise to think about comics as a way to understand how language (textual and visual) functions within specific lingual systems, offering tools and conceptual lenses that might be adapted to help students compose their own comics or inform their writing and revising processes.

Lastly, Barbara Postema focuses on the function of gaps and how they relate to meaning-making in comics in *Narrative Structure in Comics*. While the book focuses on defining the formal and material specificities of comics for critical consumption rather than production, the concepts outlined in Postema's book provide the most potential for developing product-based pedagogies for composing comics. Despite Postema's focus on semiotics and comics, much of the information culled from this text could focus on producing comics, especially the role and effect of space when composing with graphic elements. The various elements of comics—including gaps created by gutters and framed panels—work together to create meaning. Through a series of five colorful, heavily illustrated chapters, Postema demonstrates how gaps created by gutters and framed panels work together to create meaning within comics. Postema's carefully chosen excerpts in the chapters provide visual examples of how comics utilize connotative, intertextual, narrative, and temporal codes to achieve meaning, highlighting how these systems of visual representation build on one another to construct a narrative sequence. Readers must use evidence on the page, both coded and mimetic, to understand images and their implications. For example, in "Concerning the In-Between," Postema explains how frames, borders, and spaces create the structural layout of comics on a page, which is useful material for teaching composition students about creating comics. Although gutters are used to separate panels, which are laid out to create the conditions for reading, they are never devoid of meaning; reading the blank spaces causes readers to reconsider and reevaluate the meaning of earlier images.

Throughout chapters three, four, and five, Postema focuses her discussion on gaps and how they function to propel a narrative. In "All in a Row," Postema demonstrates how action is implied through the gutters and readers make "unvisualized connections" in order to fill them. Almost automatically, readers are prompted by the gaps to move back and forth in a sequence, making gaps an essential part of the reading process. Readers, and by extension composers, must consider various panels simultaneously in order to fully understand the information they provide. In literature, text propels narrative, but in comics, images must do this work. Postema explores image-text relations in "Combining Signs" and explains how text can help to fill the gaps left by images, layout, and sequence. But by adding text, Postema reminds her readers that a new gap forms—that between verbal and visual representation. A combination of text and image can smooth over gaps in signification, but together they can never quite succeed: "Comics are not inherently a hybrid form that must combine text and image. However, when the two are balanced, and image and text work together, the combination creates the possibility of bridging a gap, allowing for new forms of intricacy and nuance in the comics form" (101). Readers use prior knowledge to temporarily fill these narrative gaps, revising them as new information becomes available. Building on Postema's analysis of gaps, students can learn to consume and produce texts more critically, identifying how gaps in text and images function rhetorically and shape meaning.

In the book's final chapter, "Show and Tell," Postema deploys compelling examples to show how images provide data visually to readers, and readers participate in dialogic and recursive processes in order to understand narrative weaving: "[C]omics signal their own reading processes, creating and instructing new ways of signification as necessary" (116). To bring the controlling idea of gaps full circle, Postema reminds readers that artists choose what is said and unsaid, what is drawn and not drawn, in order to achieve clarity. Comics are engaging and immersive because on every level the reader must fill the gaps and continuously participate in the story created by the writer in order to achieve a desired effect.

Conclusion

As a whole, the three texts discussed in this review continue the work of legitimizing comics as a genre of academic study and augment our understanding of how to analyze, critique, and enjoy a wide range of comics. Furthermore, these texts expose a challenging gap in composition's use of multimodalities, multiliteracies, and visual rhetoric. Though these books do not extend their inquiries toward the production or creation of comics, composition has much at stake in creating generative production-based pedagogies. Incorporation of comics into the writing classroom should not hinge upon students' artistic abilities. Instead, emphasis should be placed on combining images and text in ways that allow the author to think differently about writing and explore new ways of composing for richer rhetorical effects. Students should pay particular attention to how text and images interact, create tension, and produce meaning that could not be generated in either by itself. In the end, comics provide a rich avenue for students to deliberate with more sophistication the rhetorical moves they employ in their own writing.

Omaha, Nebraska and Corvallis, Oregon

Works Cited

Fleckenstein, Kristie S. *Embodied Literacies: Imageword and a Poetics of Teaching.* Carbondale: SIUP, 2003. Print.

George, Diana. "From Analysis to Design: Visual Communication in the Teaching of Writing." *CCC* 54.1 (2002): 11-39. Print.

Westbrook, Steve. "Visual Rhetoric in a Culture of Fear: Impediments to Multimedia Production." *College English* 68.5 (2006): 457-80. Print.

Multimodal Literacies and Graphic Memoir: Using Alison Bechdel in the Classroom

Are You My Mother? A Comic Drama, by Alison Bechdel. New York: Houghton Mifflin Harcourt, 2012. 304 pp.

Fun Home: A Family Tragicomic, by Alison Bechdel. New York: Houghton Mifflin Harcourt, 2006. 240 pp.

Reviewed by Janine Morris, University of Cincinnati

In Dale Jacobs' *Graphic Encounters*, he discusses the importance of "[c]omplicating the view of comics so that they are not seen as simply an intermediary step to more complex word-based texts" (17). Jacobs writes that comics' readers require use of the visual, gestural, and spatial elements displayed in the panels and gutter space on a page in order to truly understand a text (14). Alison Bechdel's graphic memoirs *Fun Home* and *Are You My Mother?* further complicate the literacies needed to understand comics as she layers her memoirs with archival, literary, and psychoanalytic figures and concepts. More than a book about her family, Bechdel's memoirs look closely at sexuality, relationships, and self-realization within herself and others. As Jacobs' work attests, graphic memoirs like Bechdel's are both interesting reads and valuable pedagogical tools. Brought into the composition classroom, these memoirs provide entry points into discussions of literacy acquisition and the writing process, research and source material, and multimodal meaning-making practices.

Multiple composition theorists have argued the importance of incorporating multimodal composing into the composition classroom (e.g., Banks; Fleckenstein; Jacobs; Palmeri; Shipka). Patricia Dunn, for example, believes that we need to "take better advantage of multiple literacies, that we investigate and use whatever intellectual pathways we can to help writers generate, organize, re-conceptualize, and revise thoughts and texts" (1). Dunn challenges written texts as the primary means of communication and focuses instead on alternate ways of knowing that come from practices like sketching ideas or walking through a paper. As multimodal texts that highlight alternate ways of knowing, Bechel's memoirs serve as useful examples for students as they deal with complicated ideas and themes using visual, gestural, and spatial modes of meaning that go beyond the textual.

* * *

Bechdel's *Fun Home* and *Are You My Mother?* both center on her attempts to better understand her relationships with her parents. *Fun Home* describes the aftermath of her father's death, whereas *Are You My Mother?* focuses on Bechdel's relationship with her mother, set during the time when she was composing *Fun Home*. Both memoirs rely heavily on archival material from Bechdel's past: she recreates family photographs, drawings, letters, newspaper clippings, maps, and diary entries. Beyond the physical addition of material, the memoirs act as metatexts, offering commentary on literature, literary figures, and psychoanalytic theory. In different ways, each text becomes a collage of collected materials that ultimately allow Bechdel "to write a book about the problem of the self and the relationship with the other" (Bechdel and Chute 203). Bechdel's texts showcase the richness of the graphic memoir form and the materiality of memory as she examines issues of growth, reconciliation, self, past, and family.

Fun Home examines Bechdel's relationship with and the life of her deceased father Bruce, a high school teacher and funeral director. When she was nineteen, Bechdel's father was hit by a truck. Following his death, hidden elements of his life, such as sexual relationships with younger men, were revealed. Each chapter involves Bechdel piecing together past memories while constructing her own narrative of coming out and discovering her sexuality. In textboxes over two long panels showing first an empty road and then a young Bechdel and her father together in a car, she writes, "And in a way, you could say that my father's end was my beginning. Or more precisely, that the end of his lie coincided with the beginning of my truth" (117). Several months before her father's passing, Bechdel came out to her family. As Bechdel comes to acknowledge her own sexual truths, she also works to understand those of her father. The suspense in *Fun Home* comes from Bechdel's introspective examination of the past and the events going on around her. As she says in an interview with comics scholar Hillary Chute, "[t]here's really not much dramatic action. If you don't count the subplot of my own coming out story, the sole dramatic incident in the book is that my dad dies. Everything else is this extremely involuted introspection about it all" (Chute and Bechdel 1008).

Complementing the family narrative, each of the chapters in *Fun Home* center on a particular literary reference that comes to represent Bechdel's family, especially her father, in particular ways. Chapters revolve around the myth of Icarus, Albert Camus, F. Scott Fitzgerald, Marcel Proust, James Joyce, and Oscar Wilde, and within each chapter are multiple literary references and scenes from particular works and authors' lives. For example, chapter three, "That Old Catastrophe," examines the fantasy life created within her father's library, highlighting his love of books, particularly those by Fitzgerald. Bechdel draws parallels between Fitzgerald's biography and writing and Bruce's life and disposition by showcasing how he adopted Fitzgerald's "sentimentality" in letters to his wife Helen (63). In this section, Bechdel reproduces her father's hand-written letters in panels that show the letters themselves alongside panels of him as a young man writing them in a bunker. The graphic form of the text allows Bechdel to overlay family scenes and events with literary comparisons and commentary in the gutter of the text. For instance, in this chapter, Bechdel writes in the gutters above three long panels featuring her family cooking in their kitchen, "I employ these allusions to James and Fitzgerald not only as descriptive devices but because my parents are most real to me in fictional terms. And perhaps my cool aesthetic distance itself does more to convey the arctic climate of our family than any particular literary comparison" (67). By distancing herself from her family, using literary figures in place of confession, Bechdel is able to capture the importance literature held to her growing up while maintaining the emotional distance that seems to run through her family.

In the classroom, the literary figures that Bechdel draws on can serve as entryways to discussions on how source material and research inform composing practices. Even though Bechdel's memoirs are about her family, she frequently uses literary references and additional texts to inform her thoughts and feelings. This use of source material demonstrates to students that our work rarely exists in a vacuum and that it can be worthwhile to explore and acknowledge outside influences on our thinking. In the classroom, students could note how Bechdel uses source material, explore how literary allusions get intertwined with the family narrative, and discuss the significance of the comparisons Bechdel makes between the figures and family members. From a multimodal perspective, students might discuss the affordances of the graphic memoir for aligning literary references with moments from Bechdel's past. As an example, students might question which figures are chosen and why, how the source material is visually represented, what parts of the literary works get quoted, when and how those references appear, and how the visual representation of sources differs from source use in a predominantly textual form.

Beyond the literary references, one of the most fascinating things about *Fun Home* is the use of archival material from Bechdel's past, including letters, photographs, poetry, drawings, maps, diary entries, and newspaper clippings, which she "very painstakingly" reproduced by hand (Chute and Bechdel 1007). The memorabilia further enriches the text for readers, who with Bechdel's help, relive her memories. The archival material allows readers to recall physical reminders of their own pasts and brings to light the gestural and spatial components of memory. Within the text, the memorabilia helps anchor Bechdel in a particular time and place, reminding the reader that the events are real. The diary entries that feature prominently in chapter five, for instance, take her back in time, allowing access to what her younger self was thinking at a given moment. The memorabilia further demonstrates the material importance of objects for triggering and bringing back memories since Bechdel uses them as evidence in the text to highlight what she felt or believed. The collage-like form of the memorabilia complements the textual and visual narrative and makes visible the tactility involved in our everyday understandings of the past.

Further demonstrating the richness and physicality of memory, Bechdel also represents sensory experiences from her past, which touch on the multimodal affordances of comics that Jacobs describes above. Bechdel often brings in evidence of the senses to these texts, particularly the visual and olfactory. To represent smell, Bechdel juxtaposes panels that focus on her father gardening with ones of him adjusting floral arrangements in the funeral home, whereby "their quick, damp scent masked the odor of formaldehyde" (91). When describing a day out during her family trip to New York, Bechdel recreates a city scene in a large panel that takes up two thirds of the page. Overlaying the street corner within the panel are textboxes pointing out various smells of the city (including diesel, pastry, urine, electricity, shit, menthol, putrefaction, and Brut) along with the following written in the gutter: "In the hot August afternoon, the city was reduced, like a long-simmering demiglace, to a fragrance of stunning richness and complexity" (103). Although visually represented, the emphasis on various smells showcases the material role of the senses in triggering memories and demonstrates the affordances of the comics form for representing these senses. Even drawing itself, Bechdel says, "is a form of touch for me. When you are drawing a figure, you are touching them. You are creating this person's body. You are outlining their face. Their limbs. Their clothes" (Bechdel and Chute 211). The reader, too, is involved in the touch of the comic as she handles the book and is drawn in to the re-creation of Bechdel's memories and senses.

Both the use of archival material and visually recreated senses reinforce the complex and embodied nature of memory and literacy acquisition. Bechdel's memories are triggered by the many literary texts her family members are often depicted handling, illustrating literacy learning as a lifelong process with multiple moments of significance. As she describes the important feminist and queer writers that she encountered in university who shaped her adult views of the world, the reader sees that formative literacy experiences are not limited to childhood reading and writing. Furthermore, Bechdel describes influential reading and writing experiences both at home and in educational domains, showing how each came to influence her views of the world. Because of the multiple literacy experiences described in *Fun Home*, this text provides a useful entry point for discussing with students how our literacy learning is a lifelong process.

* * *

Are You My Mother? chronicles Bechdel's struggles while writing *Fun Home*, both professionally and interpersonally, while offering a closer examination of her relationship with her mother. More conceptual than *Fun Home*, *Are You My Mother?* involves a "search for meaning in patterns" (*Are You My Mother?* 31), which Bechdel does while connecting dreams, memories, recorded moments, and psychoanalytic theories throughout the text. More focused in literary references than *Fun Home*, *Are You My Mother?* primarily uses Virginia Woolf's diaries and autobiographical writing and pediatrician and psychoanalyst Donald Winnicott's theories as metatext underlying her work. While focusing on the writing of *Fun Home* and her mother's response to it, Bechdel weaves in past family and interpersonal memories, therapy sessions, and the biographies and works of Winnicott and Woolf to make meaning of the various patterns that she draws among identity, memory, womanhood, understanding, and creation. As Chute describes in an interview with Bechdel, more than an autobiography, the book "'is about ideas [Bechdel] was excited about'" rather than particular events (Bechdel and Chute 203). As such, this text effectively demonstrates what it is like to "work through" something—Bechdel works through dreams; relationships; the writing process; feelings of love, envy, and jealousy; as well as the past, again by collecting past materials and presenting analytic comments in the gutters overlaying illustrative panels. Along with illustrating Winnicott, Woolf, and pieces of their work, Bechdel once again brings in archival material like her grandparents' obituaries, newspaper clippings of her mother's career as an actress, telephone conversations that Bechdel transcribes, photographs, and selections from various books. These materials figure similarly to the way they do in *Fun Home*, bringing Bechdel back to a particular place and time. Instead of looking only at particular moments, Bechdel here richly offers multiple layers in the text to better understand the ideas she works through.

As the primary illustrative references within the text beyond her family, Woolf and Winnicott themselves become important characters in the story, occasionally with their lives mirroring that of Bechdel's. Chapter three, "True and False Self," for instance, draws comparisons between Woolf and Winnicott's biographies from the 1920s. Although it is "doubtful they know one another" in actuality (26), Bechdel imagines their life trajectories overlapping in England, positioning them on re-created city maps. She uses the Woolf and Winnicott narratives to explore what it means to be a writer and to apply psychoanalytic concepts that reveal understandings of the self. To the former, Bechdel uses Woolf's ideas about authenticity in biography writing, arguing that the symbolism Woolf uses in her fiction allows her to achieve "a deeper truth than facts" (29). Truthful representations are a repeated concern for Bechdel, as she justifies her choices in representing her father for her mother and herself. Bechdel also uses Winnicott, both his theories about early childhood relations and his biography, to further examine her own relationship with her mother and her adult romantic relationships. She weaves in her memories with illustrative case studies from Winnicott's texts, such as overlapping an argument between Bechdel and her mother in panels alongside Winnicott disciplining a young boy from an unnamed 1949 paper (174-78).

Because the graphic nature of the memoir allows Bechdel to juxtapose ideas about these figures and their lives with her own, she effectively creates a visual representation of how their ideas come to inform her own self-understanding. For students in the writing classroom, Bechdel's dealing with Woolf's writing and Winnicott's theories can offer an alternate approach to working with difficult concepts in the texts they read. Like Bechdel, students might visually represent ideas from theories or texts that they are currently grappling with in their own work. This approach to working with sources would allow students to draw on visual and spatial modes of meaning-making that go beyond the textual, encouraging them to consider the relevance of the sources to arguments they wish to forward.

What stands out thematically in *Are You're my Mother?* are ideas of composing. Not only is the text a composition in and of itself but also a reflection of the difficult process of writing and the challenges that accompany creative efforts. One of the narrative strands of the text involves Bechdel's professional troubles—the difficulty she has with writing *Fun Home* and staying financially afloat, the professional jealously she feels towards other queer graphic artists, and anxieties about how her family will handle the content of her book. This line of thinking in the text is useful for new writers to gain insight into the writing process of a professional writer. While writing textbooks like Elizabeth Wardle and Doug Downs' *Writing About Writing* and selections like Anne Lamott's "Shitty First Drafts" also detail the struggle writers face, Bechdel explores the emotional and physical drains that come with composing in great detail. Students reading Bechdel might recognize their own struggles with writing; the memoir can begin conversations about the nature of feedback on writing, the fear of reception, and the anxieties that surface as we compose.

* * *

Fun Home and *Are You My Mother?* offer a great deal to composition scholars with an interest in multimodal composition, literacy development, and research writing. Because both texts rely on the use of archival and source material in their composition, students mirroring Bechdel's form may begin noticing the material elements around them that come to explain and inform the writing process. As Bechdel's memories are triggered by items like photographs or journal entries, so too can our students draw inspiration from objects around them in their own composing processes. In the classroom, students might look at Bechdel's memoirs and discuss the physicality and sensory nature of memory and consider how their current interests are shaped by past events. The archival material can further serve as a starting point for examining students' own literate practices. Bechdel's memoirs discuss her reading and writing experiences as a child and again upon entering college. In many ways, while about her family, her memoirs also serve as literacy narratives with Bechdel exploring the role that reading and writing played in her home life and educational development. Students reading these graphic novels are introduced to an exploration of literacy that moves away from a straightforward chronological or linear text.

Together these two memoirs demonstrate the difficulties associated with understanding identity and the past, using outside references, and the composing process itself. By using past events and literary references to highlight feelings and ideas, Bechdel draws her readers into a world where emotions of anxiety, concern, love, disappointment, hope, betrayal, and tenderness are all too common. It is through our engagement with these texts as readers that we get to experience Bechdel's past as well as make connections with our own. As Jacobs writes, "multimodal meanings are made as people engage with comics" (9), and it is through our engagement with Bechdel that readers are brought back to their own awkward teenage years, family dramas, and anxieties about acting as professionals. For our field, Bechdel offers examples of the richness the graphic novel form provides, allowing multimodal and multidimensional texts to come to life.

Cincinnati, Ohio

Works Cited

Banks, Adam. *Digital Griots: African American Rhetoric in a Multimedia Age*. Urbana: NCTE, 2011. Print.

Bechdel, Alison, and Hillary Chute. "Public Conversation: Alison Bechdel and Hillary Chute." *Critical Inquiry* 40.3 (2014): 203-19. Print.

Chute, Hillary, and Alison Bechdel. "An Interview with Alison Bechdel." *Modern Fiction Studies* 52.4 (2006): 1004-13. Print.

Dunn, Patricia. *Talking, Sketching, Moving: Multiple Literacies in the Teaching of Writing*. Portsmouth: Heinemann, 2001. Print.

Fleckenstein, Kristie S. *Embodied Literacies: Imageword and a Poetics of Teaching*. Urbana: NCTE, 2003. Print.

Jacobs, Dale. *Graphic Encounters: Comics and the Sponsorship of Multimodal Literacy*. New York: Bloomsbury, 2013. Print.

Lamott, Anne. "Shitty First Drafts." *Language Awareness: Readings for College Writers*. 9th ed. Ed. Paul Eschholz, Alfred Rosa, and Virginia Clark. Boston: Bedford, 2005. 93-96. Print.

Palmeri, Jason. *Remixing Composition: A History of Multimodal Writing Pedagogy*. Urbana: NCTE, 2012. Print.

Shipka, Jody. "A Multimodal Task-based Framework for Composing." *CCC* 57.2 (2005): 277-306. Print.

Wardle, Elizabeth, and Doug Downs. *Writing About Writing: A College Reader*. Boston: Bedford, 2011. Print.

Re/Framing Identifications, edited by Michelle Ballif. Long Grove: Waveland, 2014. 360 pp.

Reviewed by Peter Brooks, University of Wisconsin-Milwaukee

Assembled by Michelle Ballif, *Re/Framing Identities* contains thirty-four essays and speeches from the 2012 Rhetoric Society of America (RSA) Conference that respond to RSA President Krista Ratcliffe's call to (re)consider Burkean identification "as a place of perpetual reframing that affects who, how, and what can be thought, spoken, written, and imagined" (1). Some works in the collection directly address Burke/identification, while others intuit, invent, and interpret identification/identity within various artifacts and events. Inspired by the conference theme, and after describing Ballif's "rich substrata of themes," I will re/frame the traditional purview of this review in order to demonstrate the book's value to us as teacher-scholars.

Ballif sifts essays into six "arbitrary [and] very general but thematic" sections that embody the explorative, evolving ideas presented at professional conferences (2). The first, "Re/Framing National Identity" includes Jacqueline Jones Royster's plenary address alongside essays discussing U.S. identity construction through historic artifacts, while the second, "Re/Framing Deliberative Rhetoric, Democracy, and Ethics," focuses on ethical questions culled from pop culture, politics, and economics. Contributors to section three—"Re/Framing History, Memory, and Events"—analyze how historical frames reveal new information, conceal facts, or alternately reframe events, and those in section four—"Re/Framing Embodiment and Rhetorical Agency"—unveil the ways media reframes bodies of gender, race, or sexuality. "Re/Framing Racial, Ethnic, and Class Identifications," the collection's fifth section, looks at the rhetorical symbols used to identify race, ethnicity, and class, while the sixth and final section, "Re/Framing Disciplinary Identifications and Assumptions," contains essays that show alternate ways to view our academic community's scholarly foundations.

Ballif's self-described "arbitrary" organizational grouping is accurate. Essays could crossover from section to section without thematic disruption: for example, in section three, Shawn D. Ramsey's claim that cultural historical activity theory helps us better understand rhetoric's history links just as easily with Tonya Ritola's essay on disciplinary identification in section six. Considering the liberties participants take with a conference theme, I think it is fair to say that this collection establishes itself as a discursive and circumscribed—rather than a direct or comprehensive—Burkean tome. The few essays that tackle Burke's theories (identification or otherwise) do so adequately for a conference anthology, but are not as exhaustive as one would expect in traditional edited collections.

However, this is not problematic. Ballif's intention in this collection is to introduce readers to the best thirty-four essays from the 2012 RSA Conference, and she acknowledges that the contributors have different scholarly backgrounds, varied levels of professional experience, and diverse research identities. In as much, contributors present a breadth of rich ideas in various stages of development. But if I can re/frame at least slightly Ballif's intentions for the collection, I want to argue that *Re/Framing Identifications* offers us rich pedagogical applications for first year composition (FYC), in addition to innovative analyses and re/interpretations of Burkean theoretical tenets.

Indeed, *Re/Framing Identification* begs FYC pedagogical applications through essays containing analyses of rhetorical practice found in familiar artifacts and through its use of a range of writing styles. From my perspective as a teacher-scholar, I can think of no better way to invite students into our professional community than to ask them to read such a collection. In addition to using the essays as the basis for discussion and analysis, teachers could use RSA submission guidelines (350 word abstracts for a committee; 10-15 minute readable papers for a live audience; 4500 word submissions for publication) as an activity for FYC classrooms, challenging students to identify different context and audience considerations in the development of their own conference texts.

We often ask FYC students to analyze essays where the rhetorical mechanics melt into the written word, even though students often struggle to see such rhetorical nuance. William Duffy's essay on Jon Stewart's comedic and journalistic credibility carefully delineates the rhetoric woven within verbal interactions between Stewart and political pundits, and as such, Duffy's rhetorical unpacking could aid students to do future unpacking of their own. Because students are familiar with the content of *The Daily Show*, they can follow Duffy's claim that Stewart's ethos is "audience-conscious, rhetorically precise, and completely transparent in his construction of an argument" (72). Both Duffy's and Stewart's rhetorical techniques suggest rich activities for classroom practice.

Likewise, Katherine Bridgman's contribution is accessible to students, analyzing the Facebook page "We Are All Khaled Said" in interesting ways. She reframes Facebook using Burkean identification and embodiment, and then connects the social media tool to the 2010 Egyptian protests. Her central argument—that by responding to Facebook event pages, users declare ideological support—bridges digitally native FYC students to rhetoric in real life through multimodal social media artifacts. In a similar vein, M. Elizabeth Thorpe's Pledge of Allegiance analysis demonstrates the real life rhetoric of grammar. Thorpe scrutinizes the appositive "under God" to show how its rhetorical effect encourages consideration "of the assumptions about the flag, America, and the Republic" within a determined hierarchy: first God, then nation, then flag

(36). These essays introduce FYC students to an overt rhetorical unpacking of language. In short, they are worth sharing with FYC students because most will be thoroughly familiar with the essays' content.

The collection also offers varied writing styles for student analysis. Two standout pieces are Royster's plenary address and Erik Doxtader's essay analyzing the Universal Doctrine of Human Rights (UDHR). Royster's brief speech provides context to and shares work from her upcoming book, focused on reframing women's roles in the Civil War. Doxtader's analysis of UDHR argues that "human rights discourse is simply a horde of words affording thin cover for imperial aspirations" (117). For FYC students, his essay is one to chew through, slowly: Doxtader bends and breaks language in complex yet beautiful ways. Royster's rhetorical approach is less dense, yet equally engaging. Audiences are afforded the opportunity to (re)visit her speech and read the emotionally invested narration of her walks around Atlanta that inspired her to consider the ways Civil War women "situate[d] their voices within the larger sociopolitical context of 'war work'" (18).

Teachers will also find the collection helpful in introducing notions of privilege to FYC students, who sometimes express denial or misunderstanding over this real life issue. Bryan Carr's "Reframing the Secret Identity of Whiteness" uses Burke cluster criticism to formulate three themes regarding privilege in superhero portrayals: (1) whiteness as default identity; (2) nonwhite identity stereotypes; and (3) white considered "classic" and "desirable." Carr's work is relevant in two ways. First, superhero portrayal is modally ubiquitous, presenting students with a deep pool from which to draw discussion examples. Second, Carr's possibilities and pitfalls open up space for further discourse by exploring how fan audiences react to changes in race and character identity. Specifically, he examines fan responses to comics author Idris Elba's portrayal of the Norse god Heimdall in the *Thor* series—who is drawn white in the comics—and Marvel Comics' decision to make a Hispanic version of Spider-Man. The preference for white characters as desirable, as Carr frames it, mirrors a trend in "geek culture" where young, white males communicate via social media hateful messages to those with alternate perspectives (e.g., Google the Gamergate controversy).

Carr's essay bridges us from the pedagogical possibilities within *Re/Framing Identifications* to the important theoretical tenets we should (re)consider about Burkean identification given the collection's contributions. Katherine Bridgman's essay on Islamic identity as well as Dominic Ashby's on Japanese rhetoric will educate Burkean neophytes and offer interesting, cogent examples of Burke's theory of identification. Alternatively, Burke mavens will appreciate Ashby's call "to adjust our rhetorical theories to account for those new perspectives" that challenge notions of dominant group privilege (313). Certain essays, like the ones I discuss next, challenge Burke's concept of consubstantiation, an occurrence at the end of identification where parties "acting together [result in] common sensations, concepts, images, ideas, [and] attitudes" (Burke 20-21).

Janice Odom's vocally rich critique of Burkean identification likewise addresses interesting theoretical tenets. Funneling her critique through work by feminist rhetorical theorists Dorothea Olkowski and Barbara Biesecker, Odom's resolution to Burke's conflict ridden, masculine, and submissive approach to identification is to reframe it, using Luce Irigaray's concept of the interval. With writing befit of French feminist Hélène Cixous' poetic style, Odom describes the interval as "the labia–remind[ing] us that the gap is constantly opening and closing, rubbing, touching, never becoming one, yet never fully breached" (245). Instead of using warlike tactics to surrender to an opponent and seal the gap, our key approach should be to maintain two identities instead of succumbing to one through consubstantiation, to keep the gap in various stages of openness and closeness.

Ballif includes two other writers who also explore consubstantiation to interesting ends. Nicholas S. Paliewicz discusses consubstantiation problems found in artifacts emerging from the ten-year anniversary of 9/11. He claims a capitalistic religion further drives our "national consubstantiation [and] remains centered on the dissociation of our constructed scapegoat: Muslims and Arab Americans" (295). Katie Rose Guest Pryal's essay "Reframing Sanity" also analyzes consubstantiation through media portrayals of Tucson shooter Jared Loughner. Here, the scapegoat is mental health, and we have "through the process of identification, formed a social group, those external to the group are divided, cast out, and ripe for scapegoating to protect the cohesion of the identified group" (160).

My re/frame of *Re/Framing Identifications* as both pedagogical and theoretical risks rigid closure and the consubstantiation these writers warn against. I do not wish our students to become comp/rhet teacher-scholars; yet, I suggest the benefits of sharing with them the professional conference community embodied by this anthology. Through accessible writing that re/frames traditional rhetoric, contributors to the volume show their passion for the field. If we share selections from this volume, then we share topics relevant to our students' lives, showing them that what's at stake in a written text is more than just a grade.

Milwaukee, Wisconsin

Works Cited

Burke, Kenneth. *A Rhetoric of Motives*. Berkeley: U of California P, 1969. Print.

Understanding Rhetoric: A Graphic Guide to Writing, by Elizabeth Losh, Jonathan Alexander, Kevin Cannon, and Zander Cannon. Boston: Bedford/St. Martin's, 2013. 304 pp.

Reviewed by Molly J. Scanlon, Nova Southeastern University

The authors of *Understanding Rhetoric* utilize the comics medium to present writing concepts for first-year composition courses and beyond. The title is a nod to the foundational comics theory treatise by Scott McCloud, *Understanding Comics,* in which the animated author explores how comics make meaning through image and text. Like McCloud, *Understanding Rhetoric*'s authors explain rhetoric and writing through didactic content that directly addresses the reader. Losh, Alexander, Cannon, and Cannon take form as characters Liz, Jonathan, Kevin, and Zander in the textbook as they engage students and instructors alike through compelling narrative, humor, visual metaphors, thoughtful examples, and authentic author voices.

The introduction, "Spaces for Writing," foregrounds several key writing principles and best practices: context and space, audience and purpose, writing as a process, collaboration, visual literacy, and revision. Each of these concepts is then given attention in seven "issues" (read "chapters"): (1) "Why Rhetoric?"; (2) "Reading Strategically"; (3) "Writing Identities"; (4) "Argument Beyond Pro and Con"; (5) "Research: More than Detective Work"; (6) "Rethinking Revision"; and (7) "Going Public". Each issue concludes with REFRAME and Drawing Conclusions sections. The REFRAMEs feature student characters Cindy, Luis, and Carol. Carol is Cindy's mother and a non-traditional college student. Following the REFRAME, a Drawing Conclusions section presents readers with four assignments related to the chapter's content.

Modeling Multiliteracies

Though readers may approach this text with hesitant curiosity, one strength of *Understanding Rhetoric* is the fact that the authors avoid making assumptions about students' (or instructors') literacies. Where the introductory issue presents concepts of visual representation by comparing cartoons, photographs, and symbols in multimodal texts, issue two explores signification in written texts. The authors introduce students to the kind of reading that will be expected of them at the college level. One concern I often have with college textbooks is the authors' inclination to assume that students already know what is expected of them. *Understanding Rhetoric* makes no such assumptions. In order to demonstrate critical reading for students, "Issue 2: Reading Strategically" illustrates the story of Frederick Douglass and displays how textual representation can become imagery in a reader's mind. As the story progresses, Liz and Jonathan respond, question, and engage the text in multiple ways, modeling the act of critical reading. Later, illustrators Kevin and Zander climb into the panels to help student characters make sense of the comic adaption of *The 9/11 Report*. One strength of this issue is the authors' equitable approach to analysis. Though they begin with the more literary work of Frederick Douglass, they conclude with a contemporary comics adaptation. Both texts demonstrate rich meaning-making practices in order to form arguments about serious subject matter. The content is sure to please instructors, but what about students?

No textbook compels *all* students to engage in discussions of writer identity or audience constraints, but I have had more students complete the readings in *Understanding Rhetoric* than in any other textbook I have assigned. *Understanding Rhetoric*'s unique form is memorable enough, but the clever narrative used to frame its contents also contributes to the reinforcement of these concepts, serving as a visual pneumonic for students. There are several moments throughout the textbook that my students have found particularly salient because of the ways in which they are presented through the comics form. I will present a select few.

Rhetorical Theory and Analysis

In many writing courses, rhetorical theory can be the pedagogical cornerstone. In issue one, the authors portray debates concerning rhetoric by drawing ancient thinkers in contemporary contexts. Plato's hesitations about writing as a technology, Aristotle's yearning for more educated communication among the people, and Cicero's understanding of rhetoric as visual and spatial allows students to understand the foundations of such thinking. Issue one's REFRAME section reinforces these theories as Cindy helps Luis apply what they've learned about rhetoric through a discussion of professional email correspondence with professors—a rhetorical situation incredibly relevant to first-year students.

Research Ethics

Discussions of effective argumentation are followed by the fifth issue, "Research: More than Detective Work." The issue begins with three points regarding summary, paraphrase, and quotes and then moves on to research ethics, including a section on plagiarism. Again, the content of this section is not what makes it so innovative; most of our textbooks confront the ethics of citing others' work. Rather, the execution through the comics medium is its strength. In the section "Coming Clean with Citation," Liz and Jonathan's likenesses are transformed through another artist's drawing style. The change is abrupt and obvious to readers—much like shifts in a writer's voice can be to experienced writers and writing instructors. The authors invited artist Tom Gammill to draw this section in order to illustrate, quite literally, how plagiarism is not only unethical but also damaging to an author's credibility and personal style.

Re-Vision

Many students resist revision as a necessary part of the process, but the authors present it as a uniquely transformative activity in which all writers engage. In issue six, "Rethinking Revision," the authors demystify the writing process by discussing the ways in which first drafts of canonical texts barely resemble those we know so well—namely *Pride and Prejudice* and Abraham Lincoln's Inaugural Address. The authors also share the story of Maxine Hong Kingston who lost a manuscript in a house fire. My students have identified with this loss—perhaps naively, but nonetheless—as similar to losing a paper due to a corrupted hard drive. Fortunately, the authors remind us, the work itself exists in the writer. The REFRAME that follows issue six then shows Cindy working through a rough draft that her instructor feels needs significant revision. She is frustrated but visits the writing center to work through this draft and improve her argument. Showing students utilizing resources on their campus (their peers, their instructors, and the writing center) is another strength of these REFRAME sections and the addition of the student characters.

Too Much Comic, Not Enough Textbook

Perhaps the largest drawback to this textbook is the Drawing Conclusions (DC) sections. In their attempts to make this textbook read more like a didactic comic, the authors have compromised one of the primary purposes of a composition textbook: to invite students to apply learned material through activities that include checking for understanding, engaging in discussion, practicing writing individually, etc. The DC exercises are neither titled nor divided by type or rigor of activity. Many of the activities take significant scaffolding or time to complete. For example, the DC section at the end of issue three, "Writing Identities," asks students to keep notes on their online interactions for a week. They are then asked to write an autoethnography, which the authors describe as "a brief narrative describing your own use of the sites" to understand identity in rhetorical situations (140). This activity, depending upon interpretation, could be a 250-word journal assignment or a three-page essay. It could be abridged and completed over a couple of days, or become a multi-week documentation project for students. I typically have to adapt this and other DC assignments to such an extent that I end up rewriting the assignments altogether.

The authors have certainly introduced an innovative approach to textbooks in *Understanding Rhetoric*, and for the most part, their work in the chapter content and REFRAMEs is exemplary and reflective of contemporary composition theory and pedagogy. However, the DC sections remind readers that some conventions of the textbook were lost in the convergence to a hybrid genre. The authors did release an online instructor's manual and companion website for students to serve as resources, though I suspect these are underutilized since they need to be accessed outside of the text.

Understanding Rhetoric in the Composition Classroom

The textbook's content will be comfortable and familiar to writing teachers; new to most will be the presentation of familiar concepts through a unique form. Considering comics as a medium worthy of consideration was certainly a goal of the authors from the very beginning. And that was a smart move. Because *Understanding Rhetoric* will look and work differently from textbooks students are used to reading, it seems only right to utilize that curiosity as a catalyst for discussions about argument across multiple media.

For the authors, it is clearly very important that students are being asked to intelligently engage in media, and they have created a textbook that models that engagement. Issue two's DC section includes an activity in which students are asked to consider "What evidence do you find that indicates that the writers and illustrators of this book thought carefully about the images it includes? What choices might you have made differently?" (111). In addition, the introduction's REFRAME depicts Luis and Cindy responding to having been assigned a textbook for their first writing class; Luis is excited but Cindy is not so sure.

Teachers and students of writing will engage this textbook and approach it with a particular set of expectations related to writing pedagogy. *Understanding Rhetoric*, in many ways, will challenge those expectations and present both teacher and student with broader definitions of writing, beginning with the very textbook they use to understand it.

Fort Lauderdale, Florida

DIY Citizenship: Critical Making and Social Media, edited by Matt Ratto and Megan Boler. Cambridge: MIT Press, 2014. 450 pp.

Reviewed by Jason Luther, Syracuse University

If multimodality requires us to shift the primary subjectivity of our students from "writers" to "makers," then the potential of do-it-yourself (DIY) provides both an extracurricular site and a productive (or even necessary) public and political exigence for the materiality of students' makings. Whether DIY describes an ethos, process, production, culture, or is simply a standalone noun, it carries with it a number of questions about who controls what gets made, by whom, when, where, and especially how. Put another way, it asks, what rhetorical agency do we have given our available means of production, circulation, and sponsorship, especially in the digital age? These are just some of the essential issues taken up by *DIY Citizenship: Critical Making and Social Media,* an exciting, ambitious interdisciplinary edited collection representing the fields of communication, journalism, education, sociology, women and gender studies, and, of course, media and cultural studies.

Based on revised and expanded papers from an international conference convened by the editors in 2010, the contributions to *DIY Citizenship* range in terms of the makers they consider as much as the things they make, including open source software (chapters one and two), fan sites (chapters three, seven, and twenty-two), pirate radio stations (chapter four), ID cards (chapter five), zines and comics (chapters six, twenty-four, twenty-five), spectacles and hoaxes (chapter eight), knitting and e-textiles (chapters nine and twelve), local television programs and documentary films (chapters eleven, thirteen, fourteen), games (chapter fifteen), growbots (chapter seventeen), vox pop (chapter twenty-three), and, of course, social media. Holding the collection together are the terms of the book's title—DIY and citizenship—which are consistently and thoroughly defined, explored, contested, and refreshed throughout all the chapters. Helpfully, many authors also introduce new terminology—such as Daniela K. Rosner and Miki Foster's *inscribed material ecologies* (189), Mandy Rose's *cocreative media* (207), and Joshua McVeigh-Schultz's *civic ritual* (313)—which scholars of media and multimodality might find useful in further theorizing hybrid media, participatory processes, or subjectivities crafted via maker identities that have powerful effects on what we make and who we make them with.

One term that is threaded throughout the book is co-editor Matt Ratto's *critical making,* what he defines here and previously as "materially productive, hands on work intended to uncover and explore conceptual uncertainties, parse the world in ways that language cannot, and disseminate the results of these explorations through embodied material forms" (227). In short, for Ratto, making is an important process for interrupting and influencing one's social reality through material play and circulation. Many of the chapters speak to these possibilities.

For instance, in chapter one (and in playful fashion), Steve Mann introduces the terms *maktivists*—authentic, amateur makers, who design and create material things for social change (29)—and *tinquiry*, which combines tinkering with inquiry in order to theorize a pedagogy where student hackers reverse engineer things through a three pronged process Mann calls *praxistemology*. Praxistemology combines praxis, existential reflection, and critical questioning as an "academic counterpart" to activities of making and is representative of a larger thread in the pedagogically oriented chapters of this collection that argue for reflection as an important dimension to making. For composition teachers it may bring to mind innovations such as Jody Shipka's "Statement of Goals and Choices," from her book *Toward a Composition Made Whole*, which asks students to document and detail the rhetorical, technological, and methodological choices they make as they produce multimodal compositions. Likewise, in chapter nine, Kate Orton-Johnson works with interview data from online knitters to explore practices of *craftivism*, where knitters take a historically private, domesticated hobby and translate it into a collaborative, embodied, and public act through *guerrilla knitting*—"a range of practices that employ 'vigorous' or 'militant' knitting activity in mass demonstrations, in urban interventions, and for political causes, using knitting in controversial, unusual, or challenging ways" (143). This occurs, she demonstrates, via digitally mediated maker identities that are created and maintained through online spaces that connect individuals to networks—a necessary meso-space that socializes makers within larger public structures that unite the local/physical with the global/digital. In chapter seventeen Carl DiSalvo also examines hybrid scenes of making, but rather than focus on activist contexts, he explores DIY speculative co-design though "growbots," robotic technologies meant to support small-scale agriculture. Important to this chapter is the chosen site for making—an annual maker festival in San Jose, CA called 01SJ Biennial—a context that mobilizes participants "from matters of fact to matters of concern" (per the French philosopher and scientist Bruno Latour), meaning that designers forgo precision, as would be the case in an exhibition, in order to experiment and enact "the imaginative projection of possibilities at the intersection of robotics and small-scale agriculture" in a public venue (244).

As the titular term *citizenship* suggests, the public sphere comes up early and often in this collection, illustrating several concrete ways in which multimodality might broaden participation in public life. Some of the work in the collection, for instance, attempts to bridge the gap between fandom and citizen. In chapter three, esteemed fan studies scholar Henry Jenkins traces some of the online activities of the Harry Potter Alliance (HPA), offering it as a case study for fan activism, a form of participatory politics that parlays the language and rituals of fan culture to more civic forms of engagement. As Jenkins argues early in the chapter, a recent white paper suggests that sites like the HPA, which are made up of over 100,000 members, are important because they act as "a gateway to more traditional political activities such as voting or petitioning" (65). Pushing this argument, Jenkins suggests that HPA's fandom practices—organizing local chapters, arguing via discussion boards, curating content—actually primes them for more traditional notions of citizenship, such as raising and donating over $120,000 to rebuilding efforts in Haiti after the devastating 2010 earthquake. In a more methodologically reflective account of fan studies, chapter seven finds Catherine Burwell and Megan Boler looking to the more affective and networked notions of citizenship by interviewing two bloggers for prominent fan sites dedicated to *The Daily Show* and *The Colbert Report,* concluding—experientially and methodologically—that political expression isn't always limited to rational-critical discourse.

While many contributors to the collection might agree that critical making and DIY cultural production can qualify as contributing to public life, evaluating their effects is a different story. In chapter four, for example, Christina Dunbar-Hester uses examples of media activism to remind readers that "maker cultures" that do not critically or reflectively consider their roles in the social (re)organization of their work—or that too zealously preach maker identities at the expense of historicizing them—can end up, ironically, reinforcing the same cultural scripts they are trying to resist. Likewise, in chapter six, Red Chidgey finds that even though makers announce their projects as DIY, the term can just as likely represent "an empty signifier"—left vulnerable to "depoliticized lifestyle and self-managerial branding" (107)—unless they organize around particular affective identities and progressive initiatives, such as how feminist activist networks make and share zines.

In fact, a key tension throughout the book is how, as Alexandra Bal, Jason Nolan, and Yukari Seko put it, "the DIY ethos has been absorbed by corporate culture" (163) through the cultivation of individual choice. In some ways, these authors remind us that DIY can be used to re-inscribe neoliberal capitalist logics, just as much as they can undo them. As Michael Murphy, David J. Phillips, and Karen Pollock explain in chapter eighteen, dominant companies like Apple and Google have paradoxically sustained DIY practices by offering ubiquitous spaces or freely available tools to everyday, amateur makers in exchange for compliance, capital, or personal data. In this way Rosa Reitsamer and Elke Zobl (chapter twenty-four) as well as Chris Atton (chapter twenty-five) feel that the term DIY has been so co-opted, branded, and overused to the point that it has become an uncritical term implying romantic, unbridled agency; they therefore prefer the term "cultural citizen" because it suggests that amateur production is an ongoing social and intersubjective process.

No matter what readers make of the political effects of the projects articulated throughout this collection, composition scholars will undoubtedly feel overwhelmed by the volume's capacity for redefining the public work of multimodality—and this is likely to raise familiar questions and old debates about "the fundamental boundaries of our curricular landscape and our sense of its stakeholders, interests, and purpose" (Hesse 605). But for those among us who see the rising importance of hybridity in not only the forms of composition but also the delivery systems that change them (Trimbur 190), many of the chapters in *DIY Citizenship* have much to contribute.

Syracuse, New York

Works Cited

Hesse, Douglas. "Response to Cynthia L. Selfe's 'The Movement of Air, the Breath of Meaning: Aurality and Multimodal Composing.'" *CCC* 61.3 (2010): 602-05. Print.

Shipka, Jody. *Toward a Composition Made Whole*. Pittsburgh: U Pittsburgh P, 2011. Print.

Trimbur, John. "Composition and the Circulation of Writing." *CCC* 52.2 (2000): 188-219. Print.

Contributors

Erin Kathleen Bahl is a doctoral student in English at the Ohio State University. She studies composition, digital media, and folklore, and her research investigates multimodal composition and vernacular religious practices. Her work is featured in *Computers and Composition* and *Showcasing the Best of CIWIC/DMAC*.

Peter Brooks is a teacher-scholar in the rhetoric and composition doctoral program at the University of Wisconsin-Milwaukee. His research focuses on writing transfer in simulated organizational activities in professional writing. Brooks is also involved with the Harlem Renaissance Museum project and reads poetry for Urban Spoken Word, both in Madison, Wisconsin.

John Carvajal is a cartoonist based out of White River Junction, Vermont, where he is attending the Center for Cartoon Studies. You can see more of his work at jacarvajal.com.

Kathryn Comer is Assistant Professor of English and Director of First-Year Writing at Barry University, where she also teaches professional writing and multimodal composition. Her research engages pedagogy, writing program administration, and digital rhetoric. She is one of the founding editors of *Harlot: A Revealing Look at the Arts of Persuasion* (harlotofthearts.org).

Hannah Dickinson is Assistant Professor of writing and rhetoric and director of the Writing Colleagues Program at Hobart and William Smith Colleges. She coauthored *Taking Initiative on Writing: A Guide for Instructional Leaders* (2010), and her scholarship has appeared or is forthcoming in *Praxis* and *Reading Research Quarterly*.

Franny Howes is Assistant Professor of communication at the Oregon Institute of Technology, and received her PhD in rhetoric and writing from Virginia Tech in 2014. She is the creator of the comic "Oh Shit, I'm in Grad School!" and a graduate of the Adventure School for Ladies.

Aaron Humphrey is a lecturer in the Department of Media at the University of Adelaide. He has recently completed a dissertation on comics in education.

Dale Jacobs is the author of *Graphic Encounters: Comics and the Sponsorship of Multimodal Literacy* (Bloomsbury Academic, 2013). His essays on comics have appeared in *English Journal*, *Journal of Teaching Writing*, *CCC*, *Biography*, and *ImageText*. He is the editor of *The Myles Horton Reader* (University of

Tennessee Press, 2003) and co-editor (with Laura Micciche) of *A Way to Move: Rhetorics of Emotion and Composition Studies* (Boynton/Cook 2003).

Aaron Kashtan is a Visiting Assistant Professor in the Department of English at Miami University in Oxford, Ohio.

Tammie Kennedy is Assistant Professor of English at the University of Nebraska at Omaha, where she teaches courses in writing graphic memoir, women's rhetorics, memory studies, writing pedagogy, and representations of whiteness in film. Her work has appeared in *Brevity*, *Feminist Formations*, *Rhetoric Review*, and *JAC*, among other venues.

Susan Kirtley is an Associate Professor of English and the Director of Composition at Portland State University, where she is developing a comics studies program. Her research interests include visual rhetoric and graphic narratives. Her book, *Lynda Barry: Girlhood through the Looking Glass*, won the 2013 Eisner Award for Best Academic work.

Jason Luther is a doctoral student in the composition and cultural rhetoric program at Syracuse University. His research focuses on multimodality, community publishing, and writing center theory and practice. His dissertation, "DIY as Delivery System: Re-situating the Extracurriculum," examines self-publishing since the popularization of the web.

Leah Misemer is a PhD candidate in English literature at University of Wisconsin-Madison where she is one of the organizers of the A.W. Mellon workshop on comics. Her dissertation explores how connections between authors and readers have evolved throughout the history of American comics.

Janine Morris is a PhD candidate specializing in rhetoric and composition at the University of Cincinnati. Her research interests include multimodal and digital writing and feminist rhetoric. Her dissertation explores reading practices on digital devices.

Molly J. Scanlon is Assistant Professor at Nova Southeastern University where she teaches undergraduate and graduate writing courses. She received her PhD in rhetoric and writing from Virginia Tech. Her research interests include visual rhetoric, public rhetoric, and faculty identity construction.

Gabriel Sealey-Morris is Assistant Professor of English and Director of the Writing Studio at Johnson C. Smith University in Charlotte, NC. Besides his interest in comics and poetry, he makes pottery and ceramic art, and is a passable banjo and ukulele player.

Jessi Thomsen completed her MEd at Creighton University in 2009 and MA in English at the University of Nebraska at Omaha in 2015. Her research interests include writing pedagogy, reflection in the classroom, graphic memoir, and multimodal composition. Her work has appeared in *Teaching English in the Two-Year College* and *Kairos*.

Erica Trabold (ericatrabold.com) is a writer of family and memory. Her essays and comics about the Midwest have appeared or are forthcoming in *Weave*, *Seneca Review*, *Penumbra*, and other venues. She writes and teaches in Oregon, where she is pursuing an MFA in creative nonfiction.

Shannon Walters is Assistant Professor of English at Temple University, where she teaches and researches in the areas of rhetoric and composition, disability studies, and women's studies. She is the author of *Rhetorical Touch: Disability, Identification, Haptics*.

Gary Weissman, Associate Professor of English and Comparative Literature at the University of Cincinnati, is the author of *Fantasies of Witnessing: Postwar Efforts to Experience the Holocaust* (2004). He has published articles on Holocaust literature, film, and scholarship, and on teaching and interpreting literary texts.

Maggie M. Werner, Assistant Professor of writing and rhetoric at Hobart & William Smith Colleges, teaches writing with a focus on analysis and style. Her research specialties include sexuality studies and rhetorical criticism. She has published articles and book reviews in *Feminist Formations*, *JAC*, *Rhetoric Review*, and edited collections.

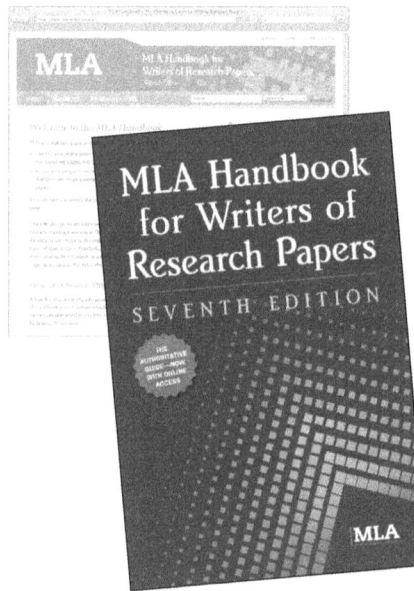

www.ingramcontent.com/pod-product-compliance
Lightning Source LLC
Chambersburg PA
CBHW031318160426
43196CB00007B/577

9781602357020